AF605860

THE CRIMEAN WAR AND CULTURAL MEMORY

The Crimean War and Cultural Memory

The War France Won and Forgot

SIMA GODFREY

UNIVERSITY OF TORONTO PRESS
Toronto Buffalo London

© University of Toronto Press 2023
Toronto Buffalo London
utorontopress.com

ISBN 978-1-4875-4777-6 (cloth)
ISBN 978-1-4875-4778-3 (EPUB)
ISBN 978-1-4875-4779-0 (PDF)

Library and Archives Canada Cataloguing in Publication

Title: The Crimean War and cultural memory : the war France won and forgot / Sima Godfrey.
Names: Godfrey, Sima, 1951– author.
Description: Includes bibliographical references and index.
Identifiers: Canadiana (print) 20230444172 | Canadiana (ebook) 20230444288 | ISBN 9781487547776 (cloth) | ISBN 9781487547783 (EPUB) | ISBN 9781487547790 (PDF)
Subjects: LCSH: Crimean War, 1853–1856 – Social aspects – France. | LCSH: Collective memory – France – History – 19th century.
Classification: LCC DK214 .G63 2023 | DDC 947/.0738 – dc23

Cover design: Alexa Love
Cover image: The pont de l'Alma Zouave statue, 4 June 2016 (6m05 Seine height). Ibex73 © 4 June 2016. CC BY-SA 4.0.

We wish to acknowledge the land on which the University of Toronto Press operates. This land is the traditional territory of the Wendat, the Anishnaabeg, the Haudenosaunee, the Métis, and the Mississaugas of the Credit First Nation.

This book has been published with the help of a grant from the Federation for the Humanities and Social Sciences, through the Awards to Scholarly Publications Program, using funds provided by the Social Sciences and Humanities Research Council of Canada.

University of Toronto Press acknowledges the financial support of the Government of Canada, the Canada Council for the Arts, and the Ontario Arts Council, an agency of the Government of Ontario, for its publishing activities.

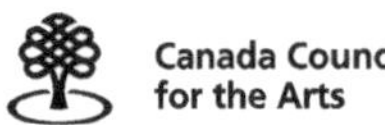

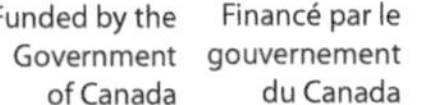

Contents

List of Illustrations vii

Acknowledgments xi

1 Introduction: *La Guerre de Crimée n'aura pas lieu* 3

2 *À la recherche de la guerre gagnée*: Crimea, the Invisible War 33

3 Spectacles of War 61

4 Crimea: The Visible War 101

5 *À la recherche de la guerre oubliée*: Crimea, the Forgotten War 143

Notes 169

Bibliography 183

Index 205

Illustrations

1.1 The Crimean War memorial, Waterloo Square, London 4
1.2 Crimean War Memorial, London 4
1.3 Notre Dame de France Puy-en-Velay 5
1.4 Funeral stele in the cemetery of the commune of Biozat 11
1.5 Transcription of the thirteen names on the funeral stele, cemetery at Biozat 12
1.6 The Sebastopol Monument, also known as the Welsford-Parker Monument 26
1.7 Monument to Maréchal Saint-Arnaud, Saint-Arnaud, Australia 26
1.8 Tour Malakoff, commune of Sermizelles 27
1.9 Chocolat Malakoff 28
1.10 The Zouave on the pillar of the Pont de l'Alma 29
1.11 The Zouave on the Pont de l'Alma, submerged in water up to his thighs 29
1.12 The *chasseur à pied* on the Pont de l'Alma, 1910. Postcard 30
1.13 The *chasseur à pied* on Autoroute 4 heading into Paris 30
2.1 Constantin Guys, "Our artist on the Battlefield of Inkerman" 58
3.1 "Meeting of Henry VIII and Francis I at Ardres – the Field of the Cloth of Gold." From a painting by John Gilbert 64
3.2 Eugene-Charles-François Guerard (1821–1866), *Queen Victoria's Entry into Paris, 18 August 1855* 66
3.3 Victor Joseph Chavet (1822–1906), *The Promenade in the Galerie des Glaces, Versailles, 25 August 1855* 68
3.4 Victor Joseph Chavet (1822–1906), *The Overture to the Ball in the Galerie des Glaces, Versailles, 1855* 69
3.5 Charles-Auguste Questel (1807–1888), *The Illuminations in the Gardens of Versailles, 25 August 1855* 70

3.6 Eugène Lami (1800–1890), *Souper Offert par Napoléon III en l'honneur de la Reine Victoria dans la Salle de l'Opéra de Versailles, 25 Août 1855* 71
3.7 Emile Lassalle (1811–1871), *Queen Victoria and Napoleon III Visit the Universal Exhibition of 1855, 22 August 1855* 72
3.8 Honoré Daumier (1808–1879), "À la Sortie du Théâtre de la Gaîté après une représentation des Cosaques" 75
3.9 Outdoor performance of *Le Siège de Silistrie* at the new Paris Hippodrome (1854) 78
3.10 *Souvenir de la Crimée. Chansonnier nouveau pour 1856* 79
3.11 Horace Vernet (1789–1863), *Zouaves at the Malakoff*, 1856 80
3.12 Roger Fenton (1819–1869), *Self-Portrait as a Zouave*, 1. Photograph 81
3.13 Roger Fenton, *Self-Portrait as a Zouave*, 2. Photograph 81
3.14 "Théâtre d'Inkermann: 'Théâtre des Zouaves,' in the French camp before Sebastopol" 84
3.15 *Le Théâtre des Zouaves, Tableau militaire, mêlé de couplets* 85
3.16 Zouave Playbill; Théâtre d'Inkermann. 26 August 1855 86
3.17 Zouave Playbill; Théâtre d'Inkermann. 30 August 1855 86
3.18 Clément Pruche (1811–1890), *Rentrée à Paris des régiments français revenant de Crimée [...] 29 Décembre 1855* 89
3.19 R. Bongean, illustrateur, *Entrée Solenelle* [sic] *dans Paris de la Garde Impériale et des troupes de ligne venant de Crimée* 91
3.20 Clément Pruche, *Retour de Crimée* 92
3.21 Léon Leymonnerye (1803–1879), *Arc Vis-à-Vis de la Colonne de Juillet élévé pour le retour à Paris de l'Armée d'Orient le 29 décembre 1855* 96
3.22 Pierre Ambroise Richebourg (1810–1875), *Inauguration du Boulevard de Sébastopol, le 5 avril 1858, en présence se l'Empereur Napoléon III et de l'Impératrice Eugénie. 1er, 2ème, 3ème Et 4ème Arrondissements, Paris* 97
3.23 *Inauguration du boulevard de Sébastopol, le 5 avril 1858* 98
4.1 Adolphe Yvon (1817–1883), *La Prise de la Tour Malakoff, le 8 septembre 1855*. 1857 102
4.2 "Bombardement de la Tour Malakoff," china plate by J. Viellard. 1857 103
4.3 "Guerre d'Orient, jeu de loto." Board game 103
4.4 "Loterie de la Guerre d'Orient." Board game 104
4.5 "Camp français devant Sébastopol no. 14." 1855 105
4.6 "Drôleries d'Orient" 106
4.7 "Guerre de Crimée." Tapestry 107

4.8 "Victoire de l'Alma, remportée sur les russes par les armées alliées, le 20 septembre 1854" 107
4.9 "Etablissement orthopédique fondé à l'occasion de la prise de Sébastopol." Handkerchief by F. Daniel et Cie 108
4.10 Jean-Auguste-Dominique Ingres (1780–1867), *l'Apothéose de Napoléon I* (1853) 108
4.11 Isidore Pils (1815–1875), *Tranchée devant Sébastopol* (1855) 110
4.12 Isidore Pils, *La Bataille d'Alma. 1861* 112
4.13 Gustave Doré (1832–1883), *Histoire de la Sainte Russie*. 1854 114
4.14 Honoré Daumier, "Un Ours contrarié." *Le Charivari*, 28 August 1854 115
4.15 Gustave Doré, "Chasseurs d'Afrique in a reconnoitring excursion headed by General d'Alloville charging the Cossacks," "Arrival of General Ulrich in the bay of Kamiesk." *Musée français-anglais*, March 1855 116
4.16 Gustave Doré, "Physiognomy of the Great Square Saloon at the Universal Exhibition of Fine Arts." *Musée français-anglais*, June 1855 116
4.17 Gustave Doré, "The Battle of Tchernaya," *Illustrated London News*, 29 September 1855 117
4.18 Henri Durand-Brager (1814–1879), "Episodes de la Campagne de Crimée." (Texte et dessins) *l'Illustration*, 27 January 1855 120
4.19 "M. Durand-Brager, correspondent de L'Illustration dessinant en Crimée." *L'Illustration*, 9 February 1856 (dessin de J. Worms, gravure de B.H. Cie) 121
4.20 Roger Fenton, "View of Balaklava from the top of Guard's Hill. Harbor with tent encampments in the foreground, ships in the harbor and, on a hill in the background, ruins of the old Genoese castle," 1855 123
4.21 Roger Fenton, "Zouaves and Soldiers on the Line," 1855 124
4.22 La Salle de Crimée in the Château de Versailles. Postcard 125
4.23 Cham (Amédée de Noé) (1818–1879), "Polissons d'enfants! Nous ne vous mènerons plus jamais à l'Exposition voir les belles batailles de M. Yvon, puisqu'elles vous font ce effet-là," *Salon de 1857 illustré par Cham* 126
4.24 Cham, "– Ah! mon Dieu! Caroline, tu fais peindre ton portrait habillée en zouave? – Que veux-tu, ma chère, le peintre n'a pas voulu me faire autrement, ce sont les seuls portraits que l'on regardera à l'Exposition de cette année à ce qu'il dit." *Salon de 1857 illustré par Cham* 128
4.25 Henri Durand-Brager, *Siège de Sébastopol: Vue de Kamiesch*. Photograph 132

4.26 Gustave Courbet (1819–1877), *Demoiselles des bords de la Seine*, 1856–57 133
4.27 Cham, "Femme du monde prise subitement de la colique à la campagne (par M. Courbet). Le peintre a voulu prouver qu'il pouvait peindre la femme comme il faut tout aussi bien que la femme commune." *Salon de 1857 illustré par Cham* 133
4.28 Constantin Guys, "Canrobert on the battle field of Inkermann. Taken on the spot." 1854 134
4.29 Constantin Guys, "General Canrobert after the Battle of Inkerman [*sic*]." *Illustrated London News*, 13 January 1855 135
4.30 Jean-Charles Langlois (1789–1870) and Léon Méhédin (1828–1905), *La Tour Malakoff* 138
4.31 Jean-Charles Langlois and Léon Méhédin, *Panorama de Sébastopol pris de la Tour Malakoff* 138
5.1 Horace Vernet, *La Prise de la Tour Malakoff*, 1858 150

Acknowledgments

This book about cultural memory, collective forgetting, and war originated in a moment of confessed ignorance. An accident of wordplay at a conference – see chapter 2 – led me out of my comfort zone of Parisian modernity, product placement, fashion, and Second Empire authors to a nineteenth-century French war on the Crimean Peninsula that I knew virtually nothing about. Baudelaire, Flaubert, Gautier, Sand, and company had little to tell me about this war. I started looking elsewhere, consulting along the way every friend and colleague I knew in French history, literature, art, and cultural studies. I am grateful to them all for their insight, their scholarly references, their encouragement, and their patience. Thank you especially to members of the Nineteenth-Century French Studies Association, who have given me over the years the opportunity to test-drive ideas about the Crimean War in formal sessions as well as informal bars. It was at meetings of the association that I invariably got the best questions, the best answers, and the best you-should-look-ats. I owe a particular debt of gratitude to Michel Pierssens and the late Jean-Jacques Lefrère, who, without knowing it, sparked the wordplay at the Colloque des Invalides that led to this book. A further debt of gratitude goes to Françoise Gaillard and Catherine Soussloff, who convinced me to follow that spark and see where it would lead me. Their readings of early drafts of this book and their advice, like their friendship, were invaluable.

Much of this book was written during a pandemic that regrettably limited access to libraries and archives in Paris but happily allowed me to give talks in New Haven, London, and Paris with marvellous colleagues but without jetlag. The feedback and lively discussions were all the more precious at that time of social isolation "in the trenches," as it were. Thank you to Maurice Samuels, Patrick Bray, and Cary Hollinshead-Strick for making this possible.

Prior to the pandemic my year as a Wall Scholar at the Peter Wall Institute for Advanced Studies at the University of British Columbia afforded me the perfect setting to pursue the research for this book in the company of an inspiring cohort of scholars. I have fond memories of the festive evening in March 2020 where all of us presented five-minute versions of our research to a roomful of guests, little knowing that this would be the last public event at the institute before Covid closed its doors. I am forever indebted to the institute for generously supporting my travel to and research in Paris once transatlantic travel resumed and libraries reopened. Thank you to all the helpful librarians at the Bibliothèques Nationale, Sainte Geneviève, Mazarine, and École Militaire. God bless Gallica.

In Stephen Shapiro at the University of Toronto Press I found an editor who was not only enthusiastic about this project but remarkably knowledgeable as well. He may well be the only editor in the English-speaking world who knows what a Minié rifle is and why it put the French army at an advantage. He gracefully shepherded this book through the editorial process and never balked at the number of images I wanted to include. For tracking down those images and securing permissions far and wide I am very grateful to Greg Gibson. I could not wish for a better or more professional assistant.

As in all research projects there were the inevitable cul-de-sacs and periods of discouragement. I feel so lucky to have had supportive friends to cheer me on. I want to thank in particular Jennifer Crewe, Celina Kates, Deena Mandell, Ronni Rosenberg, Margaret Schabas, and Rhea Tregebov, whose wine and wise words buoyed me. The dearest of supporters were my children, Ben and Lulu. There are not enough words to express to them my love and gratitude.

A version of chapter 1 of this book appeared in different form in "La Guerre de Crimée n'aura pas lieu," *French Cultural Studies* 1 (2016). Unless otherwise indicated, all translations from French are my own.

THE CRIMEAN WAR AND CULTURAL MEMORY

Chapter One

Introduction: *La Guerre de Crimée n'aura pas lieu*

La conquête du lama est dix fois plus importante que la conquête de Crimée (Saving the llama is ten times more important than the conquest of Crimea.)

Jules Michelet, *L'Oiseau* (1856)

Quelle commémoration a été faite, en France, des soldats tués à Sébastopol? (What commemoration did France make for the soldiers killed at Sebastopol?)

Pierre-Joseph Proudhon, *De la Justice dans la Révolution et dans l'Église* (1860)

Two Monuments

A visitor to London who comes to Waterloo Place, guidebook in hand, has many monuments to admire. There is first the 34-metre column erected in 1834 to honour the Duke of York, commander-in-chief of the British army against Napoleon and son of King George III. Facing the column, on the north side of the place, there is the very imposing Crimean War Memorial, cast in bronze from Russian cannons captured at Sebastopol and erected in 1861. Unlike the column this memorial presents not a high-born martial leader but rather three sombre guardsmen with downcast eyes. There is nothing triumphant about their pose. A female allegorical figure, Honour, stands atop the monument with outstretched arms holding a pair of laurels. On the back facade a plaque reads: "To the memory of 2152 Officers, Non-Com. Officers and Privates of the BRIGADE OF GUARDS who fell during the war with Russia in 1854–56. Erected by their Comrades." Adjacent are two more commemorative installations. In 1914, the memorial was moved thirty feet to allow for the erection in front of it of statues to Florence Nightingale, "the Lady with the Lamp" and mother of modern nursing, and Sidney Herbert, the Secretary of War who facilitated her work in Crimea.

1.1 The Crimean War memorial, Waterloo Square, London. Photo 107985412 / Crimean Memorial © Dmitry Naumov/Dreamstime.com.

1.2 Crimean War Memorial, London. iStock.com/Tony Baggett.

The same traveller crossing the channel to Paris, guidebook in hand, will find no such equivalent memorial in the city. They would hardly expect to. Nor would any Parisian. After all, the Crimean War (1854–56) was about Light Brigades and British nurses and Russian sieges. True enough. But it was also about French troops – three times the number Britain sent – who led the allies to victory over the Russians, brought an end to the year-long siege at Sebastopol, and lost 95,000 men. Crimea was, in fact, the only major war the French won in the nineteenth century. Yet nowhere in the French capital is there a monument to that victory, the war, or the men who died there.

To be fair, the French too erected a monument from the melted iron of Russian canons captured at Sebastopol, but tellingly, it is not in Paris, and it is a monument not to the war or its heroes but to the Virgin Mary. On the occasion of the Pope's proclamation of the dogma of the Immaculate Conception, Mgr de Morlhon, the bishop of Puy-en-Vélay, proposed erecting a colossal monument to the Virgin on a high volcanic spur in the Auvergne that could be seen from miles around. When funding from a public subscription fell short, on 5 September 1855 the bishop went to Paris to request patronage from Emperor Napoleon III.

He strategically added that the town of Puy wished to erect the statue as a prayer for France to obtain peace through victory in Crimea. The emperor promised that the Russian cannons his troops captured at Sebastopol would be melted down to build the monumental Virgin of Puy. Three days later, on 8 September 1855, the French stormed Sebastopol. The Virgin herself, some said, had intervened to fulfil Napoleon III's promise. Designed by the Jean-Marie Bonnassieux and cast in iron using 231 cannons taken at the Battle of Sebastopol, Notre Dame de France was solemnly blessed by Mgr de Morlhon before 120,000 pilgrims on 12 September 1860, one year before the inauguration of the Crimean War Memorial in London. It was the largest statue in the world until the Statue of Liberty was raised in 1886.

Monuments are symbolically charged aids to memory, "lieux de mémoire." They shape collective identity by encouraging us to remember some things and – as has become so divisive in recent years – to forget others.[1] As James Young puts it in the opening words to *Texture of Memory*, "sites remember the past according to a variety of national myths, ideals, and political needs" (1). The different uses to which the enemy cannons were put in Britain and France is emblematic of the ways in which this war entered into or bypassed national memory in the two countries and played out those myths, ideals, and needs. Whereas in Britain, the cannons were melted down to produce in the centre of the capital a national memorial and a tribute to military bravery and honour on the battlefields of Crimea, in France they were turned into a 900-ton patriotic declaration of Catholic piety deep in "la France profonde" with no reference to the Crimean War or to the cannon fire that French soldiers and officers had faced. In France the Crimean War was, to borrow an image from "Spleen III" by the poet Charles Baudelaire, the war "où coule au lieu de sang l'eau verte du Léthé" (where the green water of oblivion flows instead of blood). To the extent that the process of creating

1.3 Notre Dame de France Puy-en-Velay. W. Bulach, CC BY-SA 4.0, via Wikimedia Commons.

monuments shapes public memory and collective identity, Notre Dame de France declares the triumph of Catholic piety, not the patriotic triumph of the military.

An Anecdote

In February 2013, Agence France-Presse reports that a Ukrainian excavator bucket has stumbled upon dozens of human remains at a construction site at Sebastopol's Cane Bay. At first, people think the yellowed bones belong to Russian or German soldiers who fought in the Second World War battles for Sebastopol. But then they find fragments of a military greatcoat with buttons of the French Army's 39th Infantry Regiment, which had taken part in the siege of Sebastopol during the Crimean War. Historical documents confirmed that a huge camp housing tens of thousands of French soldiers had been stationed on that shore. What the excavator bucket had unearthed was the site of a large French hospital cemetery filled with unknown soldiers.

According to the local museum director, "the average age of the deceased does not exceed thirty years, but due to the absence of personal belongings or documents, there is 'close to zero chance' of establishing their identity." When French diplomats subsequently visited Sebastopol, "dozens of plastic bags with the bones of their countrymen had been piled up by the construction site's fence" ("Ghosts of Crimean War").

Just as Notre Dame de France hides the story of French soldiers and Russian cannons, the story of those buried bodies in plastic bags, forgotten and neglected for 150 years, is emblematic of how the Crimean War has been buried, neglected, and forgotten in French memory. For French anthropologist Pierre Malinowski, who participated in the excavations, the stakes were clear: "Il y a un devoir de mémoire car ce conflit est oublié en France" (We have an obligation to remember because this conflict was forgotten in France) (quoted in Cabourg, "En Crimée").

Anonymous as they remained, the bodies of the 155 French soldiers who had fought in the Crimean War did eventually find a resting place in a nearby nineteenth-century French military necropolis. The process, however, was far from restful. After the Russian annexation of Crimea from Ukraine in 2014, the bodies became embroiled in a new Crimean conflict between France and Russia; they would spend the next six years in the museum of Sebastopol awaiting burial. The Russians wanted to bury them, but France did not recognize the annexation and maintained that Ukraine had jurisdiction over the penninsula.

Finally, on 3 October 2020, the soldiers were buried in the French military cemetery at Sebastopol. A Russian soprano sang the Russian national anthem, followed by "The Marseillaise," and Crimean Cossacks carried the coffins draped in the French flag. No French official was present to witness or salute the service of the forgotten men, now buried a second time.[2]

Not quite a necropolis, this book is more like that Ukrainian excavator bucket. If cultural memory implies the cultivation of objectified culture – that is, texts, images, buildings, and monuments designed to recall fateful events in the history of the collective (J. Assmann, "Collective Memory," 132) – then this book represents an attempt to unearth and confront those French remains of the Crimean War and to come to terms with how it was and was not buried and forgotten in French cultural memory.

On a chilly day in March, fear of an impending Crimean war fills the front pages of newspapers throughout Europe. There is talk of Russian aggression, expansionism, and eventual control of the Black Sea. Sebastopol, home of the Russian Black Sea Fleet, suddenly figures on the cognitive maps of individuals who two months earlier would not have been able to find it on a globe. But the year is not 2014. It is 1854, and by the end of March, France, Britain, and the Ottoman Sublime Porte – three now vanished empires – would be officially at war with Russia, a fourth. For months the events that led up to and took place during the Crimean War would dominate political discussions throughout the Western world, not least of all in France, where they made headlines for three solid years.

And so begins the narrative, or rather *a* narrative, of the Crimean War, or, as it was also called, "la Guerre d'Orient," the Eastern War. It is not at all clear where this particular nineteenth-century story fits into the larger story of modern France. The Napoleonic Wars at the beginning and the Franco-Prussian War towards the end of that century constitute loud, unforgettable chapters in the collective memory and narratives of French history. But what of the Crimean War, the only one of the three that the French ultimately won? Jean Huon includes it in his French history of forgotten battles and conflicts. This, even though the names of its victorious battles are etched on towns throughout France and repeated daily on boulevards, bridges, squares, and metro stops: Alma, Malakoff, and especially Sebastopol.[3] In 1994, Jacques Perot, director of the French Museum of the Army, asked somewhat impatiently: "Quelques noms quotidiennement répétés … Sébastopol, Malakoff, l'Alma. Mais qui saurait dire ce qu'ils évoquent, au delà des hauts lieux du Paris haussmannien qu'ils désignent?" (A few names repeated daily … Sebastopol, Malakoff, Alma. But who knows what they represent, other than some well-known places in Haussmannian Paris?) (*Crimée 1854–1856*, 8). To paraphrase the art historian Ulrich Keller, the Crimean War has no place in the canon of culturally retained historical events that define modern French identity (*The Ultimate Spectacle*, ix).

A joke from the time of the war is revealing. When the brutal siege of Sebastopol (1854–55) seemed endless, a customer in a Paris café, annoyed that no one was taking his order, exclaimed: "Ah ça! Mais on ne peut donc rien prendre ici, c'est comme à Sébastopol!" (How long do you have to wait to get some action here? It's like Sebastopol!). The customer in question was Paul Grassot, a comic actor famous at the time whom no one remembers today. But just as the name Grassot no longer rings a bell, neither does the Crimean War that he referred to in his "bon mot." In the words of Antoine Bourguilleau, "presque plus personne en France ne connaît ni le nom, ni les raisons, ni la date de début et de fin" (almost no one in France anymore knows the name, the causes, the date it started or the date it ended). It would seem that for the French, the legacy of that war has been reduced to a single defiant declaration: "J'y suis, j'y reste!" (Here I am, here I stay). French lore has it that, having just taken the strategic Malakoff fort overlooking Sebastopol, General Patrice de MacMahon uttered these defiant words even as others warned him that the fort was about to explode. For all the bravura of the phrase, however, MacMahon denied ever having said it. In his memoirs he recalls his conversation with the artist Horace Vernet, who painted the victorious general in the *Prise du Malakoff*: "Je lui dis, ce qui est exact, que je ne m'étais jamais servi de cette expression" (I told him, and this is the truth, that I had never used that expression) (Sémur, *MacMahon*, 172). Ironically, the most familiar French keepsake retained from the war may well be a fake.[4]

The Crimean War was the first major armed conflict on European soil since the Napoleonic Wars at the beginning of the century. It is widely considered the first modern industrial war with its tactical use of railways, telegraphs, synchronized watches, ironclad steam-propelled battleships, rapid-fire long-range rifles, and 200-pound explosive shells. It is the war that initiated international meteorological services.[5] Its notorious trenches anticipated those of the First World War. While the scale and objectives of the two conflicts differed, the familiar stories marking our understanding of the Great War – suffering in the trenches, misguided optimism about a quick victory, military bungling, the horrors of war, fears about the balance of European power, and the need to confront a "bullying" enemy – had all been features of the Crimean War sixty years earlier.

It is a war as famous today for its displays of military incompetence as for its victories. It was also the first "media war," in that people in Britain and France, and to a lesser extent in Russia and Turkey, received news of battles at hitherto unknown speeds, thanks to photography, telegraphy, and, for the first time, the presence of war correspondents on the field of battle. From start to finish it was a war that filled the pages of British and French daily newspapers and illustrated weeklies without interruption. It is a war that today looms large in the national mythologies of Russia and England, yet in French collective memory it remains at best a postscript.

The story of the Crimean War as told from the Russian and British perspectives is primarily one of loss. For the Russians, loss of a war, loss of international prestige, and massive loss of life. For the British, loss of command from an aristocratic but incompetent officer corps and the senseless loss of life because of appalling shortcomings in medical care that aroused indignation back home. French diplomat Alexis de Tocqueville and British economist Nassau William Senior agreed that Russia and England had both lost by this war. "Russia probably the most in power, England in reputation." By comparison, France was "a gainer, by becoming head of the coalition against Russia" (*Correspondence*, 101). This, in March 1855, long before the war had ended.

In his exchange with Senior, Tocqueville was blunt: "It is an unpleasant truth, but I ought not to conceal it from you … The heroic courage of your soldiers was everywhere and unreservedly praised, but I found also a general belief that the importance of England as a military power had been greatly exaggerated; that she is utterly devoid of military talent, which is shown as much in administration as in fighting; and that even in the most pressing circumstances she cannot raise a large army … You are believed to be absolutely dependent on us" (91).

Thomas Chenery, writing in *The Times* on 12 October 1854, was laconic in his condemnation of the supply shortages and medical mismanagement on the British side, an issue that incensed the public: "It is with feelings of surprise and anger that the public will learn that no sufficient preparations have been made for the proper care of the wounded." Following the great blizzard of November 1855, British soldiers froze in the trenches; many, lacking wood to cook their food, had to eat it raw. William Russell, the war correspondent for *The Times*, declared Crimea "the most ruinous, most cruel, and least justifiable of all modern campaigns" (in Wrench, "The Lessons," 205). "Our whole medical system is shamefully bad. Here the French are greatly our superiors."[6] French soldiers, writing home from the front during that terrible winter, confirmed the press reports, as in this letter of 22 January 1855:

> Le tableau désolant que traçait dernièrement le *Times* de leurs misères [nos pauvres alliés] n'est que trop vrai … Au 18 janvier, sur les 27,000 hommes de troupes britanniques devant Sébastopol, il n'y en avait pas 13,000 en état de faire le service des tranchées. C'est ce qui explique pourquoi les Français ont été obligés de prendre la garde et de continuer la construction de la plus grande partie des travaux de siège occupés et commencés par les Anglais … Nous avons même plus d'une fois partagé nos vivres avec eux.
>
> (The distressing picture that *The Times* recently painted of the misery of our poor allies is all too true ... On January 18, of 27,000 British troops at Sebastopol, only 13,000 were fit to serve in the trenches. That explains why the French had to assume guard and complete the greater part of the siege construction begun and occupied by the English … More than once we have had to share our food with them.) (in Mullois, *Histoire* [1857], 213)

Unlike the British, the French army had recent experience in supplying and fighting a war abroad. Lara Kriegel quotes Captain Frederick Cockayne Elton, who, startled by the contrast between French efficiency and English blunder in the first winter of the war, wondered "how we ever managed to thrash them [the French]" (*The Crimean War*, 37). The French army was, indeed, well provisioned and led by professionally trained officers, many of them veterans of the French conquest of Algeria. General Saint-Arnaud, who led the expedition to Crimea, had established his career in Algeria and advanced through the ranks there between 1836 and 1851. By comparison, Lord Raglan, who headed the British expeditionary force, had seen no action since Waterloo, forty years earlier.

From the French perspective, though the story is similarly one of tragic suffering and loss of life – 95,000 of the 310,000 Frenchmen who went over died, most of them from cholera, typhus, and other diseases – ultimately it is also a story of military victory culminating in the 1856 Treaty of Paris. As Kriegel puts it, "the Treaty of Paris ended the war, hastening a French ascent in Europe, a Russian retreat to insularity, an Ottoman decline in power, and a British reorientation of interests" (7). Two weeks after Sebastopol fell, British Colonel Hugh Rose wrote to Lord Clarendon, British Secretary of State for Foreign Affairs, signalling the real and symbolic importance of that victory for France: "After 1815 the spirit of the French Army was lowered by a succession of reverses. The successes in Algiers against Barbarians, without artillery, were not sufficient to restore them the prestige they once enjoyed. But the share of successes which the French Army have had in conquering a Military European Power of the first order, in battles on the field, and in the Siege of a peculiarly strong and invested Fortress, a Siege without many parallels in History ... have raised their military feeling and confidence" (23 September 1855).[7]

The French comprised by far the largest contingent of the allied forces and set the standard for military efficiency. Their corps of engineers and medical corps had been modernized. The French were also the most technologically advanced. Of the participants in that conflict, only the French army issued a rifle to every one of its infantrymen. Around half the infantry in the British Army were outfitted with rifles, the other half with muskets. French artillery used the same calibre of ammunition for all its guns, whereas the English had nine or ten different pieces, each requiring its own ammunition, with the result that batteries could not supply one another (Senior, *Conversation*, 358).

Crimea was, indeed, France's only victorious war against a major European power in the nineteenth century with its triumphs at Alma, Malakoff, and Sebastopol, those battle sites whose names now dot French urban geography. By defeating a formidable enemy nearly forty years after Waterloo, France regained its prestige as well as its pre-eminence on the international stage. But if national memory usually revolves around collective pride, where are the lasting narratives that recount that triumph?

In the letter he wrote to Senior following the taking of Sebastopol, Tocqueville sighed: "I fear that the victory has been bought dearly. There is not a neighbouring village to which the war has not cost some of its children" (in Senior, *Correspondence*, 128). To this day, the few memorials one finds to the war are found not in large urban centres but in small towns and communes that sacrificed their youth to the campaign, in places like the commune of Biozat, not far from Vichy, with its simple stone stele inscribed with the names of the thirteen young men it lost, or the small cemetery

1.4 Funeral stele in the cemetery of the commune of Biozat. Image courtesy Jacques Lafaure.

A la
mémoire
des braves
enfants de la commune
morts pour le patrie
Guerre d'Orient 1854–1856

Beaufort Jean	Magerand Antoine
Bréchard Joseph	Méchin Gabriel
Durand Antoine	Mesples Auguste
Pillot Etienne	Roumeaux Gilbert
Georges Jacques	Saby Quintien
Grand Auguste	Véderine Jn Léon

Lafaure Antoine
Comment les forts sont-ils tombés
eux plus rapides que les aigles
plus courageux que les lions
que le Seigneur les place parmi
les chefs de son peuple.
Pse de David

1.5 Transcription of the thirteen names on the funeral stele, cemetery at Biozat.

on the Île Ste-Marguerite off the coast of Cannes, with its stele dedicated to thirty soldiers who died there as a result of injuries suffered in the Crimean War.[8]

But where are the lasting narratives of mourning or anger for the deaths of 95,000 men on a peninsula in the Black Sea? Kriegel, in *The Crimean War and Its Aftermath,* has written eloquently about the afterlife of that war in the making of modern Britain: "Afterlife is a notion that apprehends the reverberations of the conflict over the ages – its unfinished business and its unanticipated effects, its literary inheritances and its material residues, its structures of feeling and its unanswered questions. It captures the robust persistence of the Crimea's legacies and the reinterpretation of its meanings across both time and space … The persistence of the Crimean War is evident in the texture of everyday life" (4–5).

But where is the afterlife of the Crimean War in France?

If collective memory is produced through mediated acts of remembrance circulating in the form of images and stories, where are the lasting images and narratives of triumph *or* loss, commemoration *or* contestation, that would embed this event in the national psyche?

This is the question that sent me "à la recherche de la guerre gagnée."

The details of the Crimean War (1854–56) are confusing and, given the hundreds of thousands of lives it cost, baffling. Victor Hugo characterized it as "une guerre qui part du risible pour aboutir à l'horrible" (a war that starts out laughable and ends up horrifying) ("La Guerre d'Orient," 125). The origins of the French engagement in the war are found in rivalries between the Orthodox Church and the Catholic Church over the keys to holy sites in Jerusalem and elsewhere in the Holy Land, then under the rule of the Ottoman Empire. The Orthodox Church refused to share the keys to the main entrance of the Church of the Nativity with the Catholic Church, whose clergy had to use a side entrance. Xavier Tanc, lawyer to the imperial court, was shocked by the "scandalous scenes" during Easter that involved heated disputes over the sanctuaries: "Le cabinet français ne pouvait donc laisser passer inaperçues les usurpations des Grecs et des Arméniens" (The French cabinet could not let the Greeks' and Armenians' usurping go unnoticed) (*Guerre d'Orient,* 8). Tsar Nicholas I of Russia defended the rights of the Orthodox Church in the Ottoman Empire; Napoleon III of France argued on behalf of Catholic claims with reference to earlier treaties. In so doing, he was eager to rally support from French Catholics and to please his devoutly Catholic wife, Eugénie. He had succeeded in winning over the French clergy, who supported his presidential election in 1848, and as president he sought to cement that support by directing General Aupick, the French representative at the Sublime Porte – coincidentally, stepfather of Charles Baudelaire – to demand of the sultan in 1849 that he return control of the holy places to the Franciscans, who had held that privilege since 1740 (11). Reflecting on the lead-up to the war, Louis Thouvenel, French foreign minister at the time, declared: "en Orient, qui dit religion dit politique" (in the Middle East, to speak of religion is to speak of politics) (Thouvenel, *Nicholas I,* vii).[9]

For his part, the tsar was particularly attached to Jerusalem. Nicholas I was the champion of "the true Christianity and sacred tradition," and like many Russians he saw the Holy Land with its shrines as an extension of Holy Russia.[10] Under his rule, Russian pilgrimage, backed by the largesse of the Russian state and the Russian Orthodox Church, increased exponentially (Bowman, "In Dubious Battle," 382). "Palestine," wrote one Russian theologian in the 1840s, "is our native land, in which we do not recognise ourselves as foreigners" (Figes, *Crimea,* 4).[11]

In Lucien Descaves's 1901 novel *La Colonne,* a disabled French veteran of the Crimean War tries to explain the causes of that war to a young boy: "nous étions en Crimée afin de maintenir l' équilibre européen, en reprenant aux Russes la clef des Lieux Saints qu' ils avaient ravie" (We went to Crimea in order to maintain the balance of power in Europe by taking back from the Russians the key to the Holy Sites that they had seized). A republican worker sitting next to them sneers: "Mais pourquoi leur disputions-nous la possession de cette clef? Quel besoin en avions-nous?" (But why were we fighting them for possession of that key? Whatever did we need it for?) (228). Victor Hugo could barely hide his scorn for the religious pretext for the war:

> Rien de plus simple. Faire pencher à Jérusalem la balance du côté de Rome; rompre devant le tombeau du Christ l'humiliante égalité des deux croix; mettre l'église d'orient sous les pieds de l'église d'occident; ouvrir la sainte porte à l'une et la fermer à l'autre; faire une avanie au pape grec; en un mot, donner au pape latin la clef du sépulcre […] C'est ce que M. Bonaparte a compris; c'est ce qu'il a fait.
>
> (Nothing could be simpler. Make Jerusalem lean towards Rome; destroy the degrading equality of two crosses in front of Christ's tomb; put the Eastern church under the foot of the Western church; open the holy door to one and close it to the other; humiliate the Greek pope; in short, give the Latin pope the key to the sepulchre … That's what Mr. Bonaparte figured out; that's what he did.) ("La Guerre d'Orient," 101)

Religious concerns aside, Louis-Napoléon ("M. Bonaparte"), recently crowned Emperor Napoleon III, saw in the prospect of war with Russia the opportunity to restore French pride in the military, a military he had most recently used against his own people in the *coup d'état* of 2 December 1851 that placed him on the throne. A glorious war against the Russians in Crimea would perhaps override memories of the French soldiers he had sent onto the streets of Paris. To achieve that end, he even chose the general who had orchestrated the *coup d'état*, Jacques Leroy de Saint-Arnaud, to lead the troops into Crimea. Saint-Arnaud did not disappoint – though ill, he led the French troops to a decisive victory in the first major battle at Alma. Shortly after, he died of cholera, a stoic hero.[12]

There was also a matter of personal ambition and ego. Recently snubbed by the tsar, the emperor saw in the prospect of a foreign war with Russia the opportunity to redeem French glory, to settle the Napoleonic score with Russia, and to assert his own status in the shadow of his uncle Bonaparte through what Ernest Vizitelly called a "baptism of glory" (*The Court*, 79.)[13] In 1853, the Ottoman sultan adjudicated in favour of the French and handed over to them the keys to the main entrance of the Church of the Nativity.

The tsar used the sultan's decision as a pretext to invade two neighbouring Ottoman-controlled Danubian Principalities, Moldavia and

Wallachia (present-day Romania). England and France, seeking to ensure the stability of the Ottoman Empire and their own geopolitical and economic interests, sent fleets to the Dardanelles to safeguard the straits against Russian expansionism. In early March 1854, Napoleon III declared to the legislative session:

> Nous allons à Constantinople avec l'Angleterre pour défendre la cause du sultan, et néanmoins pour protéger les droits des chrétiens; nous y allons pour défendre la liberté des mers et notre juste influence en Méditerranée … Nous y allons enfin avec tous ceux qui veulent le triomphe du bon droit, de la justice et de la civilisation.
>
> (We are going to Constantinople with England to defend the cause of the sultan and nonetheless to protect the rights of Christians; we are going there to defend the freedom of the seas and our just influence in the Mediterranean … Finally, we are going there with all those who wish for the triumph of the law, of justice and of civilisation.) (Jaeglé, *La Guerre d'Orient*, 3)

On 27 March 1854, France and England joined Turkey in declaring war on Russia.

For the British, debates over holy sites were of no significance; their concern was with protecting commercial trade routes to the East and "ruling the waves." In Foreign Minister Louis Thouvenel's words, the British were "de glace" on the question of holy sites, "de feu" on any threat to the Ottoman Empire (Thouvenel, *Nicholas I*, 102). The historian George Trevelyan is far more cynical: "The Crimean War … was merely a foolish expedition to the Black Sea, because the English people were bored with peace" (in James, *Crimea 1854–1856*, 17). A war now, Queen Victoria asserted in response to tsarist aggression, would be "popular beyond belief" (Charlot, *Victoria*, 350). The popularity of the war at its beginning created an insatiable appetite for news: one government official wrote that "the excitement, the painful excitement for information, beggars all description" (in Knightley, *The First Casualty*, 2). It was just such excitement that inspired the editor of *The Times* to send a civilian correspondent to the front. And in Manchester, a city known for its pacifism, when the Seventh Fusiliers marched to the railway station on the first leg of their journey to Crimea in 1854, "they were received by crowds 'wrought up to such a pitch of excitement as almost amounted to madness'" (Myerly, *British Military Spectacle*, 104), As it turned out, the expedition that began as what many imagined would be a quick and glorious adventure ended in the long, deadly, traumatic siege of attrition before Sebastopol.

Briefly put, the Crimean War pitted the military alliance of French, British, and Turkish forces against the Russian empire. The war was fought largely on the Crimean Peninsula, where, with an eye to destroying Russian naval power in the Black Sea and curtailing any expansion into the Mediterranean, France and Britain targeted the Russian naval base at Sebastopol.[14] The march and assault on Sebastopol was marked by three main battles: Alma on 20 September 1854, an allied victory in which the French distinguished themselves; Balaclava on 24 October, known best for the disastrous Charge of the Light Brigade; and Inkerman outside Sebastopol on 5 November, where the Russian army was routed and its will to defeat the allies in the field was broken. The rest of the war was played out in the protracted siege of Sebastopol, the first modern example of extended trench warfare.[15] On 8 September 1855 the French stormed the vital Malakoff redoubt overlooking Sebastopol – where General MacMahon may or may not have made his famous declaration – and the Russians evacuated the city. The war came to a formal conclusion on 30 March 1856 with the signing of the Treaty of Paris, which returned Russia and Turkey to pre-war boundaries, demilitarized the Black Sea, and neutralized it for international trade. Russia was also forced to abandon its claim, the pretext for the war, to protect Christians in the Ottoman Empire, in favour of France. As if in response to the 1815 Treaty of Paris, which had severely penalized France following the defeat and abdication of Napoleon Bonaparte, the 1856 Treaty of Paris "raised Napoleon III from the depths to the heights … Everywhere French prestige revived by magic" (Temperly, *The Treaty of Paris*, 387).

Given the complex backstory, it is not surprising that few people today are familiar with the details of the Crimean War. It is a war that nonetheless entered almost immediately into British national mythology and deep collective memory. It even left its traces on British garments, with the introduction of the cardigan (named for Lord Cardigan, commander of the ill-fated Light Brigade), the raglan sleeve (named for Lord Raglan, commander of the British army, who had lost an arm at Waterloo), and the balaclava (the knitted helmet worn at Balaclava). There was even a new colour in women's clothing, "Alma brown" (Myerly, 150). The war also unleashed artistic and literary activity. Hours after reading an account of the Light Brigade's catastrophic charge in *The Times* in 1854, Alfred Lord Tennyson began composing "The Charge of the Light Brigade," a poem that would quickly take its place in the minds of Britons everywhere alongside the story of Florence Nightingale, the mother of modern nursing, who had attended to the sick in miserable makeshift hospitals in Crimea. The disastrous charge at Balaclava, ordered by Lord Raglan and led by Lord Cardigan, transfixed British readers. In the words of William Russell, the *Times* war correspondent, "some hideous blunder" had destroyed the British light cavalry. Tennyson would immortalize that "blunder" but especially the honour and courage of its victims:

> [...] "Forward, the Light Brigade!"
> Was there a man dismayed?
> Not though the soldier knew
>   Someone had blundered.
>   Theirs not to make reply,
>   Theirs not to reason why,
>   Theirs but to do and die:
>   Into the valley of Death
>   Rode the six hundred.
>
> Cannon to right of them,
> Cannon to left of them,
> Cannon in front of them
>   Volleyed and thundered;
> Stormed at with shot and shell,
> Boldly they rode and well,
> Into the jaws of Death,
> Into the mouth of hell
>   Rode the six hundred. ...

Thirty-six years after the event, Rudyard Kipling described the hardships faced by aging veterans of the Crimean War in "The Last of the Light Brigade," a poem that describes a visit by the last twenty survivors of the Charge to the aging Tennyson:

> There were thirty million English who talked of England's might,
> There were twenty broken troopers who lacked a bed for the night.
> They had neither food nor money, they had neither service nor trade;
> They were only shiftless soldiers, the last of the Light Brigade. [...]
>
> They laid their heads together that were scarred and lined and grey;
> Keen were the Russian sabres, but want was keener than they;
> And an old Troop-Sergeant muttered, *"Let us go to the man who writes*
> *The things on Balaclava the kiddies at school recites."* (my emphasis)

The tragic charge and the selfless service of Florence Nightingale, the "Lady of the Lamp," mother of modern nursing, amply represented in monuments, paintings, lithographs, and stories, were engraved in the public imagination.[16] The charge is even featured in Anna Sewell's bestselling children's book of 1877, *Black Beauty*. There, Captain, the old war horse who carried his master into the fire at Balaclava, recounts the events of the charge. "Do you know what they fought about?" Black Beauty asks. "'No,' he said, 'that is more than a horse can understand, but the enemy must have been awfully wicked people, if it was right to go all that way over the sea on purpose to kill them'" (168).

Cultural artefacts such as this, Ann Rigney observes, constitute "a precondition for the operation of memories across generations, for the production of collective memories in the long term" ("Plenitude," 13). In America, Henry Wadsworth Longfellow wrote a poem about the Lady with the Lamp, "Santa Filomena" (1857), and Mark Twain wrote a story about a British officer in the Crimean War, "Luck" (1886). Nor have the images and stories faded: in addition to the many films relating the Charge of the Light Brigade, there is at least one Christian rock song ("Charge of the Light Brigade" by DeGarmo and Key), one Canadian pop song ("The Thin Red Line" by Glass Tiger), one heavy metal song ("The Thin Red Line" by Saxon), a board game, a handful of video games, two rock videos commemorating the Crimean War ("The Trooper" by Iron Maiden, "Empire" by Kasabian), and more.[17] Poems, stories, images, monuments, and performances have shaped British narratives about the war and set the agenda for collective remembrance. A.L. Berridge, author of popular historical fiction, and in particular the very successful *Into the Valley of Death*, comments tongue only half in cheek, "One would expect Crimea to 'sell' like the proverbial hot cakes" ("Off the Chart," 1).[18] To the extent that memorability is culturally produced, there are no such widely disseminated equivalents in France.

Besides placing a commemorative stamp on British culture, the war ultimately transformed the British health system, both military and civilian, hence the prominence of Florence Nightingale. Following the signing of the peace treaty, medical officers in London founded the Metropolitan Association of Medical Officers of Health (later known as the Society of Medical Officers of Health), whose purpose was "to promote the advancement of public health in every branch." Initially focused on general sanitation, the organization eventually targeted preventive medicine "by practical and theoretical study of all questions connected there-within" (Seaman, "Cholera," 93).

More generally, the Crimean War had a powerful impact on the British psyche. Death rates from disease, exposure, and malnourishment – the result of archaic British military logistics – were communicated to a highly literate audience by a new species of war correspondents sending rapid, regular, detailed, and largely uncensored dispatches.[19] William Russell's reports to *The Times* put human faces on Britain's soldiers, "and the public was never again able to unsee them" (Berridge, "Off the Chart," 9). Grounded in the inarguable facts of suffering and physical injury visited on the bodies of everyman soldiers, Russell's reporting "came to connote 'the real' for middle-class readers back in England, as a new narrative came to challenge a previous myth that had been central to national identity" (Teukolsky, "Novels," 37).

Before the war, the idea of military honour was associated with aristocracy. Gallantry and valour were attained by "high-born martial leaders" like the Duke of York, son of King George III and commander-in-chief of the British army against Napoleon, who stands on the column in Waterloo Place. The press reports on negligence by senior commanders tested traditional ideals of military heroism and accelerated a shift in public perceptions of the soldier, from aristocratic dandy to brave private. "The … Crimean War witnessed the rise in stature of the rank-and-file soldier. Construed as the "'scum of the earth' in Napoleonic times, this figure took hold of the nation's hearts during the Crimean conflict" (Kriegel, *The Crimean War*, 8). After the war, the stereotypical military man defending the nation's honour would be the "unknown soldier," the everyman with whom all could identify, like the anonymous guardsmen on the Crimean War Memorial on Waterloo Place. (It is not by chance that when Russia invaded Ukraine in February 2022, in an off-guard moment, British Defence Secretary Ben Wallace declared: "The Scots Guards kicked the backside of Tsar Nicholas I in 1853 in Crimea – we can always do it again"; in Brown, "We'll Kick Putin's Backside.")

On the Russian side during the Crimean campaign, memories of the victory over Napoleon in 1812 served as a central trope of the "invincible nation" (Maiorova, *From the Shadow of Empire*, 27). The myth of invincibility was sorely put to the test at Sebastopol. Whatever their position on the war, all the major Russian poets of the time composed poems during or after it: Fyodor Tyutchev ("The Black Sea"), Afanasy Fet ("The Sebastopol Brotherhood Cemetery"), Nikolai Nekrasov ("Silence"), Apollon Maykov ("To General-Lieutenant Khrulyov," "The war is over. A vile peace is signed …"), and so on. Having served as an officer in the Russian artillery in Crimea, in 1855 Leo Tolstoy published his three memorable *Sebastopol Sketches*, which record his experiences during the siege, scenes that later informed his novel *War and Peace*. In the *Sebastopol Sketches*, Tolstoy made it clear: the battle for Sebastopol had been a battle for Russia. Even as they present gruesome scenes of suffering, the sketches express above all pride and profound admiration for the city's tenacious defenders: "Long will Russia bear the imposing traces of this epic, a hero of which was the Russian people" (*Sebastopol Sketches*, 57). The epic defence of Sebastopol inspired national pride; the eventual Russian defeat there prompted soul-searching and ultimately provided the impetus for possibly the greatest social transformation in that country's history: the abolition of serfdom.[20] For it was Russia's loss in the Crimean War, largely a consequence of its antiquated conscription system and ill-prepared serfs, that determined Tsar Alexander's commitment to military and domestic reforms and to the Great Emancipation of 1861.[21] It was the defence, not the defeat of Sebastopol that entered into national myth. That defence, which lasted 349 days, earned Sebastopol its official designation as a "Hero City," a "City of Military Glory." Respectable men of reputation who had heard about the defence wished they had been there on the ramparts, and many claimed they had been: "If any memory from our military past could restore confidence in ourselves, it was assuredly the siege of Sebastopol" (quoted in Rambaud, "Les Russes à Sébastopol," 502). It is not by chance that the subject of the first feature-length film made in Russia was the *Defence of Sebastopol* by Vasili Goncharov, who tapped actual war veterans as consultants. On 26 October 1911, the film had its premier before Tsar Nicholas II at his summer palace in Crimea. Notwithstanding the historical reality of defeat, the collective memory of the siege was shaped by a narrative of heroism, steadfastness, and military glory.

It is telling that nearly a century after the Crimean War, when Nazi Germany bombed Sebastopol and laid siege to the city, it was Tolstoy – rather than any Soviet voice from the Revolution – whose words resonated. His writings produced a narrative that constituted the backbone of national identity. The "second great defence" against Nazi Germany was thus decisively linked to the "first great defence" of Sebastopol during the Crimean War (Qualls, "The Crimean War's Long Shadow," 3–5). Today in Sebastopol one can still visit the Panorama Museum of the Defence of Sebastopol 1854–1855, which houses a 115- by 14-metre panorama painted by Franz Roubaud to mark the fiftieth anniversary of the siege, and one can watch re-enactments of Crimean War battles at the military-themed Park of Living History, Fedyuchiny Heights.[22] In Julia Brown's words, Sebastopol is "a city of military defeats that have been recast as glory" ("Great Patriotic War Memory," 400). Yet if military glory there was at Sebastopol in 1855, it went to the French, who took the city after the deadly year-long siege. That story was, however, neither cast nor recast.

In 1954 the Soviet Union transferred Crimea to the Ukrainian Soviet Socialist Republic. The transfer was not without controversy. Writing in 2000, Serhii Plokhy asserted that "every 'strong man' in the Kremlin would exploit the issue of Sebastopol, thereby appealing to the nationalistically-oriented electorate" ("The City of Glory," 371–2). When in 1996 the status of Sebastopol was under discussion in the Russian parliament, Russian newspapers published an appeal to return the city to Russian control, signed by A.P. Nakhimov, G.V. Kornilov, and A.P. Istomin – three supposed descendants of Admirals Nakhimov, Kornilov, and Istomin, the celebrated commanders of the fleet and defenders of Sebastopol during the Crimean War. (It is noteworthy that Admiral Nakhimov was never married and had no children.) The invocation of those three names illustrates perhaps better than anything else the tenacious grip that Sebastopol and the Crimean War have in contemporary Russian myth-making (372).

The deep collective memory of the war was reactualized in March 2014 when Russia invaded, reclaimed, and annexed Crimea. The incursion was routinely referred to as the "third defence" of Sebastopol.[23] In his speech to the State Duma justifying the invasion, President Vladimir Putin made clear the link to the war in 1854: "Everything in Crimea speaks of our shared history and pride ... This is also Sevastopol – a legendary city with an outstanding history, a fortress that serves as the birthplace of Russia's Black Sea Fleet. Crimea is Balaklava and ... Malakhov Kurgan. Each one of these places is dear to our hearts, symbolising Russian military glory and outstanding valour ... Residents of Crimea and the city of Sevastopol, the whole of Russia admired your courage, dignity and bravery" ("Address," 2014).

The cornerstone of Russian claims to Crimea and Sebastopol is, indeed, the myth of Sebastopol as the city of Russian glory. Never mind the outcome – for President Putin the Crimean War of 1854 was a moral and religious victory. And indeed, despotic Tsar Nicholas I is one of Putin's heroes because he fought for Russia's interests against all the Great Powers; his portrait now hangs in the antechamber of the presidential office in the Kremlin (Figes, *Crimea*, 2014).

In short, in both Britain and Russia, this war generated major cultural and memorial significance that resonates to this day.

The same does not hold true in France, where the war was not emplotted in any national narrative and was quickly forgotten. Not suppressed, not censored, but forgotten, like a bag of bones. Already in May 1857, Alfred de Vigny, the French poet and former army officer, derided French indifference to a war that had concluded just one year earlier: "On n'y pense plus. ... Cent mille hommes perdus sont pour la France comme une coupe de cheveux" (People don't think about it anymore ... A hundred thousand men lost; for France it's like a haircut) (quoted in Sabourin, *Alfred de Vigny*, 683). Some years later the popular historian Firmin de Croze called it "cette grande expédition qui … passe assez inaperçue" (that great expedition … that passed quite unnoticed) (*Nos Zouaves*, 8). As playwright Jean Giraudoux might say, "La Guerre de Crimée n'aura pas lieu" (the Crimean War will not take place).[24] The official site of the French Ministry of Foreign Affairs, France Diplomatie, sums it up succinctly: "Guerre de Crimée, guerre oubliée" (Crimean War, forgotten war). If collective memory is based on selection and exclusion, on the separation of relevant from irrelevant memories, in France the Crimean War, all evidence to the contrary, belongs to the irrelevant.

Even for some historians of nineteenth-century France, the Crimean War is back-page news. For Alain Gouttman, a historian of the Second Empire, indifference to or ignorance of the Crimean War is almost a joke (*La Guerre de Crimée*, 5). In her preface to a special issue of *Revue d'histoire du XIXe siècle* on the cultural history of war in nineteenth-century France, editor Odile Roynette complains about the dearth of work by historians on the topic. It is true, she notes, that the trauma of the Great War of 1914–18, by virtue of its overwhelming impact, as well as the vast amount of source material, eclipsed all preceding nineteenth-century wars, including the Franco-Prussian War. By the same token, one understands that the trauma of the Franco-Prussian War eclipsed memories of the Crimean War. None of this, however, explains the silence surrounding this war prior to 1870. In the face of the relative silence of nineteenth-century scholars, Roynette insists, "Tout justifie … que l'on questionne le XIXe siècle en restituant à la guerre une place … plus conforme à celle qu'elle a réellement tenue dans la vie des Français" (Everything compels us … to revisit the nineteenth century by questioning the place of war … that conforms more to the place it occupied in the lives of Frenchmen) ("Pour une histoire culturelle," 12–13). Yet despite this call, in that same special issue on the cultural history of French wars in the nineteenth century there is not a single mention of Crimea. Even for French nineteenth-century cultural historians, it would seem, it is as if that war did not happen. Cultural memory – like personal memory – is clearly selective about the battles it picks.

Anne Rigney has described cultural memory as a "working memory" that is continuously performed by individuals and groups as they recollect the past selectively through various media ("Plenitude," 41). As retained in monuments, novels, paintings, and poems, cultural memory offers defences against oblivion. It has "fixed points" on its horizon: "fateful events of the past whose memory is maintained through a body of reusable texts [and] images … whose 'cultivation' serves to stabilise and convey that society's self-image" (J. Assmann, "Collective Memory," 129–32). But while cultural memory participates in the shaping of identity by *cultivating* specific events of the past, it does so only "by *forgetting* what lies outside the horizon of the relevant" (J. Assmann, "Communicative"; my emphasis). In the narratives of French collective identity, the Crimean War is clearly not one of those "fixed points" on the horizon. On the contrary, lying as it does outside the horizon of the "relevant," it has been largely forgotten.

Forgotten, but not gone. For just as there are active and passive forms of memory, there are active and passive forms of forgetting, what Paul Ricoeur calls "un oubli de réserve" (back-up forgetting) ("Memory," 414), what Anne Rigney describes as "forgetting by default" ("Toxic," 13). In this instance, the information has not been wilfully destroyed or silenced; rather, it exists in a state of latency or transitory forgetfulness. Simply put by philosopher Jeffrey Barash: "Each epoch chooses to remember in relation to its present preoccupations. Nonetheless, the forgetfulness that this involves does not invalidate the claim of historical understanding to retrieve the meaning of the past, for what is neglected in one epoch may be revived at a later time" (*Collective Memory*, 14). Aleida Assmann expresses the dynamic with an architectural metaphor: "What is lost, may be discovered by accident at a later time in attics and other obscure depots" ("Canon and Archive," 97–8). Or in excavations …

It is in such attics that we are obliged to rummage for lost traces of a Crimean War, passively stored in French cultural memory. And as this book demonstrates, there is no shortage of traces packed away. In the world of virtual space, we would say that the forgotten file is stored somewhere in the Cloud. Significant events may recede into the background and fade out of social awareness; others may be retrieved as needed from the dark attic and moved into the spotlight. Nevertheless, anthropologist Paul Connerton reminds us, "to say that something has been stored – in an archive, in a computer – is tantamount to saying that, though it is in principle always retrievable, we can afford to forget it" ("Seven Types of Forgetting," 65).

Contemporary circumstances can provide cues for retrieving images and information from the past. Such was the case in 2014 when the Crimean Peninsula suddenly reappeared on the cognitive horizon as Kremlin-backed Russian military forces seized control of it. Once again, Sebastopol and its strategic importance figured in the political headlines. And just as suddenly, memories of French participation in the Crimean War were downloaded so as to re-enter the French social imaginary. Articles appeared with titles like "Drôles de guerres de Crimée" ("Strange Crimean Wars") (Philippe Leymarie, *Le Monde diplomatique*,

6 March 2014) and "L'Autre guerre de Crimée" ("The Other Crimean War") (Davide Maria De Luca, *Courrier international*, 12 March 2014) and "Souvenir de la guerre de Crimée. Musée Clément Ader" ("Souvenir of the Crimean War: Clément Ader museum"). The latter drew the attention of readers in the Haute Garonne to two objects that Maréchal Niel, Napoleon III's Minister of War, had brought back from the Crimean War and that were on display in a regional museum in Muret (Évelyne Encoyand, *La Dépeche.fr*, 13 April 2014). But just as suddenly, as other world events crowded out the modern-day battle over Crimea in which France had no direct stake, memories of the nineteenth-century war that the French had fought and won receded back into the "oubli de réserve" and fell off the map. It remains unclear whether the Russian invasion of Ukraine in 2022 will have revived any of those passive French memories of Crimea.

Active and passive memory are for Aleida Assmann much like two distinct spaces in a museum. The main galleries display precious artefacts selected for the edification or education of visitors. The objects the museum displays are sustained by a fiction that they somehow constitute a coherent representational universe (Donato, *The Museum's Furnace*, 223). Pushed further, the museum operates as a vault of traditions and canons, a site of appreciative, unproblematic dialogues with the past that can in many instances serve to legitimate the state. This is the case with the collective memory of the Crimean War: a memory that Napoleon III carefully tried to curate in the form of public spectacles and commissioned artworks – works we will return to – but whose impact did not outlast his ambition.

Peripheral spaces, by contrast, like an attic, are crammed full of heterogeneous objects that do not form part of that coherent fiction, objects not on view: a place of remembered experience that has fallen into oblivion and no longer circulates in the reserve of collections and recollections – much like Maréchal Niel's atlas, housed at the Clément Ader museum in Muret. Assmann calls these latter spaces the "archive" – the passive reference memory of a society. The display in the museum, by contrast, represents the "canon," that is, the active working memory of a society that defines and supports the cultural identity of the group. It is made up of cultural messages that are addressed to posterity and includes works of art intended for continuous repetition and appreciation – works, for instance, such as the much memorized "Charge of the Light Brigade" – "*the things on Balaclava the kiddies at school recites*." The active memory of the canon, Assman explains, "perpetuates what a society has consciously selected and maintains as salient and vital for a common orientation and a shared remembering; its institutions are the literary and visual canon, the school curricula, the museum, and the stage" (Assman, "Reframing Memory," 43).

This is not to say there are no literary or artistic traces of the Crimean War in France, no material objects, no paintings, no poems, no plays. Indeed, much of this book is about the many texts and cultural artefacts that did *not* achieve canonical status and instead have remained boxed up in the archive, cultural objects that have become decontextualized from the frames that formerly determined their meaning. The messages have lost their immediate addressees as well as their direct meaning and function and do not circulate as common knowledge. In Aleida Assmann's words, the information "has not passed the filters of social selection nor is it transformed into a living memory supported by public awareness and validation by cultural institutions and the public media" ("Reframing Memory," 43–4). These works exist in a state of latency, waiting to be rediscovered as fragments of relevant information.

In short, while the cultural memory of the Crimean War has been actively circulating in the canon of British and Russian national identity, this has not been the case in France, where the war that was actively won on the battlefield was then passively lost in the archives. Like a dusty old reference book, it does not circulate as common knowledge.

After the fall of Sebastopol, Britain sent captured Russian cannons to cities throughout its empire to commemorate the victory and to honour those who had served. In my own country, they are spread across Ontario, Quebec, and the Maritime provinces. In "French Canada," there is one on the Quebec City ramparts, one in Montreal on the Place du Canada opposite the statue of Sir John A. Macdonald, Canada's first prime minister, and even one in the city of Trois-Rivières with the following inscription: "Victorieuse lors de la campagne de 'Crimée' (1854–1856), la Grande-Bretagne a voulu remercier les villes de son empire qui avaient participé à l'effort de guerre. Ainsi Trois-Rivières a reçu un canon enlevé à l'armée du Tsar" (Victorious in the Crimean campaign (1854–1856), Great Britain wished to thank the cities of its empire who participated in the war effort. Trois-Rivières has thus been honoured with a cannon taken from the Tsar's army) (*War Monuments in Canada*). In Halifax, the grand Sebastopol monument, also known as the Welsford-Parker Monument (1860), is a triumphal arch that commemorates the British victory in the Crimean War and two Nova Scotians who fought there.

Four Russian cannons were presented to Gibraltar in 1858, and two sit outside the parliament buildings in Georgetown, Guyana. Yet another is in Saint Peter Port, Guernsey, and has a plaque that reads: "Presented by Her Majesty's Government to the Island of Guernsey as a trophy of

1.6 The Sebastopol Monument, also known as the Welsford-Parker Monument, at the entrance to the Old Burying Ground in Halifax, Nova Scotia. Photo 84906489 © Jiawangkun/Dreamstime.com.

1.7 Monument to Maréchal Saint-Arnaud, Saint-Arnaud, Australia. Monument Australia (www.monumentaustralia.org.au).

the Russian War 1856," and so on. In France, no town or park or public square commemorates Jacques Leroy de Saint-Arnaud, the French general who led the French troops to victory at Alma, yet there are towns in both Australia and New Zealand named after him, as well as a range of mountains on New Zealand's South Island. In Australia, there is a monument to him in the town that bears his name.

In London, as noted, the Crimean War Memorial occupies pride of place down the street from the Duke of York Column in one of the city's principal squares. Towns and villages throughout Great Britain maintain imposing memorials to the local men who gave their lives in the Crimean War. A Russian cannon taken at Sebastopol that once topped the Crimean War Memorial in Cheltenham was given to the government during the Second World War to provide metal for armaments, but the memorial with its now phantom cannon still occupies a prominent place in that town's Imperial Square.[25] And the highly prized Victoria Cross – created by the queen to honour acts of valour during the Crimean War and bestowed by her on ordinary soldiers as well as officers – is said to still be made from the bronze of a captured cannon used by the Russians at Sebastopol.

If collective memory provides content for political commemoration and historical representation of the Crimean War, it is not evident in France, where there are no enduring mnemonic icons and where the cannons of Sebastopol occupy no equivalent spectacular place in the capital. To the extent that "Paris claims to stand for the whole of France" and that "the plethora of Parisian sites of public remembrance … [open] up a complex politics of memory in the capital," there is certainly no plethora of Parisian sites commemorating the Crimean War and the politics of memory about that war are not particularly complex (Benjamin, "Places and Spaces," 1). There the war was discreetly inscribed in the pavement of the Haussmann's Paris, where Sebastopol became the street sign on a new boulevard. It is deep in "la France profonde" that one has to go to find monuments to the French victory at Malakoff that ended the siege of Sebastopol: "Tours de Malakoff" such as one finds in Sivry-Courtry (Seine-et-Marne), Toury-Lurcy (Nièvre), Sermizelles (Yonne), and Saint-Amand-Montrond (Cher). There is also the Chocolat Malakoff,

1.8 Tour Malakoff, commune of Sermizelles. Patrick89, CC BY-SA 3.0, via Wikimedia Commons.

1.9 Chocolat Malakoff. Photo courtesy Malakoff & Cie.

To celebrate the French victory at Malakoff, Napoleon III asked the prize *chocolatier*, Jean-Louis Pupier, to create a sweet to commemorate the event. Pupier came up with a rectangular bar, wrapped in gold metallic paper with the date 1855 prominently displayed below the name Malakoff.

created in Lyon in 1855 at the request of Emperor Napoleon III to celebrate the victory. There is even a highly scented rose that was bred in 1857 named Tour de Malakoff.[26] In Paris, on the other hand, Malakoff figures as half of two hyphenated Métro station names: Malakoff–Rue Étienne Dolet and Malakoff–Plateau de Vanves.[27]

Thousands of Parisians walk down the Boulevard de Sébastopol every day, oblivious to the victory it commemorates that ended a costly war. Some of them take the Métro and get off at one of the Malakoff stops; others take the RER to the Pont de l'Alma. Perhaps some of the *flâneurs* among them will stumble upon a short, narrow, gated street called the Cité de l'Alma, so private as to go unnoticed. There is a Boulevard d'Inkermann on the edge of Paris in Neuilly. The Crimean War is invisibly inscribed in the rhythms and traffic patterns of modern Paris. Perhaps, after inspecting the site of the historic event most often associated with the Pont de l'Alma – the fatal car crash that killed Princess Diana in August 1997 – a *flâneur* will walk across the bridge to admire the 5-metre-high sculpture of the valiant Zouave soldier who stands on one of its pillars: he of legendary courage on the battlefields of Crimea.[28] The bridge was built between 1854 and 1856 by Napoleon III to commemorate the first battle of the Crimean War and was decorated with statues of French soldiers from different regiments on its four pillars. Of all the regiments – *zouaves, grenadiers, voltigeurs, chasseurs à pied, artilleurs* – it was the Algerian-born Zouaves in their exotic uniforms who captured the imagination. William Russell, war correspondent for *The Times*, declared the Zouaves "probably the most perfect soldiers in the world" (*Despatches*, 422). Even the Russians who were defeated at Alma could not hide their admiration for the prowess of the Zouaves, calling them "hearts of bronze" and "vampires of the shadows."[29] Once celebrated for his valour in Crimea, the Zouave on the bridge is now best known for serving as a measure of the water level of the Seine. During the great floods of 1910, the water reached his shoulder. Since then, Parisians measure rising water levels against his ankles, knees, and thighs.

Downgraded for service as he may be, he has, nevertheless, fared better than his colleagues who were on the three remaining pillars of the bridge, the *chasseur à pied*, the *grenadier*, and the *artilleur*, who were removed from the Pont de l'Alma and scattered around France when the bridge was widened in 1970. Today the *chasseur* occupies a spot on the side of the A4 autoroute coming into Paris, his story lost on the highway, if not in the archives.

The Zouave on the Pont de l'Alma has become something of the visual equivalent of General MacMahon's "J'y suis, j'y reste!" – shorthand for the vague memory of a war that happened not-sure-when,

1.10 The Zouave on the pillar of the Pont de l'Alma. Georges Diebolt, CC BY-SA 3.0, via Wikimedia Commons.

1.11 The Zouave on the Pont de l'Alma, submerged in water up to his thighs. Ibex73, CC BY-SA 4.0, via Wikimedia Commons.

1.12 The *chasseur à pied* on the Pont de l'Alma, 1910. Postcard. Author collection.

1.13 The *chasseur à pied* on Autoroute 4 heading into Paris. Image courtesy Denis Gradel.

not-sure-why, but clearly colourful. He has inspired popular songs, most notably "Le Zouave du pont de l'Alma" by Serge Reggiani, "Les Ricochets" by George Brassens, and "Ne pleure plus" by Thomas Fersen. Only the first of these songs references the war at all, as Octave le Zouave, quoting MacMahon, tells us of his fall from glory from Sebastopol into the dirty waters of the Seine:

> Je m'appelle Octave
> Et je fais le zouave
> Sur le pont de l'Alma …

On nous redoutait comme le feu, comme la peste
De Sébastopol à Magenta à Palestro
Comme Mac Mahon je suis parti: "J'y suis, J'y reste!"
Pour en arriver finalement à: "Que d'eau, que d'eau!" ...[30]

... Car j'ai de la flotte
Jusqu'à la culotte

(My name is Octave
And I am the Zouave
on the Pont de l'Alma.

We were as feared as fire, as feared as the plague
From Sebastopol to Magenta to Palestro
Like MacMahon I declared: Here I am, here I stay!
Only to end up sighing: So much water! Too much water!

... For now I've got water right up
To my underwear.)

To be sure, the Zouave who scaled the cliffs at Alma did enter the French collective imagination – not as a fearless fighter, though, but as "le zouzou," a water gauge under a bridge, stripped of his Crimean credentials in ways the guardsmen on the memorial in Waterloo Place could never be. Certainly not with British "Honour" and the statue of Florence Nightingale watching over them. As Ray Ventura and his Collégiens sang in their popular 1936 song, being the Zouave on the Pont de l'Alma is right up there with having scarlet fever, swallowing rat poison, and sucking mothballs.[31] In the end, the brave French Zouave of the Pont de l'Alma who was destined to carry the weight of memory now simply carries the weight of a bridge.

Bridges like Alma and physical monuments are forms of memory production designed to spectacularize and communicate moments of national significance in public space. But strategies of memorialization can, as we have seen, be short-lived. Whereas the Zouave whose wet feet signal an approaching flood is alive and well in the active canonical memory of the French – he is one of those objects society has consciously selected for a shared remembering – the Zouave who carried the French flag at Alma in September 1854 is sleeping in the archive. Both Zouaves inhabit the same statue on the same bridge, but monumental as he is, Crimea's "most perfect soldier in the world" did not make it into the gallery of public awareness. The nature of collective remembering is, as Magdalena Abel notes, restless (Abel and Roediger, "Collective Memory," 361).

If one has to look under a bridge to find the heroic Zouave of the Crimean War, looking for other traces of that war in French culture is a bit like looking for his military companions who disappeared overnight. Like those missing soldiers standing on a roadside, the traces, in all their diversity, have not disappeared. Collective memories are, in Wulf Kansteiner's apt metaphor "multi-media collages" ("Finding Meaning," 190). There are countless traces buried in the archives, various combinations of discursive, visual, and spatial elements: poems and stories, art and theatre, eloquent objects in storage like the remains of French soldiers that were unearthed in Ukraine. That is the paradox at the heart of this book, in which I identify many cultural markers of the Crimean War in France only to note their disappearance from memory. The Crimean War is clearly not a "lieu de mémoire" in French culture even though many are the "mémoires de lieu," like the Pont de l'Alma, that were meant to commemorate it.

In the chapters that follow we look to the "oubli de réserve" to examine the multimedia of memory that serve the constitution and continuation of cultural identity. And we consider the role aesthetic forms played in generating – or not – memorability. For this we now take our cue from the Roman poet, Horace, who declared the most lasting monuments to be made not out of bronze but words. With that in mind, we open the archive of French literature of the Crimean War.

Chapter Two

À la recherche de la guerre gagnée: Crimea, the Invisible War

Literature as part of cultural memory translates and transcends the other memory formats.

A. Assmann, "Four Formats of Memory"

As a scholar of nineteenth-century French literature I have spent a great deal of time hanging around the decade of the 1850s, the decade of Baudelaire, Flaubert, Gautier, the decade of Courbet, Degas, Manet, the decade of Haussmanization, the opening decade of Napoleon III's Second Empire with its garish tastes, enormous crinolines, and so much more. For a number of years I also participated in a one-day event in Paris, the annual Colloque des Invalides, a quirky, captivating conference at which scholars were given exactly five minutes to address the theme of the conference from an unexpected angle in an erudite and preferably witty way. In 2011 the theme of the conference was, in French, "Crime." In a moment of impulse I proposed a talk titled "Crime et Crimée" ("krimékrimé"), simply because I liked the play on words. I figured I would refer to the fact that first chapter of Hells Angels in France was located on the rue de Crimée in the 19th *arrondissement* of Paris; I imagined myself then weaving images of "anges d'enfer" throughout passages of Paris and French literature. I did not get very far. Beyond noting the address of the club, there wasn't a lot to say. I did learn though that there was a rival chapter, Hells Angels Malakoff, and thereby stumbled onto the fact that both locations referenced the Crimean War. This is how the Crimean War in France first entered my consciousness, down a twisting path whose circuitousness I now see was not accidental.

I quickly realized that I knew virtually nothing about the Crimean War, short of "The Charge of the Light Brigade," Florence Nightingale, and the *Sebastopol Sketches*. I didn't know, for instance, that the French, with triple the number of troops the British sent over, had played a central role in the war, and that the French had lost almost as many men as the British had sent over in total. I was startled and embarrassed by my ignorance of an important war that fell square in the middle of "my decade." This was a major gap – and gaffe – in my knowledge. How could I, who spent my time reading French works written or published in the 1850s, have missed a three-year war the French had fought and won? After a certain amount of self-shaming, I returned to the same question, this time less rhetorically. How indeed did I miss a war? The truth was that this war did not feature in any of the works I was reading. I could not in fact think of a single work of French literature that referred to the Crimean War. In other words, it was not that I had overlooked the Crimean War in my reading – it wasn't *there* in all that I had read. I went back to the correspondence of "my authors" of the 1850s to see if the war figured in their private conversations. And that's when I stumbled across a letter from Flaubert that I had read before, the letter of 17 September 1855 addressed to his friend Louis Bouilhet in which he announces his plan to poison the heroine of his novel, Emma Bovary, in about a month: "J'espère que dans un mois la *Bovary* aura son arsenic dans le ventre. Te l'apporterai-je enterrée? J'en doute" (I hope to have the arsenic in Miss Bovary's stomach in a month. Will she be buried by the time I bring her to you? I doubt it) (Flaubert, *Correspondance*, 30–1). The letter goes on to discuss Flaubert's and Bouilhet's literary ambitions. And then I came to the final paragraph, which opens with "J'ai appris avec enthousiasme la prise de Sébastopol" (I was delighted to hear about the taking of Sebastopol). There it was: the Crimean War, nine days after the defeat of the Russians at Sebastopol, buried in the archives of a letter from Flaubert writing about one of the most canonical novels in French literature. It is to just such archives of *oubli* that we have to go to retrieve the memory of the Crimean War. For just as the cannons of Sebastopol did not find a place in public squares in France, neither did they find it in the canon of French literature.

There are, of course, works of French literature that reference the Crimean War. But scouring the fiction, theatre, and poetry of the time, one is hard pressed to find, for instance, literary characters of consequence associated with it. When looking for such characters, aside from brief references to the occasional veteran or *bonne soeur*, one always comes back to Moutier, the dedicated French soldier, and Dourakine, the colourful Russian general, veterans of the Crimean campaign in two bestselling children's novels of 1863 by the comtesse de Ségur, *L'Auberge de l'ange gardien* and *Le Général Dourakine.* The countess was born Sophie Rostopchine, daughter of Count Fyodor Rostopchin, who had been governor of Moscow in 1812 during the invasion by Napoleon's army. In 1817 the family went into exile in France, where Sophie converted from Orthodoxy to Roman Catholicism. Her Russo-French persona embodied many of the contradictions and ironies of the Crimean War itself. Moutier, the principal character in *L'Auberge de l'ange gardien* (*The Inn of the Guardian Angel*), is a kind and brave French soldier who saves the life of the Russian General Dourakine on the battlefield in Crimea. In return, the wealthy Russian general helps the impoverished but heroic French soldier marry a young French innkeeper whose bookshelf contains "*Imitation de Jésus-Christ, Nouveau Testament, Parfait Cuisinier, Manuel des ménagères*" (*The Imitation of Christ, The New Testament, The Perfect Cook, The Housewife's Manu*). Moutier notes with pleasure: "Voilà des livres que j'aime à voir chez une bonne femme de ménage!'" (These are the kind of books I like to see in a good homemaker's house) (50). In these novels, Christian charity and good housekeeping triumph over nationalism and military victory. As in the case of Notre Dame de France, the giant Virgin of Puy cast from 231 seized Russian canons, the Crimean War is transformed into a story of Catholic triumph.

If literature plays a central role in the construction of cultural memory, in the case of the Crimean War its absence from canonical literature played a role in its disappearance. Yuval Harari contends that literature is what enables us to imagine things collectively. In Britain it took only a single poem, "The Charge of the Light Brigade" by Alfred Lord Tennyson, to inscribe it indelibly (*Sapiens*, ch. 2). The Tsarina of Russia herself cried when she read Tolstoy's account of the war in *Sebastopol Sketches*. Where do we go to find the Crimean War in French literature?

References to the war in the canonical prose literature from the late 1850s onward are, to be sure, slim. As a young man, Émile Zola witnessed the deployment of French soldiers to Crimea. In *Nouveaux contes à Ninon* (1874), he recounts his adolescent excitement at seeing French soldiers passing through his town on their way to Crimea: "Mais je me souviens mieux encore de l'autre guerre, de la campagne de Crimée [...] La petite ville du Midi que j'habitais fut, je crois, traversée par presque tous les soldats qui allèrent en Orient [...] Ah! les beaux hommes! et les cuirassiers, et les lanciers, et les dragons, et les hussards! Nous avions un faible pour les cuirassiers" (But I remember that other war even better, the Crimean campaign ... Almost all the soldiers going east to the front, I think, passed through the little town in the Midi where I lived ... Ah! The handsome men! The cuirassiers, the lancers, the hussars! We especially liked the cuirassiers).

The dazzle gives way to the realities of war as the mature Zola recognizes that the festive march past he admired as a young man was in fact, a death march. For those who limped back, there were no excited adolescents cheering them on: "Un jour on les vit repasser en sens inverse, éclopés, saignants, se traînant sur les routes. Ce n'étaient plus nos beaux soldats. Ils ne valaient pas le moindre pensum" (Then one day, we saw them coming back in the opposite direction, crippled, bleeding, crawling along the route. These were no longer our handsome soldiers. They were hardly worth a thought) (207).

Zola's poignant memories notwithstanding, in his twenty-volume saga of the Second Empire, *Les Rougon-Macquart,* there are only the briefest of brief passing allusions to the war. The most "extended" is a reference in *La Curée* (1872) that speaks to the indifference of Parisian speculators – "Les mois s'écoulèrent, la guerre de Crimée venait d'être declarée. Paris, qu'une guerre lointaine n'émouvait pas, se jetait avec plus d'emportement dans la spéculation et les filles" (Months passed, the Crimean War had just been declared. Paris, unmoved by a faraway war, was enthusiastically carried away with real estate speculation and beautiful women). In another reference in *Le Ventre de Paris* (1873), Gavard the poulterer denounces the Crimean War as that "expédition aventureuse," "faite uniquement pour consolider le trône et emplir certaines poches" (An adventurous campaign … designed only to consolidate the Emperor's throne and to line certain pockets) (Zola, *La Curée,* 97; *Le Ventre de Paris,* 128).

Similarly, in her memoir, *Souvenirs d'une petite fille,* the novelist "Gyp" (Sibylle Riquetti de Mirabeau) recalls in detail her childhood fascination with the Crimean War. She complains to her grandfather that she needs more Crimean toy soldiers. "Grand-père, j'ai pas assez de zouaves ... donnez-m'en pour finir la guerre" (Grandpa, I don't have enough zouaves… give me some so I can finish the war):

> … j'écoute les conversations des vieux officiers de la grande armée … Ils parlent de l'expédition de Crimée, qui dure depuis si longtemps; du choléra qui décime l'armée ... Canrobert a lui-même planté le drapeau sur la plage au débarquement. J'ai, depuis que j'entends raconter ça, l'idée fixe de voir Canrobert. Je rêve de lui, je me l'imagine aussi beau que mon empereur sur son cheval blanc.
>
> (I listen to the conversations of old army officers … They talk about the campaign in Crimea that has dragged on for so long; about the cholera that is decimating the army ... Canrobert himself planted the flag on the landing beach. I've been obsessed with the idea of seeing Canrobert ever

since I heard that story. I dream about him, I picture him as handsome as my emperor on his white horse.) (Gyp, *Souvenirs*, 47–8)

But neither dreamy Canrobert nor the war will figure in her fiction.

Elsewhere in French literature references to the Crimean War are just as fleeting. In Alexandre Dumas's *Bric-à-brac* (1861), the last heroic act of a harbour master is to save a cargo of wine destined for the soldiers in Crimea from a sinking ship. In Edmond About's society novel *Maître Pierre* (1858) an irritated gentleman complains: "On disait … que la jeunesse s'ennuyait, et qu'il lui fallait une guerre. On leur en a donné, de la guerre, et de la bonne encore! Combien y en a-t-il qui aient eu la curiosité de voyager en Crimée?" (They said that young people were bored, that they needed a war. So we gave them one, a good war at that. But how many had the curiosity to travel to Crimea?) (211). The Crimean War figures again in About's *Le Mari Imprévu* (1863), in which a young, profligate aristocrat is threatened with being sent to Crimea. In "L'Agonie de la Sémillante" by Alphonse Daudet, first published in 1866 and based on a true story, 600 troops on their way to Crimea are not so lucky: they die eerily in the shipwreck of "La Sémillante." In George Sand's *Césarine Dietrich* (1871), Madame Feron, a lace-mender, receives a small pension as the widow of a non-commissioned officer killed in Crimea. A secondary character in Zola's *L'Assommoir* (1877), le Père Bru, lost his three sons in the Crimean War. A nun in Maupassant's tale "Boule de Suif" (1880) announces that her "speciality" is treating soldiers wounded at the front. "Elle avait été en Crimée, en Italie, en Autriche ... " (She had served in Crimea, Italy, Austria …). In *Chérie* by Edmond de Goncourt (1884), the father of the heroine is fatally wounded in the taking of the Malakoff Tower. The Crimean War is central to the plot of *Le Sergent Renaud* (1898), a popular novel in the *Aventures parisiennes* series by Pierre Sales. Here the marquis Jean de Villepreux, who is hiding his aristocratic identity, falls in love with a poor orphaned linen maid whose father, he learns, Sergent Renaud, was the man who died protecting him during the assault on the Mamelon Vert. In *Pour Cause de bail* (1899) by the humourist Alphonse Allais, two veterans at the Hôtel des Invalides, one an amputee from the Crimean War, the other an amputee from the war in Italy, argue about the relative superiority of "their" wars. The list of minor Crimeania goes on.

Already in 1857, the war was fair game for satire. In Henri Monnier's spoof of bourgeois manners *Mémoires de M. Joseph Prudhomme* (1857), the Crimean War is placed on equal footing with the latest theatre reviews: "Les amis de la maison sont venus; il faut ranimer le whist et la conversation qui languissent. De quoi va-t-on causer? De l'Opéra, du Vaudeville, de la question d'Orient? Mademoiselle Cravelli était-elle en voix hier? – Grassot est-il amusant dans son dernier rôle? A-t-on des nouvelles de Sébastopol?" (Some friends came over. We had to liven things up; the whist and the conversation had petered out. What should we talk about? The Opera, Vaudeville, the Crimean question? Was Mademoiselle Cravelli in good voice yesterday? Is Grassot funny in his latest role? Any news from Sebastopol?) (vol. 1, 59).[1]

A soprano, a comic actor, and bulletins from the war provide topics for light banter. In volume 2 of the *Mémoires*, the main character, Joseph Prudhomme, a man of neither conviction nor competence, is selected as editor of the newspaper *Le Progressif.* The following day a journalist comes to see him requesting an increase in pay because he had to spend 500 francs of his own money to buy books about military strategy in order to report on the operations of the war: "Le siège de Sébastopol m'a ruiné" (The siege of Sebastopol left me broke) (vol. 2, 259).

In subsequent decades there were novels that occasionally referenced the war, but most often it served as a pretext or context for the plot. In Jules Verne's 1872 novel *Aventures de trois Russes et de trois Anglais dans L'Afrique australe* (*The Adventures of Three Russians and Three Englishmen in South Africa*) the Crimean War serves as a distant backdrop and occasion for an ethical dilemma for three English and three Russian astronomers on a joint mission to measure the arc of a meridian in the Kalahari Desert. Despite a bitter rivalry between the leaders of each team, for the most part things go well, that is, until the six men arrive at a missionary station, where they find some dated European newspapers. Colonel Everest, leader of the English team, picks up a copy of the *Daily News* dated 13 May 1854. His hands start to tremble. "Gentlemen," he announces, "war has been declared between England and Russia": "Les dernières paroles du colonel Everest produisirent l'effet d'un coup de foudre … Ce n'étaient plus des compagnons, des collègues, des savants unis pour l'accomplissement d'une œuvre scientifique, c'étaient des ennemis qui déjà se mesuraient du regard, tant ces duels de nation à nation ont d'influence sur le cœur des hommes!" (Colonel Everest's last words left the men thunderstruck … They were no longer friends, colleagues, scholars united in a scientific project, they were enemies who already started sizing each other up. Such are the duels between nations that transform the hearts of men) (161).

As the scientists proceed on their mission, they wonder about this war that has suddenly redefined their personal, if not their scientific, relationship. The novel ends with the men arriving in a large town where the British consul informs them that Sebastopol is still under siege by the French and British. The war is not over. While they prepare to board the ship that will take them to Suez, Colonel Everest addresses the men as his Russian counterpart, Mathieu Strux, listens. They have lived together and worked together as friends on a project of great interest to the scientific community of Europe, but, he continues, as the war is not over, they must still consider each other enemies.

The novel ends with the British and the Russians parting as friends. A British scientist turns to his Russian friend and asks: "'Toujours amis, Michel?' – 'Oui, mon cher William, toujours et quand même!'" ("Friends always, Michel?" – "Yes, my dear William, always, whatever happens!") (202).

The Crimean War provides an important plot twist for Verne's *Aventures*. That said, the narrative clearly is not about that war, which is presented as a war between England and Russia. No specifics are given about it aside from the very few general references to the siege at Sebastopol. In fact, references to the war occupy a scant five pages of the 200-page novel. The rest is devoted in great detail to "l'Afrique australe" and to the scientific and interpersonal challenges the astronomers face on their joint mission. The ethical dilemma that enters the novel midway could have been generated by any political upheaval that pitted colleagues from two countries against each other. Verne's purpose is to reinforce the superiority of the universal bonds of science and intellectual curiosity that bring men together over the artificial bonds of nationalism that divide them. It is telling that Verne chose to single out British scientists as the foil to the Russians; there is scarcely a mention of the French.

The novel *La Colonne* (1901) by Lucien Descaves, a prolific journalist and novelist as well as a founder and one-time president of the Académie Goncourt, although not a novel about Crimea, contains perhaps the most detailed and precise references to the war, which, as in the case of Verne's novel, provides a background for the action. The novel is set at the time of the Paris Commune of 1871, and the column in question is the Vendôme column, erected in 1810 by Napoleon to commemorate the French victory at Austerlitz and toppled during the Commune.[2] At the start of the novel, Republican Communards have just issued a call for the demolition of the column, "un monument de barbarie, un symbole de force brute et de fausse gloire … une affirmation de militarisme" (a monument of barbarism, a symbol of brute force and false glory … a statement of militarism) (3). Thimothée Prophète, the central character of the novel, is a patriotic veteran of the Crimean War, where he lost his hand in the battle for Sebastopol. He lives at the Hôtel des Invalides with other veterans of Crimea, whom he rallies to protect the column. Prophète's ideological counterpart in the novel is a committed antimilitarist and Communard, the natural father of Prophète's great-nephew, Adrien, for whom they are rival father figures. Young Adrien is enthralled with his great-uncle's stories of the Crimean War. Midway through the novel, Prophète shares with him in twelve pages of painstaking detail the events of a war that was more often waged against deadly illnesses and harsh elements rather than enemy soldiers. Adrien's response echoes the frustrations of Fabrice del Dongo in Stendhal's *Chartreuse de Parme*, who, raised on etchings of Napoleonic battles, is disappointed by chaos on the fields of Waterloo and keeps asking, "Is this a *real battle*?" Descaves's exasperated child, wanting to hear about heroic combat, similarly punctuates his uncle's tale throughout with the question "Et l'ennemi?":

> Et l'oncle commence: – Apprends donc, … que nous avons enduré, cette année-là, en l'espace de cinq mois, les plus grands supplices auxquels la chaleur et le froid puissent condamner des hommes … Vers le milieu de juillet, les premiers cas de choléra se déclarèrent et aussitôt tout changea de face …
>
> – Et l'ennemi? répéta Adrien, tenace, trop gâté par son oncle de batailles véritables, pour se contenter … de luttes contre les éléments […]
>
> – J'aime mieux quand c'est les Russes qui vous font du mal.

> (The uncle began: "Listen then … that year we endured in the space of five months the most harrowing extremes of heat and cold imaginable … Then in the middle of July, the first cases of cholera appeared and suddenly everything changed …"
>
> "And the enemy?," Adrien insisted, too spoiled by his uncle's stories of *real battles* to be happy with … battles against the elements …
>
> "I like it better when it's the Russians who make you suffer.") (165)

The unprecedented extremes of weather and the outbreak of cholera during the Crimean War were indeed more deadly than Russian bullets. Fourteen years after the war's end, another veteran in the novel rebukes a young man for his ignorance:

> – … aurais-tu déjà oublié cette guerre de Crimée qui a coûté près de 800.000 hommes à l'Europe? Mais comptons nos morts seulement: 95.000. Apprends donc, puisque tu parais l'ignorer, que si 20,000 hommes ont péri sur le coup ou des suites de leurs blessures, le reste a été la proie des fièvres, du choléra qui frappait surtout les jeunes, du scorbut plus funeste aux vieux, et du typhus qui, moins exclusif, ne choisissait pas ses victimes. Mais oui, 75.000 de tes camarades sont morts de maladie, mort sans gloire,

dans la boue, l'ordure, le vomissement et l'infection; morts sans avoir vu les Russes …

(Have you already forgotten that the Crimean War cost Europe close to 800,000 men? Let's just count our own dead: 95,000. Listen up since you know so little: if 20,000 men perished at the front or from the injuries they sustained, the rest died of fever, of cholera that was particularly deadly for the young, of scurvy that was deadly for the older soldiers, and of typhus, that did not discriminate among its victims. Yes, damn it. 75,000 of your comrades died of illness, a death without glory, in the mud, in the filth, in vomit and infections; dead without having seen any Russians …) (150–1)

It would seem that in the long run the French public, like young Adrien, was not stirred by stories of a military campaign that was short on "real battles" and that did not conform to narrative conventions of war. What kind of war was this? The image of soldiers freezing in trenches, vomiting and dying of infection, did not square with images of heroes on horseback attacking uniformed enemies armed with rifles and bayonets.

The British story of the Crimean War was built around just such an image: the famous Charge of the Light Brigade, in which 600 brave cavalrymen advanced directly into enemy fire on the senseless command of an incompetent officer. French General Bosquet, who observed the charge, described it as magnificent but mad: "C'est magnifique, mais ce n'est pas la guerre: c'est de la folie." The Charge of the Light Brigade was a hideous, reckless "blunder," yet it was elevated to a story of wartime courage and sacrifice, moving "beyond concerns of rights and wrongs and responsibilities to higher realms of dedication and devotion to duty" (Dereli, *A War Culture*, 91). Tennyson immortalized it, and Disraeli called it "a feat of chivalry, fiery with consummate courage, and bright with flashing valour." The emphasis was not on blame or mismanagement, but on bravery of epic dimensions that could ultimately be translated into a heroic image for the nation. National memory, Aleida Assmann reminds us, is receptive to historical moments of triumph and defeat "provided they can be integrated into the semantics of a heroic narrative" ("Four Formats of Memory," 28). By contrast, in French fiction and poetry that heroic narrative was absent, even as poets strained to echo the epic grandeur of Homer.

Young Adrien craved just such a story of "real battles," a heroic story much like the one that Gustave Marchal would offer in his illustrated *Guerre de Crimée* (1888), a book that was produced to raise the spirits and "rebuild the confidence" of children in the wake of the disastrous

Franco-Prussian War. As Ann Rigney notes, memory cultures until the First World War strongly emphasized triumphs and victories as well as the heroic individuals deemed responsible for them ("Remembrance," 244). Not until sixty years later would images of soldiers dying without glory in trenches constitute the narrative rhetoric of war. In *La Colonne,* Descaves's description of the gruesome material realities of the Crimean War far exceeds anything else one can find in French novels. The campaign is presented in all its gory detail with an eye to reinforcing the antimilitaristic message that runs through many of Descaves's novels: there is nothing glorious about war, least of all the Crimean War.[3]

For all the enthusiasm French soldiers may have expressed on their departure for the war, the memoirs and letters they later wrote are filled with the sadness and disenchantment Descaves invokes. Artillery officer J.B. Bedarrides describes in his journal the creeping disillusionment of the soldiers as they resign themselves to the bitter realities of the siege of Sebastopol in November 1854:

> Déjà la vie de bivouac décolorait de tout ce qui en fait le charme et le prix ... Il fallait dire adieu aux promesses et à la gloire, au brillant soleil des batailles, renoncer à l'espoir d'un retour prochain au pays. Les tueries ténébreuses du siège, au milieu des frimas de la Russie, ne séduisaient même pas les plus chevaleresques. Sans doute, la guerre a sa poésie et sa beauté, quand on se bat, comme nos pères ... Mais nous, soldats ...jetés sur le désert de la Chersonèse, nous devions ... voir couler le sang sans cesse et avec indifférence, peut-être mourir du choléra au camp, et, à la tranchée, mourir broyés par une bombe. En face de cet horizon, l'armée d'Orient se résigna, et cette résignation l'honore plus que ses victoires.
>
> (Life in the bivouac quickly lost its charm and appeal ... Farewell to the promise of glory, to the brilliant sunshine of battle, to all hopes of a speedy return home. The darkness of death in a frozen Russian siege could not seduce even the most romantic warrior. War, when it is fought the way our fathers did, has its own kind of poetry and beauty ... As for us ... thrust into the desert of Chersonese ... we had to watch indifferent as blood flowed endlessly, perhaps we would die of cholera in the camp, or in a trench, crushed by a bomb. The army in Crimea resigned itself in the face of these circumstances. That resignation of the army is a greater tribute to its honour than its victories.) (*Journal,* vol. 2, 3–4)

Bedarride's journal belongs to a class of letters and memoirs of the Crimean War that were published well after the war. In other non-fiction genres – independent of the specialized books on military tactics and engineering – there was no shortage of books in the 1850s. Books such as *Histoire des causes de la guerre d'Orient d'après les documents français et anglais* (*The History of the Causes of the Eastern War Based on French and English Documents*) by Eugène Forcade (1854); *La Guerre d'Orient. Pourquoi la guerre aux Cosaques?* (*The Eastern War: Why Wage War against the Cossacks?*) by Émile Jaeglé (1854); *Comment finira la guerre. Exposé de la question d'Orient dégagé de tous les faux bruits et envisagé sous son véritable jour* (*How the War Will End: A True Exposé about the Eastern Question, Distinct from All the Fake News*) by E.-Ch. Bourseul (1854); *Mensonges et réalités de la Guerre d'orient* (*Lies and Truth about the Eastern War*) by Victor Joly (1855); and the anonymous *La Comète et le croissant. Présages et prophéties relatifs à la question d'Orient, par un astrologue contemporain* (*The Comet and the Crescent: Omens and Prophecies relating to the Eastern Question by a Contemporary Astrologist*) (1854).

Writing in Alexandre Dumas's journal *Le Mousquetaire*, Alfred Asseline was complaining already in July 1854 about the glut of books on the Crimean War that had so quickly taken the place of literature on French bookstore shelves:

> Depuis six mois que voyez-vous à toutes les vitres? Rien que des mémoires sur la guerre contre la Russie. La librairie a exploité la question d'Orient et n'a fait que cela; et quel acharnement sans exemple, et quelle littérature ennuyeuse! Je ne sais pas si le public a digéré tout cela, mais je crois qu'il aurait préféré le moindre petit livre écrit en français, imprimé en caractères neuf sur papier blanc, et digne de figurer sur son meilleur rayon.
>
> (For the past six months what do you see in bookstore windows? Nothing but memoirs about the war against Russia. The bookstores are milking the Eastern question – and nothing but the Eastern question – for all it's worth. And what boring reading! I have no idea if the public has digested all of this, but I am sure it would have preferred any other little book written in French, freshly printed on white paper and worthy of the best display.) (2)[4]

Predictably, after the war such books were removed from the shelves as quickly as they had appeared, to make space for military memoirs such as those by Bédarrides, as well as military tales such as those by ex-army officers: Félix Maynard's *Souvenirs d'un Zouave devant Sebastopol* (1855), Charles Bocher's *Lettres de Crimée, Souvenirs de guerre* (1877), and Charles Rabourdin's *Contes du bivouac* (1881) and *Nouveaux Contes du bivouac* (1888).

As for French poetry of the Crimean War, one has to dig deep in the attic to find it. Alfred de Vigny, the philosophical poet, ex-military officer, and member of the Académie Française, complained in 1857 that the French public had already forgotten the war: "La Guerre d'Orient a été en France comme un duel. L'affaire est arrangée. On n'y pense plus" (In France, the Eastern war was like a duel. It's all done. No one thinks about it any more) (quoted in Sabourin, 683). Nevertheless, although he did not forget the war he did not commemorate it in prose or poetry either. His 1863 poem "Wanda, Histoire russe," in *Les Destinées,* is about the brutality of the tsar, who has sent Russian Princess Wanda's husband to Siberia and turned the family into virtual slaves. Ten years after the family's exile, Wanda writes from Siberia shortly after the fall of Sebastopol. In the poem's final lines she speaks of the French victory as God's vengeance on the tsar. Vigny in *Les Destinées* invokes the familiar trope of the French as agents of God's will. The "Dieu du ciel" is served by the French eagle, who acts as divine intercessor:[5]

> Sébastopol détruit n'est plus. – L'aigle de France
> L'a rasé de la terre, et le Czar étonné
> Est mort de rage. – On dit que la balance immense
> Du Seigneur a paru quand la foudre a tonné.
> – La sainte la tenait flottante dans l'espace.
> L'épouse, la martyre a peut-être fait grâce,
> Dieu du ciel! – Mais la mère a-t-elle pardonné?
>
> (Sebastopol, destroyed, is no longer. – The French eagle
> Razed it to the ground, and the Tsar dumbfounded
> Died of rage. – They say that the great scales of the Lord
> Appeared with thunder and lightning.
> – A saint, floating in space held them in her hand.
> God of heaven! The wife, the martyr perhaps showed grace,
> – But the mother how could she forgive?) (163–4)

Despite the allusion to the fall of Sebastopol, this is above all a poem about state-sanctioned cruelty, tyranny, and a mother's pain, not Crimea.

Charles Rabourdin, a lesser-known author, wrote stories of the war (*Contes du bivouac, Nouveaux contes du bivouac*) as well as a lengthy poem in homage to his brothers-in-arms, *Le Siège de Sébastopol, poème en six chants* (*The Siege of Sebastopol: A Poem in Six Cantos*). The result was not brilliant. The author lamented in his preface that he could not overcome the challenge of adequately capturing history in verse, and he regretted not being able to throw in a few gods and goddesses to produce a true epic. The large number of names with foreign endings generated unfortunate rhymes to go along with names such as Kornilof, Nakimof, Tchernaïa, Zagorodnaïa, and so on. As one laconic critic noted: "Cependant, impossible de les éviter dans un 'Siège de Sébastopol' … Peut-être l'auteur l'aurait-il rendu plus vivant en l'affranchissant des entraves de la versification" (However, it's impossible to avoid such names in a "Siege of Sebastopol" … Maybe the poem would have been more lively if the author had freed himself from the shackles of rhyme).[6] Joseph Autran, a Catholic poet from Marseille, elected to the Académie française in 1868, though hardly a supporter of Napoleon III, waxed proud in his poems on the Crimean War and elegiac in a poem on the death of General de Ponthèves during the attack on Sebastopol:

Ton âme en son espoir n'a pas été trompée
Soldat mort en baisant la croix de ton épée,
Mort pour la France et pour la foi.

(Your hopeful soul was not deceived,
Soldier. You died kissing the cross of your sword.
You died for France and for faith.)

(in Lénient, *La Poésie patriotique,* 372)

However successful Autran may have been during his lifetime, it was not for his poems on the Crimean War but rather for his Catholic fervour.

Then there is the seventy-five-page poem by L. Touillon, author of military poetry dedicated to the French army in the Crimea, *La Chute de Sébastopol.* The sixteenth and final canto is addressed to "Orgueilleuse Russie" ("Proud Russia") and ends with images of shameless Russian tyranny and Siberian mines (77).

Surely the French voice of the Crimean War cannot belong to the father of French Canadian poetry, Octave Crémazie, and the forgettable verses he composed in 1855, "Sur les ruines de Sébastopol":

Peuples, inclinez-vous, c'est la France qui passe!
Du despote du Nord tu réprimes l'audace …
Aux murs Malakoff, c'est encore ta bannière
Que le Russe vaincu vit flotter la première …
Sous le ciel canadien nous redisons ta gloire.

(People, bow down. Here comes France!
You have slashed the Northern despot's daring …
Your flag waving on the walls of Malakoff

Is the first thing that Russia, defeated, observed …
Under Canadian skies, we sing your glory.)

(Crémazie, *Œuvres*, vol. 1, 288–95)[7]

To be fair, patriotic Canadians aside, in the face of the heroic exploits of its soldiers in Crimea, French writers of poetry were not indifferent. Some, though admired and well-known, are (and were) not known for their poems on the war or its triumph. To quote Charles Lenient, author of *La Poésie patriotique en France*, "la Muse nationale … était restée à peu près muette, indifférente à nos victoires de Crimée" (The national Muse of France … remained pretty much silent, indifferent to our victories in Crimea) (393).

Though overtly hostile to Napoleon III's empire, the much read but now largely forgotten Parnassian poet of the Académie Française, Victor de Laprade, rose to the national and Catholic glory of the Crimean War with his poem "L'Hymne à l'Épée" ("Hymn to the Sword"):

Fils des Francs, aimons notre Épée,
Son acier nous va mieux que l'or,
Et Dieu, qui l'a si bien trempée,
Veut par nous s'en servir encor.
[…]

Mais toi, France, …
Ta croisade n'est pas fermée;
Sois toujours la parole armée,
Et frappe en criant: *Dieu le veut!*

(Sons of the Francs, let us cherish our Sword,
Its steel is more precious than gold,
And God, who baptised it
Wants us to use it once more.
[…]

But you, France, …
Your crusade is not over,
Yours will always be the mighty word
That attacks and cries out: *God's will be done!*")

(*Oeuvres poétiques*, 119–24)

Once again, the war is justified here in religious rather than political terms, as a crusade for the Holy Land. For these authors, the Crimean

War was not just a test of might, it was a test of faith. Better-known to modern readers, in part thanks to the article dedicated to him by Charles Baudelaire, is Pierre Dupont, the popular socialist poet and *chansonnier* of the people, who composed patriotic poems and songs such as "La Nouvelle Alliance" (1854), which celebrated the new solidarity between France and England:

… Cette fois, sur mer et sur terre
Les Cosaques nous les tenons!
La France est avec l'Angleterre
Le droit est avec nos canons.

(This time, on the sea and the land
The Cossacks are in our hands
France is with England
And justice is with our canons.)

(*Chants*, vol. 3, 220)

In 1855, he composed "Le Siège de Sébastopol":

… Dans ces lamentables batailles,
Quel mutuel acharnement!
Les Russes comme des murailles
Résistaient au bombardement.
Les zouaves comme des chèvres
Escaladaient les défilés …

(... In these terrible battles
What relentlessness on both sides!
The Russians resisted the bombardments
Like fortified walls.
And the zouaves like mountain goats
Scaled them...)

(*Chants guerriers*, 303)

And then, on the occasion of "La Prise de Sébastopol, 8 septembre 1855," a song of triumph:

… En plein midi, le clairon sonne;
A l'assaut! et que chacun donne!
Les morts aplanissent le sol:
Nos soldats sont comme une trombe;

La tour de Malakoff succombe,
Et nous avons Sébastopol!

Victoire!

(At the height of noon, the trumpet sounds:
Begin the assault! Each man to his post!
The dead cover the ground;
Our soldiers advance like floodwaters,
The Malakoff tower is overrun
And Sebastopol is ours!

Victory!)

(*Chants guerriers*, 323)

Rousing as they were, Dupont's Crimean poems do not figure prominently in his corpus. And however popular they were, as with most topical songs, their impact was short-lived.

For the most part, though numerous, the poets writing about the Crimean War were poets neither by profession nor by reputation. Even so, they composed a significant body of patriotic poetry that fed France's Crimean War effort. Many wrote songs and poems on specific battles or significant moments in the war. The lengthy poem "L'Ovation" by C. Lys, for instance, recalls the memorable entry into Paris of the troops returning from Crimea on 29 December 1855:

Hourra! vivat! hourra! Comme leur front rayonne
De fierté, de bonheur, de cet orgueil que donne
Quelque grand devoir accompli!
Plus tard, lorsqu'ils diront, au foyer domestique,
"Je suis de la Crimée une vieille relique!"
Ils seront sauvés de l'oubli.

(Hooray! Hooray! Their faces are radiant with
Honour, happiness, and the pride that comes from
Performing a great duty!
Years later when they sit around the fire and announce
"I am an old relic of the Crimean War!"
They will be saved from oblivion.)

(Lys, 1855: 2. My emphasis.)[8]

Poetry notwithstanding, the soldiers, alas, were not "saved from oblivion."

Hundreds such poems were written at the height of the war to celebrate the courage of the French army, the rightness of its cause, the glory of God, and the glory of the Emperor. Like "L'Ovation," most are jingoistic, passionate, and clumsy. Many were written by provincial notables: "Chanson sur la Guerre d'Orient" by A. Caillebotte-la-Vente, avocat à Gers (1854); "La Vérité aux Français, épisode sur la guerre d'Orient" by M. L'Abbé Deshayes, prêtre, aumônier de l'hospice civil et militaire de Vendôme (1855), and so on. The French public was not indifferent. As one reads through these poems certain tropes emerge. Some invoke the Homeric epic to capture a patriotic national feeling, others the Bonapartian epic, with Napoleon III standing in for his uncle. Once again it is as if this strange new war, whose action (or inaction) took place in trenches, could only be represented through the conventions of battle epics that seem incongruous with the nature of the events they translated.

Finally, in a deliciously ironic twist, there are the poets who presented the Crimean War, in which French Catholics fought alongside Turkish Muslims, as the new Crusade for the Holy Land. No one was more aware of the ironies behind this association than Karl Marx and Friedrich Engels: "To drive the Moslems out of Europe would once have roused the zeal of England and France; to prevent the Turks from being driven out of Europe is now the most cherished resolve of those nations. So broad a gulf stands between Europe of the nineteenth and Europe of the thirteenth century! So fallen away since the latter epoch is the political influence of religious dogma" (*The Russian Menace*, 24 October 1854, 149).

Perhaps the most stunning example of poetry in the service of the Crimean War comes from the Académie Française, which in 1857 set "La Guerre d'Orient" as the topic of that year's *Concours de poésie* (poetry contest). A surprising 150 poems were submitted to the competition that year – between forty-five and fifty was the norm – but, quite exceptionally, none was crowned by the jury; two were acknowledged as "promising."

When the individual authors subsequently published their poems, many used the occasion to air sour grapes. Submissions to the competition could not exceed 300 lines. Hippolyte de Charlemagne complained about the constraints to Abel-France Villemain, Secretary of the Académie, with reference to his own *La Guerre d'Orient, Souvenir de Béranger*: "300 vers c'était bien peu pour un sujet qui eût demandé une Iliade entière ... J'espérai du moins une mention" (300 lines of verse is hardly enough for a subject that calls for an entire Iliad ... I was hoping for at least an honourable mention) (10).

Adolphe Dumas, a protégé of Alphonse de Lamartine, whose submission to the 1853 *concours* had won him a medal, had even more to complain about. His poem *La Guerre d'Orient*, written as a tribute to the emperor, with proud nods to both Homer and the Crusades, was interrupted fourteen times and booed in the Académie Française when Alfred de Vigny read it aloud:[9]

Muse des temps anciens, muse de la Troade,
Au nom d'Homère, encore un chant de l'Iliade!
Esprit des temps nouveaux, esprit des temps chrétiens,
Encore une Croisade et chante pour les tiens!

(Muse of ancient times, muse of the Trojan war
Here, in the name of Homer, is another song of the Iliad!
Oh spirit of modern times, spirit of Christian times,
For this new Crusade sing for your people!)

(Dumas, *La Guerre d'Orient*, 1)

Neither the "temps chrétiens" nor the "muse de la Troade" could capture the "temps nouveaux" of this modern war. Clearly, having one's poem read by an Immortal to the Immortals did not guarantee immortality.[10]

For that matter, even the poem of an Immortal did not enter the collective memory of Crimea. In October 1854, on the occasion of the death of Jacques Leroy de Saint-Arnaud, the *maréchal* who had led the French army into the war, Victor Hugo composed his poem "Saint-Arnaud." Celebrated as a military hero by the army and the state, Saint-Arnaud died not in battle but of cholera shortly after the battle at Alma in which he had led his soldiers to victory. For Hugo, this was a fitting death for the criminal "jackal" who had orchestrated the bloody massacres that followed Louis-Napoleon's *coup d'état*, events he would recount in detail in his vehement *Histoire d'un Crime* (1877).

Saint-Arnaud had built his military reputation on the role he played in the conquest and colonization of Algeria, where he distinguished himself in a ruthless campaign of burning Algerian villages and massacring their inhabitants. For his success he was recalled to France by Louis-Napoléon, who at the time was the French president, and rewarded with the position of Minister of War. And it was in that capacity that he engineered the *coup d'état* in December 1851 that placed Louis-Napoléon on the throne as Emperor Napoleon III. Subsequently appointed senator, he left the Ministry of War in 1854 to take command of the Crimean campaign. On 20 September 1854 he led the French to their decisive victory at Alma, despite the stomach cancer he had been suffering from and the cholera he had recently contracted. He left Crimea nine days later and died on-board ship, his bravery honoured and his glory secured. The emperor had him buried in Les Invalides.

Hugo wrote "Saint-Arnaud" in Jersey, where he had gone into exile to continue his attacks on the traitorous "Napoléon le Petit." He had published his volume of poetry indicting the Emperor, *Les Châtiments*, in 1853 before the outbreak of the Crimean War. The long poem on Saint-Arnaud was added to its second edition in 1870, allowing the *maréchal* to be memorialized as a supporting actor in both Paris and Crimea, in both "Crime" and "Châtiments."

The poem begins with Saint-Arnaud's bloody record of achievement during the *coup d'état*: "Il était le vainqueur des passants de Paris" (He was the man who attacked Parisians in the streets). Soon after, rumblings of a war with Russia rouse Saint-Arnaud:

> Or, voici que la guerre à l'orient se lève!
> Je ne suis que couteau, je puis devenir glaive. […]
> Vainqueur, dans une illustre et splendide fumée,
> Et duc de la mer Noire et prince de Crimée,
> Et je ferai voler ce mot: Sébastopol,
> Des tours de Notre-Dame au dôme de Saint-Paul!
>
> (Now stirrings of war arise in the east!
> I am just a blade, now I will become a sword. […]
> Conqueror rising out of the splendid smoke of battle,
> Duke of the Black Sea and prince of Crimea,
> I will sound the word: Sebastopol!
> From the towers of Notre Dame to the dome of Saint Paul!)

The poem details events of the war as well as Saint-Arnaud's ambitious actions and inglorious death – "Il voyait, pâle, amer, l'horreur dans les narines, / Fondre sous lui sa gloire en allée aux latrines" (Pale and bitter, inhaling horror, he saw his glory melt away on the path to the latrines) – and ends with the avenging angel "Châtiment" turning to the poet and asking: "Est-ce assez?" (Is that enough?) (*Oeuvres poétiques*, vol. 2, 240–7).

Like the poems submitted to the Académie Française, "Saint-Arnaud" is the poem of a patriot. Unlike them it forcefully denounces the emperor and condemns his military leader. Hugo presents Saint-Arnaud as an extension of Napoleon III and the Crimean War as both an extension of his illegitimate government and a calculated distraction from that government's illegitimacy. One of five poems added to the 1870 edition and set outside the main events of the *coup d'état*, nevertheless, this is not a text that readers of *Les Châtiments* commonly turn to.

It is all the more interesting therefore that, writing on the occasion of Hugo's death in 1885, the British poet and contemporary of Tennyson, Algernon Swinburne, should have singled out this particular poem in *Les Châtiments*. For him it represented not just another example of Hugo's poetic genius, nor another instalment in Hugo's indictment of Napoleon's crime, but a chapter in the Crimean War that had so marked the British imagination:

> Then, in the later editions of the book, came the great and terrible poem on the life and death of the miscreant marshal who gave the watchword of massacre in the streets of Paris, and died by the visitation of disease before the walls of Sebastopol. There is hardly a more splendid passage of its kind in all the *Légende des Siècles* than the description of the departure of the fleet in order of battle from Constantinople for the Crimea. (*Victor Hugo*, 77)

However deep Swinburne's appreciation, the poem by France's most prolific poet of the nineteenth century did not, to borrow Rolph Trouillot's term, "retrieve" the event as had Tennyson's poem. There are texts by Hugo that might well have done so, although in them, once again, Hugo subordinated the Crimean War to the greater crime, the *coup d'état* of December 1851. In "La Guerre d'Orient," a speech written from exile on 29 November 1854, the rivers of blood, Hugo insists, all lead back to 2 December and Louis-Napoléon, "Mister Bonaparte."

The rhetoric is more impassioned still in Hugo's speech of 24 February 1855, on the occasion of the seventh anniversary of the Revolution of 1848, in which he pauses in his vision of a future Europe to summon up the horrors of the trenches in one hallucinatory, unstoppable sentence:

> Qu'est-ce que c'est que cette tranchée qu'on ouvre devant cette ville tartare? cette tranchée à deux pas de laquelle coule le ruisseau de sang d'Inkermann, cette tranchée où il y a des hommes qui passent la nuit debout et qui ne peuvent se coucher parce qu'ils sont dans l'eau jusqu'aux genoux; d'autres qui sont couchés, mais dans un demi-mètre de boue qui les recouvre entièrement et où ils mettent une pierre pour que leur tête en sorte; d'autres qui sont couchés, mais dans la neige, sous la neige, et qui se réveilleront demain les pieds gelés, d'autres qui sont couchés, mais sur la glace et qui ne se réveilleront pas; d'autres qui marchent pieds nus par un froid de dix degrés parce qu'ayant ôté

leurs souliers, ils n'ont plus la force de les remettre, d'autres couverts de plaies qu'on ne panse pas; tous sans abri, sans feu, presque sans aliments, faute de moyens de transport, ayant pour vêtements des haillons mouillés devenus glaçons, rongés de dyssenteries et de typhus, tués par le lit où ils dorment, empoisonnés par l'eau qu'ils boivent harcelés de sorties, criblés de bombes, réveillés de l'agonie par la mitraille, et ne cessant d'être des combattants que pour redevenir des mourants; cette tranchée, où l'Angleterre â l'heure qu'il est, a entassé trente mille soldats, où la France, le 17 décembre, – j'ignore le chiffre ultérieur, – avait couché quarante-six mille sept cents hommes, cette tranchée où, en moins de trois mois, quatre vingt mille hommes ont disparu, cette tranchée de Sébastopol, c'est la fosse des deux armées.

(What is the trench they have dug around this Tatar city? The trench next to a stream of blood flowing from Inkermann, the trench where men spend the night on foot and cannot lie down because the water comes up to their knees; where others are lying down in a half a metre of mud that covers their whole body, propped up on a rock so their head can stick out; others have lain down in the snow, under the snow, and will awake tomorrow with frozen feet; still others lie down on the ice and will not awake at all; and others who march barefoot in cold 10-degree weather because, having taken off their shoes, they no longer have the strength to put them back on, men covered in wounds that no one will dress; all of them without shelter, without fire, almost without food for lack of transport, clothed in damp tatters turned to ice, plagued with dysentery and typhus, killed by the very bed they sleep in, poisoned by the water they drink, overwhelmed by attacks, crippled by bombs, tormented in their agony by grapeshot, fighting to the end unless they are dying; this trench where as of today thirty thousand English soldiers are heaped, where on December 17 – I don't have the previous numbers – France laid to rest forty six thousand seven hundred men, this trench where in less than three months eighty thousand men disappeared: this trench at Sebastopol is the grave of two armies. (Hugo, *Actes et paroles*, vol. 2, 126)[11]

Some fifty years later in *La Colonne*, Descaves would have his central character, Prophète, the Crimean War veteran, relive just such scenes of living death, with frozen trenches turned to tombs.[12]

If securing this war in the canon of culturally retained events required some form of literary commemoration, then turn up the rhetorical volume as he may, Hugo's anguish in 1855 at the unspeakable conditions that soldiers endured did not do so. For unlike the image of tragic, if heroic, battle that Tennyson had painted, Hugo's images of dysentery, typhus, and cold muddy trenches connoted ghastly, "unmanly" suffering, but not war.

Nor do we find the commemoration of this strange war in the works of the other major canonical poet who referenced the Crimean War at the time, Charles Baudelaire.

Baudelaire had personal reasons to sidestep all things military. His relationship with his stepfather, General Jacques Aupick, was notoriously rocky. A man whose political allegiances swung with the times, Aupick had served under every French régime in the nineteenth century, up to and including the Second Empire. As chance would have it, in 1848 he was appointed "envoyé extraordinaire et ministre plénipotentiaire" at the French embassy in Constantinople. There, in 1849, at the request of the foreign minister, he was instructed to protest Russia's occupation of the Danubian Principalities and demand the restoration of France's "religious protection" of sacred sites in the Holy Land as guaranteed by treaty. For this he was personally thanked by Louis-Napoléon, then President of the Republic.[13] By all accounts, Baudelaire was unaware of and uninterested in his stepfather's diplomatic activities at this time. By 1851, the Aupicks were back in Paris.

Within a few years, however, it was difficult to ignore the emerging tensions involving France, Britain, the Ottoman Empire, and Russia. During the mid-1850s, like all French readers, Baudelaire was surrounded by news of Crimea everywhere in the press. Between 1854 and 1856 one of his favourite artists, Honoré Daumier, filled the "Actualités" pages of the satirical journal *Le Charivari* with caricatures from the Crimean War; eighty-six of these were speedily published in two separate albums of lithographs: *Les Cosaques pour rire* and *Chargeons les Russes!* This was a period of great productivity for Baudelaire. Besides composing poetry, between July 1854 and April 1855 he published translations of twenty-nine tales by Edgar Allan Poe in fifty-five issues of the daily newspaper *Le Pays (Journal de l'Empire*). His translations of the *Histoires extraordinaires* appeared regularly on the bottom half of page three. During that same period, page one was always devoted to the latest news from the Crimean War. Baudelaire had literally to go through Crimea to get to his own stories. The war figured similarly on the front pages of almost every other newspaper and filled pages of the more literary *Revue des deux mondes*, including the issue of 1 June 1855, in which eighteen poems by Baudelaire appeared for the first time under the title "Les Fleurs du Mal." In the page immediately following the last of those poems, the "Chronique de la quinzaine" describes "le redoublement de l'activité en Crimée": "Nos soldats après deux sanglans [*sic*] combats de nuit, sont restés maîtres d'une place d'armes qui les rapproche de Sébastopol …

etc." (the doubling of activity in Crimea: Our soldiers, after two nights of bloody skirmishes, maintained the armed site that brings them close to Sebastopol ...) (1 June 1855, 1094). The exit from the "Fleurs du Mal," that is, led the reader directly to Sebastopol.

Crimea was visible everywhere in print. While French press coverage of the war was far more censored than the British press reports from the front, it was, nevertheless, extensive and ubiquitous. If it was invisible in the literature of the time, it was not for want of information. Some of that literature, as in the case of Baudelaire's poems, rubbed shoulders with the war.

Images of death, spectres, and tombs run through several of the eighteen poems by Baudelaire featured in the 1 June 1855 issue of *Revue des deux mondes*. In the context of the articles about and images of Crimea surrounding Baudelaire's poems there, the final image of a dying soldier in poem XI, "La Cloche" (later retitled "La Cloche Fêlée") conjures up scenes of war not unlike those of the trenches Hugo described in February of the same year:

> II arrive souvent que sa voix affaiblie
> Semble le râle épais d'un blessé qu'on oublie
> Au bord d'un lac de sang, sous un grand tas de morts
> Et qui meurt, sans bouger, dans d'immenses efforts.
>
> (It often happens that her [the bell's] weakened voice
> Resembles the death rattle of a wounded man,
> Forgotten beneath a heap of dead, by a lake of blood,
> Who dies without moving, striving desperately.)[14]

"La Cloche fêlée" is not, however, a poem about Crimea, nor does Crimea figure anywhere in Baudelaire's poetry. If one is looking for that place in Baudelaire's writing, one needs to go rather to his writings on art and, in particular, on a French artist working for the English press.

Constantin Guys, the artist celebrated by Baudelaire in 1863 as the very Parisian "Painter of Modern Life" – the eagle-eyed observer who extracts poetry from history – spent the war years in Crimea as a visual correspondent on the ground producing hundreds of drawings for the *Illustrated London News*.[15] Guy was a skilled draughtsman and illustrator and was particularly well-suited to be a roving military artist. Born in 1802, he had joined the French army in 1824 and pursued a military career until 1830. Throughout the war Guys's Crimean drawings were quickly dispatched to London engravers for mass publication in the illustrated weekly alongside reports from the front. The war drawings, by an artist not widely recognized in his home country, were little-known in France outside a small circle of artists. Baudelaire, however, avidly collected and actively championed Guys's work and was unusually familiar with these drawings, to which he would dedicate a chapter in "Le Peintre de la vie moderne" titled "Les Annales de la guerre."[16] Baudelaire's enthusiasm for the artist was well-known among his friends; he owned about one hundred of his drawings.[17] He referred to these quite strategically when he solicited a French government stipend for Guys, whose job and livelihood had terminated with the sudden death of the founder of the *Illustrated London News*. In his letter of January 1861 to Jules Desaux, at the French Ministry of State, Baudelaire praised the artist, who was, he notes, "fils d'un Amiral de la République et de l'Empire" (son of an Admiral of the Republic and the Empire). For the government bureaucrat he singled out the Crimean drawings as central to Guys's *oeuvre* and of particular interest: "J'ai vu toute la Campagne de Crimée dessinée par lui, au jour le jour pendant qu'il suivait l'expédition à la suite de l'armée Anglais, chacun de ses dessins accompagnés des notes les plus curieuses" (I have seen the entire Crimean campaign as illustrated by him day to day while he followed the movement of the British army; each of his drawings is accompanied by the most interesting notes). Along with his letter of support, Baudelaire sent dozens of Guy's war drawings for the consideration of the ministry.[18] Baudelaire wrote to Desaux three times, but to his regret the request fell on deaf ears.

For Baudelaire, the story of Crimea was best told not in words but in images, for there was no adequate language to describe the sinister sweep of that war:

> Je puis affirmer que nul journal, nul récit écrit, nul livre, n'exprime aussi bien, dans tous ses détails douloureux et dans sa sinistre ampleur, cette grande épopée de la guerre de Crimée ... En vérité, il est difficile à la simple plume de traduire ce poëme fait de mille croquis, si vaste et si compliqué, et d'exprimer l'ivresse qui se dégage de tout ce pittoresque, douloureux souvent, mais jamais larmoyant, amassé sur quelques centaines de pages.
>
> (I can affirm that no newspaper, no written account, no book has so readily expressed in all its painful detail and grim entirety, this great military epic of the Crimean war ... In truth, it is difficult for a simple pen to translate this poem made of a thousand sketches, a poem so vast and so complicated, or express the intoxication released by all this picturesque, often painful, but never sentimental material compiled in several hundred pages.) (OC, vol. 2, 701–3)

This was a war that belied familiar tropes, one in which French soldiers sat waiting – much as Hugo would describe them – in cold, damp, muddy trenches, dying ingloriously. Conventional models for writing about war – as exemplified by 150 failed submissions to the Académie Française – had been drawn from the Iliad, the Crusades, and Napoleon I; such models no longer sufficed for the realities of a differently waged modern war, however victorious its ending.

Maxime du Camp, the well-known traveller and author, put it bluntly in the very terms that disappointed young Adrien in *La Colonne*: "l'ennemi réel, ce n'est pas l'armée russe, c'est le choléra" (the real enemy was not the Russian army, it was cholera) (Du Camp, *Orient et Italie*, 303). If this war had anything Homeric about it, it was only with reference to the evil pestilence that opens the Iliad: "Involontairement on pense au premier chant de l'Iliade: un dieu vengeur lance des flèches mortelles sur l'armée" (One cannot help but think of the first canto of the Iliad, where a vengeful god hurls mortal arrows upon the army) (304). Beyond that, there was little in this war that translated into the language of the epic.

Accordingly, for Baudelaire, whatever "grande épopée de la guerre de Crimée" there might be, it would have to be conveyed in visual images. Not the spectacular battle scenes of popular state-commissioned painters like Horace Vernet, but the rapidly sketched drawings and eyewitness renderings produced by Guys and published in the (British) press.

While quietly turning the pages of an album of Guys's drawings from Crimea, a particular image catches the poet's eye, and he stops to reflect:

> Quel est ce cavalier ... qui, la tête relevée, a l'air de humer la terrible poésie d'un champ de bataille, pendant que son cheval ... cherche son chemin entre les cadavres amoncelés, pieds en l'air, faces crispées, dans des attitudes étranges? Au bas du dessin, dans un coin, se font lire ces mots: *Myself at Inkermann.*
>
> (Who is this cavalry officer ... head raised, who seems to be taking in the terrible poetry of the battlefield, while his horse ... finds its way around heaps of corpses, legs in the air, faces contorted, in weird positions? In a corner at the bottom of the drawing, the words: *Myself at Inkermann.*) (OC, vol. 2, 702)

The "terrible poetry" of battle is translated in the visual expression of the artist and his horse making their way through a field of corpses. The caption is in English: "Myself at Inkermann." For Baudelaire the narrative of the Crimean War and its poetry is filtered through the Eng-

2.1 Constantin Guys, "Our artist on the Battlefield of Inkerman [*sic*]." *Illustrated London News,* 3 February 1855. Author collection.

lish language. And for him the Battle of Balaclava, as told in several of Guys's drawings, is further refracted through Tennyson's "Charge of the Light Brigade," whose poetic echoes reverberate in a way no French poem has. It is an English story, told in an English newspaper, as commemorated by an English poet:

> La bataille de Balaklava se présente plusieurs fois dans ce curieux recueil, et sous différents aspects. Parmi les plus frappants, *voici l'historique charge de cavalerie chantée par la trompette héroïque d'Alfred Tennyson, poëte de la reine*: une foule de cavaliers roulent avec une vitesse prodigieuse jusqu'à l'horizon entre les lourds nuages de l'artillerie.

> (The Battle of Balaclava appears several times, viewed from different aspects in this curious collection. Among the most striking images, *here is the historic charge of the light brigade heroically trumpeted by Alfred Tennyson,*

> *poet to the queen;* a throng of cavalry officers gallop at prodigious speed into the horizon surrounded by heavy smoke clouds of artillery.) (*OC*, vol. 2, 702. My emphasis)

For Baudelaire it is perhaps Guys, after all – extractor of poetry from history, distiller of the eternal from the ephemeral – who is the French poet of the Crimean War.[19] It is not a general or a soldier we see in the drawing but the artist himself who is present in his own sketch, offering us a synthesis of a subjective view of that war constructed from outside by the reporter's eye. Commenting on this sketch, Ulrich Keller notes: "There is no more … 'real' reality than such an assortment of corpses contorted in agony; and it is the Special Artist whose eye-witness mandate brings him face to face with the danger and the horror of this reality … For the first time in history, someone appears on the battle-field who is neither a soldier, nor a doctor, camp follower, friend or relative of the combatants, but an eye-witness pure and simple" (Keller, *The Ultimate Spectacle*, 72). And it is this eyewitness who, for Baudelaire, tells the story. Where there was conceivably no adequate paradigm in place to describe this new kind of war, Guys's rapidly sketched drawings, and the widely disseminated journalistic engravings they inspired, offered a modern form of visual representation of war that Baudelaire admired and celebrated.

And yet … Whereas, with Baudelaire's endorsement in *Le Peintre de la vie moderne*, Guys's paintings and drawings of Parisian modernity have taken their place in the canon, even the praise of France's greatest poet of the nineteenth century, in one of his most famous essays, could not imprint Guys's Crimean drawings on French cultural memory. They are a curiosity overshadowed by the fashionable parasols of elegant women promenading in the Bois de Boulogne in his well-known paintings of modern life: pictures that celebrate memorable parades of Parisian fashion as opposed to forgotten parades of Crimean soldiers.

The two seemingly incongruous worlds of Crimean battlefields and Parisian boulevards are juxtaposed in the work of Constantin Guys and in the essay by Baudelaire. During the heady years of the war those two worlds crossed paths on the boulevards of Paris. There, under the presiding eye of the emperor, the reality of a deadlocked and deadly war was transformed by glamour and performed as theatre. And it is with the twinning of the very visible life of modern Paris and the invisible Crimean War that we now turn to the inescapable, if ephemeral, spectacles of war.

Chapter Three

Spectacles of War

The "spectacular" memorial event is created in order to produce a certain kind of collective memory, generally at the scale of the city and in relation to the production of the nation.

Katharyne Mitchell, "Monuments, Memorials, and the Politics of Memory"

As societies of spectacle go, it is hard to beat the Second Empire in France. Widely known as "la fête impériale," this régime was characterized from start to finish – that is, from 1852 to 1870 – by a staging of power and lavish display. Under the presiding eye of Napoleon III, it was a period noted for oversized appetites, oversized dresses, and garish furniture: "un vaste spectacle du pouvoir en représentation" (a vast spectacle representing power) (Mauduit, *Les Souverains au théâtre*, 21).

When the emperor ventured forth from court, it was with drama. As the daily newspaper *La Presse* commented: "L'Empereur a la coquetterie des équipages; les attelages de la cour changent à chaque excursion, comme la toilette des dames d'honneur" (The Emperor has a coquettish taste for horse-drawn carriages, and he changes them each time he leaves the court, much like ladies-in-waiting change their gowns) (15 August 1855). There was often more than a touch of theatricality to the emperor's own performance and to the military costumes he liked to wear. From across the English Channel, the British magazine *Punch* gleefully observed:

> On the occasion of the review in the Champ de Mars, [Louis-Napoléon] wore the uniform of a General of the Infantry – or of a Colonel of the National Guard – for, as he has never served in either, it is extremely doubtful which uniform he wore, or in fact, what rank in the French army

> he has gained at all, beyond that, from never having been in it, of a Rank Imposter. (*Punch, or the London Charivari*, 22 May 1852, 223)

Under Napoleon III, spectacular entertainments became an industry, with state balls, imperial receptions, military parades, state visits, and gala performances of opera and ballet. To be sure, during his reign the distance between power and spectacle was never very great. And the gruesome deaths of tens of thousands of French soldiers in cholera-infected trenches, far from the glitter of Paris, were not going to get in the way of imperial gaiety. Instead, back in the metropole the foreign campaign was camouflaged in crowd-pleasing displays. In Lucien Descave's *La Colonne*, a disaffected working-class Parisian taunts Prophète, the veteran of the Crimean War, with his depiction of the merry goings-on in the capital: "Ça vous aurait peut-être réjoui le coeur d'apprendre que jamais, à Paris, la saison n'avait été plus brillante, plus gaie. Tandis que vous enduriez devant Sébastopol mille privations, la fête battait son plein. … On dansait, on s'amusait, on était tout au plaisir de vivre et à la vie de plaisirs" (It would have warmed your heart to know that in Paris, the social season was never more brilliant or gay. While you suffered thousands of privations at Sebastopol, it was party time … People danced and enjoyed themselves, it was all about living a life of pleasure) (229).

If the Second Empire was known for its theatrical public displays, Napoleon III, its principal producer, came by his stagecraft honestly. Jean-Claude Yon reminds us that as indifferent as the Emperor was to the arts and letters, he was keenly aware of the cultural politics of theatre: "Napoléon III sait … qu'un souverain ne peut se détourner d'un loisir si apprécié à la fois du peuple et de l'élite. Avec opportunisme, il utilise parfois le théâtre pour faire passer ses idées … L'Empereur sait qu'une pièce à succès peut avoir beaucoup d'effet" (Napoleon III knows ... that a sovereign cannot overlook this leisure activity that is so appreciated by common people and the elite alike. The Emperor knows that a successful play can have great effect) (*Les Spectacles*, 11–12). The duc de Conegliano, a chamberlain to the emperor, reports in his memoirs that Napoleon III went to the theatre once a week (*Le Second Empire*, 200). Allowing for various breaks during the summer, he would thus have attended more than 750 theatrical representations, as a leisure activity, a social obligation and, one might say, a form of work-study.

Theatre – whether on or off stage – was central to the "fête impériale" and was fully integrated into visits by foreign heads of state. It was on just such an occasion that Napoleon III designed and produced one of his most dazzling spectacles: the week-long visit (18–25 August 1855) of Queen Victoria, the first British monarch to set foot in France since Henry VIII met with François Ier at le Camp du Drap d'or" (the Field of the Cloth of Gold) in 1520, a fact politicians and journalists were quick to underscore. The royal visit had been planned to coincide with the Universal Exhibition of 1855 – French counterpart of the 1851 Great Exhibition in London. The true purpose of the visit, however, was to celebrate and cement the historic military alliance between old enemies, Britain and France, who were at that very time fighting the Russians alongside each other in Crimea. The historical importance of the occasion could not be understated, as made evident in the hyperbolic language of the cover article of the *Illustrated London News* on 18 August 1855, the day of the queen's arrival in Paris:

> This day... her Majesty the Queen of Great Britain will make her triumphal entry into the city of Paris. The annals of modern times offer no event so remarkable; – few more important. The splendour of the ceremonial itself, the international courtesy and friendship of which it is the visible sign, and the influence that it cannot fail to exercise over the whole current of contemporary history ... The traditional glories of the Field of the Cloth of Gold fade into insignificance compared to the material, no less than the moral, splendour of the occasion.

On the following page, the *ILN*'s correspondent from France offered a cultural gloss on the historical moment. He couldn't resist opening with a military metaphor to emphasize a certain English upper hand:

> Paris is at present not only invaded, but occupied, by the English who have nearly put the inhabitants to flight. The theatres, the restaurants, the cafés, the boulevards, the promenades swarm with our compatriots; lodgings have become impossible to find ... In addition to the other preparations made to do honour to the Royal guest, the Emperor has selected from the public galleries – the Louvre included – some of the finest specimens of the old masters to decorate St. Cloud during her Majesty's residence there ... For the fête at Versailles fifteen thousand invitations have been issued. (18 August 1855, 194)

Poems celebrated the excitement of the occasion, and Paris was decorated and transformed by the grandeur of the visit.[1] Ernest Vandam, an Englishman who was present at the arrival of the queen, described the drama of her entry and the magnificent decor designed by the Paris Opera:

3.1 "Meeting of Henry VIII and Francis I at Ardres – the Field of the Cloth of Gold." From a painting by John Gilbert. *Illustrated London News*, 18 August 1855. Author collection.

> Among the notable features of the decorations in the main artery of Paris was the magnificent triumphal arch, erected by the management of the Opéra between the Rue de Richelieu and what is now the Rue Druout. It rose to the fourth stories of the adjacent houses, and looked, not a temporary structure, but a monument intended to stand the wear and tear of ages. No description could convey an idea of its grandeur. The inside was draped throughout with bee-bespangled purple, the top was decorated with immense eagles, seemingly in full flight, and holding between their talons proportionately large scutcheons, bearing the interlaced monograms of the Imperial hosts and the Royal guests. (*An Englishman in Paris*, 159–60)

The queen's own description of her entry into Paris similarly conveys the theatrical *mise en scène* of that moment; it is almost as if the emperor had designed the city's natural lighting to show off his most recent urban projects. "Imagine ... this beautiful city ... decorated in the most tasteful manner possible, with banners, flags, arches, flowers, inscriptions, and finally illuminations ... The approaching twilight rather added to the beauty of the scene; and it was still quite light enough when we passed down the new *Boulevard de Strasbourg* (the Emperor's creation)." The strategy clearly worked. The following evening the queen wrote (in French) to her uncle, the King of the Belgians:

> Notre entrée dans Paris a été une scène absolument *feënhaft*: il serait difficile de voir ailleurs quelque chose de semblable; c'était tout à fait *écrasant*; les décorations, les illuminations étaient prodigieuses. Il y avait une foule immense, et 60 000 soldats formaient la haie depuis la gare de Strasbourg jusqu'à Saint-Cloud, dont 20 000 gardes nationaux venus de très loin pour me voir.
>
> (Our entry into Paris was an absolutely *fairy-like* scene: it would be hard to imagine anything like it anywhere else: it was absolutely *staggering;* the decorations, the illuminations were extraordinary. The crowds were huge and 60,000 soldiers lined the route from the gare de Strasbourg to Saint-Cloud, including 20,000 national guard who had come from very far to see me.) (*La Reine Victoria d'après sa correspondance inédite,* 264)

The painter Eugène Delacroix, trying to get home that evening from working on the murals at Saint Sulpice, was astonished by the crowds and traffic, which he found particularly bothersome: "Paris est fou, ce jour-là" (Paris went crazy that day) (*Le Journal,* 294).

In the course of her one-week visit, the queen would, in the company of the emperor, attend no fewer than three plays and two operas. Having attended a production of *Les Demoiselles de Saint-Cyr* by Alexandre Dumas in London, she was eager to see it again, and the emperor obliged her by having actors of the Comédie Française perform it for her at the Château de Saint-Cloud, where she was residing (Vandam, *An Englishman in Paris,* 164.)[2] There was a gala evening at the Opera, where the queen was moved by a rendition of "God Save the Queen," and a visit to the Opéra Comique to see *Haydée*. Goupil et Cie, the Paris-based art dealership that specialized in art prints, advertised lithographs of the event: "La Reine d'Angleterre au Théâtre de l'Opéra, Grande planche représentant la Reine d'Angleterre, le prince Albert, l'Empereur,

3.2 Eugene-Charles-François Guerard (1821–1866), *Queen Victoria's Entry into Paris, 18 August 1855*. Royal Collection Trust / © Her Majesty Queen Elizabeth II, 2017.

l'Impératrice, etc., etc., dans leur loge à l'Opéra, le 21 août 1855. Dessiné et lithographie d'après nature, par Alophe. Prix, sur papier de Chine, en noir. 6 fr. En couleur, 12 fr." (The Queen of England at the Opera Theatre, large plate representing the Queen of England, Prince Albert, the Emperor, the Empress, etc. etc. in their box at the Opera, 21 August, 1855. Drawn and lithographed from nature by Alophe. Price on papier de Chine, 6 fr. In colour, 12 fr.) (*Feuilleton du Journal de la Librairie*, 25 August 1855, 429).

But this was, in many ways, the *least* theatrical part of the queen's visit. Every leg of the royal visit, from the moment she set foot in France until the moment she boarded the ship home, was staged, followed, recorded, and commented on.

Ernest Vizitelly, an English journalist, described the military grandeur of the queen's departure from France for British readers. "There was a dazzling escort of Carabineers and Guides and Hussars commanded by Marshals and Generals arrayed in full uniform, and mounted on milk-white chargers, all going in pompous procession towards the railway station ... The Emperor and Prince Napoleon accompanied the royal visitors to Boulogne, where 50,000 troops were reviewed before the farewell dinner at the imperial pavilion. At last, at eleven o'clock that night, the Queen, amid the crash of artillery, went on board the *Victoria and Albert,* and the memorable visit was at an end" (*The Court of the Tuilleries*, 87–8.) Between the daily press and illustrated weeklies, in France – as in England – media coverage of the royal visit reached the broadest audience. The "nouvelle alliance" that was being forged in the trenches of Crimea was celebrated in the streets of Paris as one big party.

Of all the various productions Napoleon III planned for the historic royal visit, the grandest by far was the state ball, held at the Château de Versailles on 25 August 1855. "Jamais le château de Louis XIV, au plus beau temps des royaux carrousels, n'a vu de pareilles magnificences" (The château of Louis XIV was never more magnificent, even during the great days of royal carousels). So reported Charles Brainne in *La Presse* on 26 August.

Celebrations such as this were key tools for projecting powerful images of the imperial regime before a mass audience, all the more so during an endless, deadly war, from which the public might be conveniently distracted. Katharyne Mitchell notes that spectacular memorial events like these are in fact created in order to produce a certain kind of collective memory, "often heightened ... through actual physical monuments and architectural grandiosity" ("Monuments," 444). The celebration at Versailles was meant to be just such an unforgettable event.

So many people came from Paris to witness the arrival of the sovereigns and the fireworks at Versailles that extra trains had to be added and there was concern about how everyone would be able to return home that night. The extravagance hearkened back to spectacles of pre-Revolution days. In her diary entry that night Victoria wrote: "It was quite one of the finest and most magnificent sights we have ever witnessed. There had not been a ball at Versailles since the time of Louis XVI and the design of this one had been taken from a print of a fête given by Louis XV."

3.3 Victor Joseph Chavet (1822–1906), *The Promenade in the Galerie des Glaces, Versailles, 25 August 1855*. This painting was presented to Queen Victoria by the Emperor and Empress on Christmas 1855. Royal Collection Trust / © Her Majesty Queen Elizabeth II, 2017.

Napoleon III loved pomp, and he loved Versailles. Twelve hundred guests attended the ball; four orchestras conducted by Strauss and Dufresne were positioned in the four corners of the room; there were hundreds of chandeliers in the Galerie des Glaces, and garlands of flowers hung everywhere. *Le Journal des Débats* counted more than 5,000 candles (26 August 1855).

Queen Victoria found the effect dazzling: "We … went into another room, from the balcony of which we witnessed the fireworks, which were magnificent; rockets and bouquets of girandoles, the like of which I have never seen … *Guns were fired the whole time* … The Emperor had, I believe, ordered the guns, as he thought … that one always required something to keep up the excitement. The finale was a representation in fireworks of Windsor Castle, – a very pretty attention" (*Leaves from a Journal*, 122–5).

3.4 Victor Joseph Chavet (1822–1906), *The Overture to the Ball in the Galerie des Glaces, Versailles, 1855.* Royal Collection Trust / © Her Majesty Queen Elizabeth II, 2017. The Emperor took his inspiration for the ball from the eighteenth-century French royal court.

To add to the drama of the dinner at the Opera, the table at which Napoleon III and Queen Victoria sat was in the box said to have been "la loge … de Marie Antoinette" (*La Presse*, 26 August 1855).

Such lavish celebrations all but eclipsed the official reason for the queen's visit to France – the Universal Exhibition of 1855 and, more significantly, the military alliance in Crimea. For that one night, the continuous sound of gunfire in the gardens of Versailles provided an ironic diversion from the reality of deadly gunfire in Crimea.

Indeed, the day after the report of "le plus émouvant des spectacles," the arrival of Queen Victoria, *Le Pays* announced: "Le bombardement de Sébastopol a recommencé" (The bombing of Sebastopol has recommenced) (20 August 1855, 1). On 26 August *Le Pays* juxtaposed details of the royal itinerary with news of the war in the same paragraph: "S.M. la reine d'Angleterre, le prince Albert et la famille royale, quitteront

3.5 Charles-Auguste Questel (1807–1888), *The Illuminations in the Gardens of Versailles, 25 August 1855*. Royal Collection Trust / © Her Majesty Queen Elizabeth II, 2017.

Paris lundi prochain … Une dépêche du general Pélissier, datée du 23, annonce qu'ils [les Russes] ont fait sauter plusieurs mines en avant de notre batterie no. 53" (Her Majesty, the Queen of England, Prince Albert and the royal family will leave Paris next Monday … A dispatch from General Pélissier, dated August 23, announced that the Russians detonated several landmines near our Battery no. 53) (25 August 1855, 1).

The one pretext for the visit, the Exhibition, went along with the other. Though mostly invisible, the war was never far from the glittering surface. As exceptional and theatrical as the royal visit was, after a long and tangled history of enmity between the two nations, it was the "nouvelle alliance" that was especially historic and truly exceptional. Looking for more drama still, Napoleon had hoped for an Anglo-French victory before the royal visit, but the final taking of Sebastopol after a year-long siege would happen only two weeks later, with the French leading the assault. The visit thus represented a strategic demonstration of diplomacy with decidedly military overtones. Even as the emperor and

3.6 Eugène Lami (1800–1890), *Souper Offert par Napoléon III en l'honneur de la Reine Victoria dans la Salle de l'Opéra de Versailles, 25 Août 1855*. Wikimedia Commons. Four hundred people attended the dinner for Queen Victoria in the Salle de l'Opéra. At the back of the hall one sees the Queen and Prince Albert sitting with the Emperor and Empress in the box said to have belonged to Marie-Antoinette.

the queen were being entertained, reports from the front were being telegraphed by the Minister of the Interior to prefects throughout the country.

Accordingly, the effusive cover article in the *Illustrated London News* that celebrated the queen's momentous visit to Paris emphasized the significance of this journey as a gesture of *military* alliance between "two nations – the greatest, the most powerful, the most civilised, and

3.7 Emile Lassalle (1811–1871), *Queen Victoria and Napoleon III Visit the Universal Exhibition of 1855, 22 August 1855*. Chronicle/Alamy.

the most generous in the world ... Queen Victoria did not wait for victory in the Crimea ... In the very heat of conflict – while the guns were still booming at Sebastopol ... she resolved to ... proceed with her illustrious Consort and children to the dominions of her friend and neighbour, in order that she might testify to the French that the amity of the nations is not one of parchments and protocols – but of hearts" (18 August 1855, 193–4).

In France, the same newspapers that thrilled to the visit of the queen and celebrated the Universal Exhibition routinely dedicated their front pages to the latest news from the Crimean front. Typically during the week of the visit, columns dedicated to the queen's activities and the Universal Exhibition followed the war bulletin. For all the festive pageantry, Queen Victoria's visit was literally prefaced by the war. Thus, on 21 August 1855, page two of *La Presse* contained the daily report of the queen's visit, describing in great detail her exact route through Paris from Sainte-Chapelle to the Place de la Bastille. The first item on page one, though, the "Bulletin du jour," refers to the bombing of the Malakoff tower and a report from General Simpson taken from the English press. On the front page of *Le Constitutionnel* on 23 August 1855, the association of the queen's spectacular visit and the spectacle of war is even more evident. Column one begins: "Le feu de l'artillerie recommence contre Sébastopol." Several lines later: "La foule est toujours la même sur les points que la reine Victoria doit honorer de sa visite" (Artillery fire on Sebastopol has resumed… The crowd is as large as always at the locations which the Queen will grace).

Beyond the press reports, reminders of the war and of the military alliance were never far from view. Hundreds of brigades, batallions, squadrons, and divisions of soldiers honoured the queen during her eight days in France. Press accounts of the royal visit routinely commented on the ubiquitous military presence surrounding the queen in Paris and the war that united France and Britain abroad. Maréchal Canrobert himself, recently returned from Crimea, participated in many of the ceremonial events. The accounts of the queen's fairytale visit were lavish, but it was ultimately the Crimean War that made the news. The juxtaposition of Parisian splendour and Crimean warfare could not have been more jarring. Just two months before the queen's visit to France, as French troops readied themselves to storm the Mamelon, a strategic Russian fortification, French General Bosquet had turned to the wife of a British officer, his eyes full of tears: "Madame, à Paris on a toujours l'Exposition, les bals, les fêtes; et dans une heure et demie la moitié de ces braves seront morts" (Madame, in Paris people are enjoying the Exhibition, balls, parties; and, in an hour and a half, half of these brave men will be dead) (Duberly, *Mrs. Duberly's War*, 187).

Victor Hugo could not hide his outrage at the coverage of fairytale balls in Versailles that the press was gushing over while bodies of young men were being thrown into Crimean pits:

> Oui, c'est le bruit d'un orchestre que nous entendons dans le pavillon de l'Horloge; oui, *le Moniteur* enregistre et détaille le quadrille où ont "figuré leurs Majestés"; oui, l'empereur danse, oui, ce Napoléon danse, pendant que, les prunelles fixées sur les ténèbres, nous regardons, et que le monde civilisé, frémissant, regarde avec nous Sébastopol, ce puits de l'abîme …
>
> (Yes, it's the sound of an orchestra that we hear in the Pavillon de l'Horloge; yes, the newspaper *Le Moniteur* is describing in detail the quadrille in which "their Majesties starred"; yes, the Emperor is dancing, yes, this

> Napoleon is dancing while, our eyes fixed on the darkness, we observe, and the civilised world trembles and observes with us, Sebastopol, that bottomless abyss …) ("Sixième anniversaire de 1848," 127)

On the same pages of the same paper, readers in France and readers outside France – like Hugo himself – were able to follow side by side the details of the war and the details of the Parisian festivities that so enraged the poet. The press and especially the illustrated press combined to create a war that readers could follow like an illustrated serial novel. The Crimean War was ultimately transformed into a cultural production, a spectacle for consumption, whether in newspapers, in the galleries of the Universal Exhibition, or in the arena of spectacle par excellence: the theatre.

If, as Aleida Assmann, argues, plays are among the significant cultural products that mediate events in collective memory, then there was no shortage of theatrical productions related to the Crimean campaign. Like most wars, the Crimean War did not make it to the stage of the Comédie Française or assume the form of a "pièce bien faite"; it did, however, find its way quickly and easily onto the popular stage. There were dozens of topical entertainments: *vaudevilles, pantomimes, à-propos, drames comiques, drames militaires,* and equestrian entertainments. On 7 May 1854, for instance, Parisian theatregoers could attend the Théâtre impérial du Cirque – previously known as Le Cirque Olympique – to see *L'Armée d'Orient, drame militaire en 3 actes et 20 tableaux* by Messieurs Albert et de Lustière (CHF, 320). The following evening one could then attend the Théâtre du Vaudeville to see *La Foire de l'Orient. Bouffonnerie-parodie en un acte,* by Messieurs Cogniard frères et Bourdois (CHF, 318). Virtually all the secondary theatres in Paris offered Crimean-related stage productions, such as the five-act drama *Les Cosaques,* which played at the Théâtre de la Gaîté (CHF, 312) and the parody of that play by Charles Chabot and Alphonse de Jallais: *Les Cosaques, drame plein de gaîté en huit tableaux … avec coups de sabre, de théâtre, de fusil et de tam-tam, rempli de coeur; le tout orné d'un chien"* (*Cossacks, a gay drama in eight tableaux … with sabres, guns, and heartfelt drumming; with the addition of a dog*) (BF, 151) If one wished, following on the Anglo-French victory at Alma on 20 September 1854, one could attend at the Théâtre des Délassements-Comiques *L'Alma, à-propos patriotique mêlé de couplets, en deux tableaux et un acte* by Messieurs Adolphe Guénée et Amédée de Jallais (CHF, 322). A year later, in honour of the taking of Sebastopol on 8 September 1855, Paris theatres opened their doors for free on 14 September. At the Théâtre impérial de l'Opéra-Comique one could enjoy the cantata "Victoire!!!" by Michel Carré and M.A. Adam in an exceptional free performance offered by

3.8 Honoré Daumier (1808–1879), "À la Sortie du Théâtre de la Gaîté après une représentation des Cosaques." Leaving the play, *The Cossacks,* theatregoers mistake a French Chasseur for a Russian general. *Les Cosaques pour Rire.* 1854. Reproduced with permission of La Bibliothèque nationale de France.

order of the emperor on the occasion of the taking of Sebastopol (CHF, 330). George Sand, delighted at the news of the victory, happily notified her son Maurice about the free matinée performance of her own play, *François le Champi,* on the 14th. (Sand, *Correspondance,* vol. 13: 345.) That same day a *Te Deum* was sung at Notre Dame for the edification of the Parisian public.

After the Treaty of Paris that formally ended the war in March 1856, predictably, Crimea faded from the stage. One finds occasional brief references in subsequent plays, though most often they serve as temporal indicators for the action of a play or the age of certain characters. One curious play stands out: *Le Conscrit ou le Retour de Crimée, drame en deux actes,* written in 1878 by Ernest Doin, an expatriate Frenchman living in Montreal. In Act I of the play, Lavaleur, an old sergeant, visits French villages to recruit young men to fight in Crimea. To inspire them, Lavaleur recounts a recent battle in which the French came to the aid of the outnumbered English, who could no longer hold out against the Russians. "Les Anglais se mettent a crier: Voici les Français! Hourrah! Vive la France!" (The English begin to shout: Here come the French! Hurray! Vive la France!) (6).

In the wake of the French victory in Crimea, it is hardly surprising that the play presented an unabashed celebration of French bravery and heroism. But in truth the Crimean War was more a pretext for this play than its subject. Despite the title, the Crimean War stands, one quickly comes to realize, as a transparent reflection on and contrast to the traumatic Franco-Prussian War that the French had lost seven years earlier, in 1871. For Doin the glorious victory of French soldiers on the Crimean fields of battle hung on the Catholic faith that had pitted the French with their brave army chaplains against Orthodox Russians: "Oui, mes amis, il n'est rien de si grand, de si touchant en voyant ces braves et bons prêtres parcourir le champ de bataille… c'est qu'aussi tous nos soldats portent la médaille de Marie" (Yes, my friends nothing is so grand, so touching as seeing those good brave priests roam the battle field ... as well as all our soldiers wearing the medallion of the Virgin Mary) (7). By extension, if the French were humiliated in the Franco-Prussian War, it was from lack of piety.

Doin's play recalls the Catholic investment in this war and dramatizes the extent to which, by the 1870s, the trauma of the Franco-Prussian War had overshadowed the Crimean War. The memory of defeat on home territory quickly erased the memory of victory on foreign soil. But the cultural memory of that victory had clearly begun to fade years earlier despite the theatre and drama that had represented it both on and off stage.

Setting aside small stage productions, on the big stage the Crimean War lent itself particularly well to grand spectacles at the Théâtre Impérial du Cirque, such as *Constantinople, drame militaire en 4 actes et 20 tableaux*, which opened on 11 April 1854 (CFH, 317) and *La Guerre d'Orient, drame militaire en 3 actes et 20 tableaux,* which premiered on 10 July 1854. Reinforcing the actuality of the events represented, Hippolyte Demanet, who wrote the program for the play, included in it biographies of the principal "defenders of Turkey" (CFH, 320).

Then there were the extraordinary equestrian extravaganzas at the Hippodrome that celebrated military victories, such as *Silistrie,* which recreated the siege of the fortress on the banks of the Danube. In the September 1854 issue of *Le Moniteur de la Mode,* A. de Braguelonne, the theatre critic, reported with enthusiasm that

> le grand succès du moment au Théâtre [c'est] la guerre que M. Arnault vient d'inaugurer à l'Hippodrome par la représentation du *Siège de*

> *Silistrie.* Infanterie, cavalerie, artillerie, uniformes français, anglais, russes, ottomans, fusillades, coups de canon, que sais-je? rien ne manque à cette pantomime militaire, pas même les morts et les blesses.
>
> (the great theatrical success of the day [is] the war that M. Arnault has just staged at the Hippodrome with his representation of the *Siege of Silistria.* Infantry, cavalry, artillery, French, English, Russian, Ottoman uniforms, gunfire, cannon shots, the works. Nothing is missing from this military pantomime, not even the dead and wounded.) (191)

In 1855 one could catch a similar extravaganza in *La Crimée, grand pantomime militaire en deux actes, avec intermèdes equestres représentant le débarquement des troupes à Vieux-Fort et la bataille d'Alma.*

The Théâtre Impérial du Cirque but more especially the Hippodrome were particularly well suited to the staging of military exploits. From 1845 to 1855, the 12,000-seat Hippodrome de l'Étoile (at the Arc de Triomphe), with an arena 104 metres long and 68 metres wide, featured historic military epics that might include chariot races, parades, tournaments, steeplechases, and so on, with as many as 300 horses and 700 performers.

Until that time most such military spectacles celebrated moments of past national glory, such as that great summit of Henry VIII and François 1er in 1520, "Le Camp du drap d'or," which was performed in 1847 with an orchestra of 100 musicians and an audience of 12,000 (Bratton, "Theatre of War," 121). In the same vein there were many Napoleonic epics at the Cirque Olympique during the July Monarchy.

Re-enactments flourished as military pantomimes, historical tableaux, and hippodromes became the dominant genres used for the staging of reality (Pao, *The Orient of the Boulevards*, 113.) Now, with the impact of telegraphic communication and the new time scale of journalism, events on the foreign front could command immediate public attention: with little time lag, spectators could enjoy a staging of a war-in-progress. The siege of Silistria ended on 24 June 1854; a first version of the equestrian spectacle was performed on 15 August 1854 on the Champ de Mars to celebrate the *fête nationale.* With a stage decoration 1,500 metres wide and populated by whole battalions of actor-soldiers, twice that day artists from the Théâtre Impérial du Cirque performed the great military pantomime representing *La Levée du Siège de Silistrie et la mort de Mussa-Pacha, tué au moment où il rend grâce à Dieu de la delivrance de la ville.* "The encounter must have been hot for the fifteen hundred volunteers who conscientiously massacred each other right down to the end," quipped *l'Illustration* (Keller, *The Ultimate Spectacle*, 67). Between shows, a hot air balloon bearing the names of France, England, and Turkey in large gold letters lifted off from the Champ de Mars, its gondola bedecked with allegorical figures of the three empires, and a flotilla of 300 balloons, each bearing the name of one of the ships from the three allied fleets, was released (Maindron, *Le Champs de Mars*, 364–5).[3] With the Crimean War, René Dalisson observes, the regime had invented a tradition of victory celebrations that outstripped those of the *ancien régime* ("La Commémoration," 1),

Spectacles such as *Le Siège de Silistrie* were meant to glorify the empire, to promote a new national narrative, and to communicate the emperor's ability to restore France's place as the pre-eminent continental power. The Second Empire brashly celebrated its military adventures. The *Siège de Silistrie*, an extraordinary production mounted in the thick of a war, had a profound effect on the French public. By 27 August 1854 the show was entertaining thousands at the Hippodrome.

3.9 Outdoor performance of *Le Siège de Silistrie* at the new Paris Hippodrome (1854). *L'Illustration*, 16 September 1854. Reproduced with permission of La Bibliothèque nationale de France.

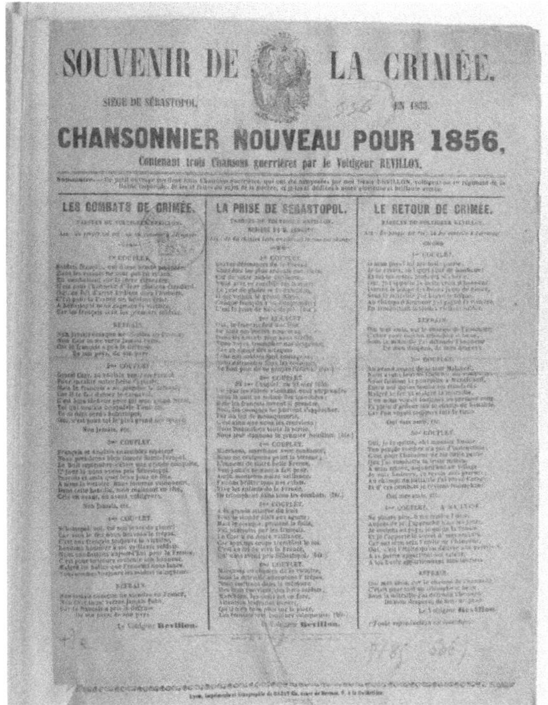
SOUVENIR DE LA CRIMÉE.

CHANSONNIER NOUVEAU POUR 1856,

LES COMBATS DE CRIMÉE.

LA PRISE DE SÉBASTOPOL.

LE RETOUR DE CRIMÉE.

3.10 *Souvenir de la Crimée. Chansonnier nouveau pour 1856.* Reproduced with permission of La Bibliothèque nationale de France.

By the time it closed, more than 200,000 spectators had seen *Silistrie* ("Les Hippodromes des spectacles à Paris au XIXe siècle").[4]

Following the victory of the French over the Russians with the taking of Sebastopol on 8 September 1855, hundreds of odes and epics were written, cantatas were sung, and plays were staged all over France, well beyond the Hippodrome and the boulevard theatres of Paris. Such is the case, for instance, of *Sébastopol, ou la revanche de Moscou, tableau militaire et patriotique en deux actes, suivi d'une apothéose,* performed at the Grand Théâtre de Marseille on 17 September 1855, nine days after the taking of the city. Popular entertainments about the Crimean War were performed not only throughout France but also in its colonies.

Just as Parisians could enjoy *Le Théâtre des zouaves, tableau militaire mêlé de couplets* at the Théâtre des Variétés,[5] citizens of Constantine, in Algeria, had the opportunity to attend performances of a one-act vaudeville, *Les Zouaves en Crimée,* at the Théâtre de Constantine.[6] It is not insignificant that the Zouaves were at the heart of that particular play, for only were the Zouave soldiers in the French army legendary for their courage, but their regiment at the time was made up of

Algerians, who were serving outside of Algeria for the very first time in the Crimean War. Moreover, if there was one cultural legacy that lived on beyond the war, it was the association of Zouave soldiers and theatre.

It is safe to say that the Zouaves were the most spectacular soldiers in the French army with their distinctive uniform: a short open-fronted jacket, baggy trousers, white leggings, sashed waist, and oriental head gear. In *Commentaires d'un Soldat*, Paul de Molènes recalls the romance of the Zouave for young Parisian recruits: "Les régiments de zouaves exercent sur la jeunesse parisienne une séduction particulière. Leur poétique uniforme, leurs libres et audacieuses allures, leur célébrité déjà légendaire … en font de nos jours la plus vive expression de cette chevalerie populaire qui date de Napoléon" (The *zoauve* regiments exude a particular appeal for Parisian youth. Their poetic uniform, their free and audacious allure, their already legendary reputation … have made them the most vivid expression of popular cavalry since Napoleon) (58). Reports of the fearlessness of the Zouaves at Alma, Balaclava, and Sebastopol spread among enemy and ally alike and were documented in the *Illustrated London News* by the British cameraman Roger Fenton. The photogenic Zouaves quickly gained international attention. Fenton's decision to not only photograph Zouave soldiers but also pose as a Zouave himself in his self-portraits merely reinforced the theatrical appeal of Zouave iconography (Wasserman, "Transcultural Cross Dressing," 12).

3.11 Horace Vernet (1789–1863), *Zouaves at the Malakoff*, 1856. Royal Collection Trust / © Her Majesty Queen Elizabeth II, 2017.

An anonymous article on "Les Zouaves" in the *Revue des Deux Mondes* from March 1855 gives a sense of the mythical reputation of these exotic soldiers from Algeria, cultural icons of the French army. "Quel Français peut lire sans joie et sans orgueil ce qu'en disent les correspondances anglaises, soit qu'elles les suivent 'grimpant comme des chats' sur la falaise de l'Alma, soit qu'elles nous les montrent 'bondissant comme des panthères' dans les broussailles d'Inkermann!" (What Frenchman can read without joy and pride what English journalists say about

3.12 Roger Fenton (1819–1869), *Self-Portrait as a Zouave*, 1. Photograph. Library of Congress, LC-USZC4–9167.

3.13 Roger Fenton, *Self-Portrait as a Zouave*, 2. Photograph. The J. Paul Getty Museum, Los Angeles, 84.XM.1028.17.

them, whether it is about them scampering up the cliffs of Alma 'like cats' or 'pouncing like panthers' in the brush of Inkermann!) ("Les Zouaves," 1127). Many poems composed on the occasion of the war celebrated the myth of the "fantastic" Zouave – part lion, part mountain goat.[7]

If Zouaves were obvious, colourful characters to portray in plays about Crimea, the association of Zouaves and theatre during the war was multifaceted. There is hardly a French memoir about the Crimean War that does not mention the remarkable theatre that the Second Regiment Zouaves built at Inkermann, the site of a major battle and allied victory on 5 November 1854. "Ce théâtre, établi en Crimée, à deux kilomètres des Russes, en plein vent, peint le caractère français on ne peut mieux" (This theatre, set in Crimea in the wide open, two kilometres from the Russians, paints the true picture of French spirit) (Gelé, *Guerre d'Orient*, 23). So renowned was the theatre that it inspired a play of its own. First performed in Paris at the Théâtre des Variétés on 1 September 1855, one week before the taking of Sebastopol, *Le Théâtre des zouaves (tableau militaire, mêlé de couplets)* represents happy-go-lucky Zouave soldiers preparing for and performing a play at their theatre. As the female canteen keepers offer them a drink before the show, they break out in song:

Le zouave est un vrai lion
Bronzé par le soleil d'Afrique;
Pour enfoncer un bataillon, (*montrant sa baionette*)
Il possède un' bagett' magique ...
Viv' le zou zou... vive le zou...
Vive le zouave!

(The zouave is a real lion,
Tanned by the African sun;
To pin down a batallion (*showing his bayonet*)
He has a magic wand...
Viv' le zou zou ... vive le zou ...
Vive le zouave!)

While one of the soldiers on stage puts up a poster for the upcoming play, an out-of-work actor from the metropole rushes in looking for the director. "Excusez-moi, monsieur. Le théâtre de guerre, s'il vous plaît?" (Excuse me sir, the theatre of war, please?). The sergeant looks confused. Delighted by his clever play on words, the actor explains that he is looking for the Zouave theatre. He is recruited for the play, which, while he is on stage, is suddenly interrupted by the sound of gunfire. He has no problem with the fire of the stage lights, but battle fire, he says, never! And he breaks into song.

Soon after, the Zouave soldier-actors who have raced off stage, weapons in hand, return victorious from a heated skirmish with the Russians. They are eager to take the stage and resume the play. The Parisian announces that he is giving up his role and returning to France. As he leaves, the Zouave soldiers cry out: "Au théâtre! Au théâtre!" The play ends with the company singing: "Viv'nt les zou zou ... viv'nt les zous ... Vivent les zouaves" (Cormon et Grangé, *Le Théâtre des Zouaves*).

E. Perret in *Récits de Crimée* recalls the prodigious reputation of the Zouave theatre all across Europe (312). Like the fearlessness of the Zouave, the Zouave theatre acquired legendary status, and the two legends were all but inseparable. In his children's book *Histoire de la Guerre d'Orient des enfants*, the abbé Mullois, first chaplain to the house of the emperor, reduced the legends to economical stereotypes: "Se battre et s'amuser, voilà tout le zouave, en deux mots" (To fight and to have fun, that's the Zouave in two words) (Mullois, *Histoire de la Guerre d'Orient*, 10).[8]

In his memoir *Nos Zouaves: historique – organisations – faits d'armes – les régiments – vie intime (1888),* reinvoking the stereotypes of bravery and *gaieté,* Paul Adolphe Laurencin-Chapelle recalls how the Zouaves came to build their theatre in the midst of the endless siege of Sebastopol. War business and show business were inextricably linked in these accounts:

> Renommés déjà par leur brillante valeur … [les zouaves] ne perdirent jamais, même aux jours les plus tristes du siège, cette gaîté et cet entrain qui les avaient caractérisés en Afrique. Aux salles de bal qu'ils avaient ouvertes dès le début du siège, les zouaves du 2e régiment ajoutèrent bientôt un théâtre … Le feu de l'ennemi n'était pas un obstacle aux représentations et la chansonnette sentimentale comme le vaudeville burlesque eurent souvent pour accompagnement la basse du bombardement ou le sifflement de quelques boulets que lançait la batterie russe."
>
> (Famous already for their brilliant valour … [the Zouaves] never lost, even during the grimmest days of the siege, that gaiety and enthusiasm that had characterized them in Africa. To the ballrooms that they had built at the start of the siege the Zouaves of the second regiment soon added a theatre … Enemy fire was no obstacle for their shows; sentimental songs as well as vaudeville slapstick were often accompanied by the sounds of bombardments or the hissing of Russian bullets.) (106–9)[9]

Memoirists and generals alike noted with pleasure that even their dour allies, the British, enjoyed the entertainment. British officers typically sat front and centre (Bapst, *Le Maréchal Canrobert*, 426). On 18 August 1855, the same issue of the *Illustrated London Times* that heralded the queen's visit to France featured an article on the "Théâtre des Zouaves, before Sebastopol," complete with the correspondent's review of the play, a reproduction of the playbill from 8 July 1855, and a half-page illustration of the theatre itself. Here, from that article, is the special correspondent's account:

> The passage into the theatre, as I entered it last Sunday, in a dark moonless night, was very striking … A few broad paper lanterns, stuck on the ends of poles, lighted up in dusky outlines the forms of the spectators, whilst the footlights threw out in bold relief the forms of the Zouaves who played in the orchestra …
>
> … the whole of the inner space was filled with officers of all nations, commissioned and non-commissioned … Jokes of a somewhat gross tendency were flying about the pit as the audience contemplated the buxom charms of *Mademoiselle Camomille*, a sergeant of Zouaves.[10]

196 THE ILLUSTRATED LONDON NEWS August 18, 1855.

"THEATRE DES ZOUAVES," IN THE FRENCH CAMP, BEFORE SEBASTOPOL.—(SEE PRECEDING PAGE.)

were immediately closed, as though the disorders of 1848 were about to be renewed. The fact is that clouds of smoke were seen rising up from

chased by the Sicilians in England during the last revolution. As it was, that part of the Castle buildings was blown into the air, and a

were found without their heads, others without arms or legs. Some were so blackened as to be beyond power of recogni-

3.14 "Théâtre d'Inkermann: 'Théâtre des Zouaves,' in the French camp before Sebastopol." *Illustrated London News,* 18 August 1855. Author collection.

The acting, the correspondent goes on to say, was very good, and the audience, accustomed to the sounds of battle in the background, did not pay much attention to them:

> But just as the sallies of the actors caused the most merriment, our ears were greeted with such a terrific outburst of flashes and explosions that the performance suddenly came to a stand-still. The curtain dropped as the audience almost by enchantment disappeared. The soldiers glided away like ghosts from the sides of the outer wall of the theatre … The roar of artillery, the crash of shells of all dimensions, the din of human voices, and a supernatural light … greeted us as we made our way to Cathcart's

LE THÉATRE DES ZOUAVES

TABLEAU MILITAIRE, MÊLÉ DE COUPLETS,

MM. CORMON ET GRANGÉ.

3.15 *Le Théâtre des Zouaves, Tableau militaire, mêlé de couplets*. Play by Eugène Cormon and Eugène Grangé. Author collection.

Hill where the best view was known to exist. (*ILN*, 18 August 1855, 195)

In an eerie *mise en abyme* of the theatre of war, the officers sitting in the pit observing the forms of Zouaves illuminated by footlights and acting out a farcical "petite Guerre d'Orient" moved onto the hill with "the best view" to contemplate those same Zouave soldiers fighting the Guerre d'Orient against a supernatural light.

As the war dragged on French officers relied on the celebrated Zouave theatre at Inkermann to entertain and distract French and the British alike from the deadly environment that surrounded them; more than one general never missed a performance. In a touching a letter to his superior, General Canrobert, General Bosquet commended the success of the Zouave theatre and asked Canrobert to see that the funds raised by the theatre be directed to the needs of French prisoners of war.

Such gestures did not go unnoticed. Early on in the play *Le Théâtre des zouaves*, an officer passing by the theatre asks: "à propos, cette fameuse représentation c'est donc pour aujourd'hui? … une représentation au bénéfice des prisonniers! …nous y serons tous! (By the way, that famous show, is it today? … A show to benefit prisoners of war? … We'll all be there). He bursts into song: "Des prisonniers vous soulagez les maux. / Acteurs, soldats, oui, vos rôles sont beaux" (You relieve the suffering of the prisoners. / Actors, soldiers, you play fine roles).

While the productions at the Zouave theatre were light and humorous, the cause it supported was deadly serious. In his memoirs, Charles Fay, former aide-de-camp to General Bosquet, recalls several occasions when programs had been printed for the next day's show and word then came about impending military action. The actors had to quickly change costumes and roles. Young "soubrettes" traded in their skirts for muskets. Two days later the same theatre program – there was no time to revise – would circulate around the camp. In his book, Fay reproduces one such program and comments on programs that were amended at the last minute because some of the actors died the day before:

> Je ne puis jamais le regarder sans une profonde émotion; car derrière ces comédies, il y a tout un drame; ce programme, raturé en plusieurs endroits, parce qu'on avait dû changer quelques pièces, débute ainsi: "*Lundi 11 juin 1855. Au bénéfice des blessés du 7 au 8 juin. Représentation extraordinaire.*" – Puis suivent ces simples et bien touchantes lignes: "Deux amateurs ayant été tués, et plusieurs blessés, on a été obligé de changer le spectacle qu'on se proposait de donner."

> (I can never look at it without being profoundly moved; for behind these comedies there is great drama; this program is scratched out in several places because they had had to change some of the plays. It begins this

3.16 Zouave Playbill; Théâtre d'Inkermann. 26 August 1855. Reproduced with permission of La Bibliothèque nationale de France. "La Petite Margot et les bienfaits de l'éducation." "Un Monsieur et une dame." "La Course à la veuve."

3.17 Zouave Playbill; Théâtre d'Inkermann. 30 August 1855. Reproduced with permission of La Bibliothèque nationale de France. "La Petite Margot et les bienfaits de l'éducation." "Michel et Christine." "Vaudeville en un acte." "Le Gobe-mouche. Scène comique."

way: *"Monday, June 11, 1855. For the benefit of soldiers wounded on the June 7–8. Special performance"* – Then come these simple, touching lines: "As two actors were killed and several wounded, the show originally announced has been changed.") (*Souvenirs,* 264)

Of the many accounts of the Théâtre des Zouaves, perhaps the most poignant comes from Paul de Molènes, novelist, chronicler, dandy, and soldier. Molènes was enthralled by the glory of war and the poetry of battle. He served as an officer in the Crimean War under Maréchal Saint-Arnaud and later Canrobert and wrote about his experiences in *Les Commentaires d'un soldat sur la Guerre de Crimée et le siège de Sébastopol* (1860). He describes the eerie atmosphere in the empty theatre following the disastrous premature attack on Sebastopol on 18 June 1855 that ended with the loss of thousands of French soldiers:

> Le jour où je le vis pour la première fois, en me rendant à notre nouveau bivouac, ce lieu destiné au plaisir était en deuil ... La matinée du 18 juin avait détruit en quelques heures, presque tout entière, la troupe des soldats artistes. Les boulets russes avaient enlevé le père noble; l'amoureux; le comique, et jusqu'à la jeune première elle-même ... Le théâtre des zouaves ne fut point fermé longtemps. Une nouvelle troupe se reforma bien vite.
>
> (The first time I saw it, when I came to our new bivouac, the theatre that was designed for pleasure was in mourning ... The dawn of 18 June had destroyed in a few hours almost the entire troop of soldier artists. Russian bullets had killed the "noble father," "the lover," "the comic," right down to "the young ingenue," herself ... But the Zouave theatre was not closed for long. A new troop formed very quickly.) (180)

However comic the plays, the drama that transpired on and off the stage of the Théâtre des Zouaves – the theatre built on a battlefield – gives a whole new dimension to what we call the "Theatre of War."

Molènes enjoyed a double career as an officer and a man of letters. His death in 1862 was mourned by authors and critics alike, most notably Charles Baudelaire. In the obituary notice that he wrote for Molènes the poet expressed his admiration for the dashing officer and inspiring author he had known: "les *Commentaires d'un soldat sur le siège de Sébastopol* sont des morceaux dignes de vivre dans la mémoire des poètes" (His *Commentaires d'un soldat sur le siège de Sébastopol* are works that should live on in the memory of poets) (OC, vol. 2, 215–16). Baudelaire knew Molènes's work well and in 1859–60 was inspired by one of his short stories, "Les Souffrances d'un houzard," to write a play for the boulevard theatre, *Le Marquis du 1er houssards*.

As with his other theatrical projects, *La Fin de Don Juan* and *L'Ivrogne, Le Marquis du 1er houssards* would never be completed or staged. Baudelaire only got as far as a draft scenario, which follows Molènes's tale closely. It tells the story of Wolfgang Cadolles, son of a French émigré, who joins Bonaparte's army out of enthusiasm for military glory. Act II opens in 1809 on the eve of the battle at Wagram. The French army has crossed the Danube, and the emperor does his march past the 1st Houssards. Here is Baudelaire's summary of what follows: "Napoléon, étendant le bras droit, montre aux soldats les plateaux de Wagram où sont échelonnées les troupes de l'archiduc. Tonnerre et applaudissements. Wolgang se sent envie de pleurer comme s'il était enlevé par un puissant comédien" (Napoleon, stretching out his right arm, shows the soldiers the plateaux of Wagram where the Archduke's troops are lined up. Thunderous applause. Wolfgang feels like crying, as if moved by a powerful actor) (OC, vol. 1, 639).

Wolfgang is moved to tears by Napoleon's performance, and Baudelaire is quick to note what a "puissant comédien" the emperor was. To be sure, Baudelaire had been able to observe only several years prior the theatrical effects of another Napoleon who moved crowds to tears. And it is here that we come back to the boulevards of Paris where we began and to the grandest theatrical production of the Crimean War, one produced not by soldiers or poets, but by an emperor who was neither.

Nothing was more typical of Second Empire spectacle than the presence of large numbers of soldiers. There was a pervasive ceremonial militarism about the regime. Though he had never served in the military, the emperor often wore a general's uniform, even at civilian events such as legislative openings. It had more to do with his claim to his uncle's heritage and "the emotionally resonant place of the military in the symbolic construction of the French nation in the nineteenth century" (Baguley, *Napoleon III*, 163). Anxious to revive the pageantry of his uncle's great army, he re-established the Imperial Guard shortly after the Crimean War broke out, complete with military music to accompany it.

In an effort to capitalize on the memory of the Grande Armée, which still inflamed the imagination and patriotic ardour of the French masses, Napoleon III sought to revive the military spectacle that the first Napoleon had inspired. It was in Paris, far from the fields of battle, that the Crimean War offered the emperor the opportunity to put on the greatest military show of his career. Collective memory is, after all, not something

3.18 Clément Pruche (1811–1890), *Rentrée à Paris des régiments français revenant de Crimée [...] 29 Décembre 1855.* Reproduced with permission of La Bibliothèque nationale de France.

that just happens. It is often orchestrated by elites, in this case sovereigns, who control powerful modes of representation. The emperor's military spectacle was performed for a popular audience made up of the entire citizenry of Paris. It was four hours in length, it had a cast of thousands, it entranced the crowds, and the tickets were free. This was a model case of the state, in the person of the emperor, using a commemoration in the interest of fashioning a national mythology. Vicomte De Beaumont-Vassy in his *Histoire de mon temps* called it "un spectacle dont la population parisienne devait garder longtemps le souvenir et qui avait, en effet, une grandeur inusitée" (a spectacle that the Parisian population would long remember and that truly possessed extraordinary grandeur) (217).

But would Parisians long remember this spectacle, as Napoleon III surely hoped they would?

The emperor's power was on full display in the plein-air Crimean War production he staged on the afternoon of 29 December 1855. Known as the "Rentrée triomphale des troupes" or "L'Entrée solennelle à Paris des soldats revenant de Crimée," it heralded the entry into Paris of thousands of French troops returning from Crimea. Early in his regime the emperor had declared: "certaines personnes se disent: l'Empire, c'est la guerre, moi je dis: l'Empire, c'est la paix" (Certain people say: The Empire means war. As for me, I say: The Empire means peace) (Napoléon III, vol. 3, *Discours, Proclamations, Messages*, 342). Three years later, he was staging a tribute to a war waged in the name of that same peace-seeking empire. The celebration of military success and restored glory clearly invoked the Grande Armée and the Napoleonic legacy, and that called for commemoration. There was even a song composed for the event.[11]

The pageantry began at the Place de la Bastille. From a spot below the July Column, under an enormous triumphal arch built for the occasion with gold letters "À la Gloire de l'Armée d'Orient," and with the statue of the Spirit of Liberty hovering above him, the emperor read a short address of welcome to the soldiers: "Soldats, Je viens au-devant de vous comme autrefois le sénat romain allait aux portes de Rome au-devant de ses légions victorieuses. Je viens vous dire que vous avez bien mérité de la patrie." (Soldiers, I come before you the way the Roman senate used to go to the gates of Rome to face the victorious legions. I come to tell you that you have earned the honour of your fatherland) (Hamel, *Histoire du Second Empire*, 349).

Once he had completed his patriotic declaration, the emperor rode back along the *grands boulevards* to the Place Vendôme, where he positioned himself beneath the column bearing the statue of his uncle, the same column that sixteen years later Communards would topple: "La Colonne, admirable et digne piédestal de notre demi-dieu … du soldat-fondateur de notre dynastie" (The Column, admirable, worthy pedestal for our demi-god … for the soldier-founder of our dynasty) (Coti, *La Guerre d'Orient*, 82).[12] The long parade of troops followed the emperor to the Place Vendôme, where they filed past him in review.

The 6 January 1856 issue of *L'Illustration* described the extraordinary scene in words and pictures, including one impressive centre-spread of the soldiers and crowd at the Place Vendôme. If there were any scene to rival the entry into Paris of these heroes, it was surely the entry into Paris of Queen Victoria four months earlier. However, this parade,

3.19 R. Bongean, illustrateur, *Entrée Solenelle* [sic] *dans Paris de la Garde Impériale et des troupes de ligne venant de Crimée.* Reproduced with permission of La Bibliothèque nationale de France.

celebrating a war that had not yet officially ended, played to very different sympathies, as injured and mutilated soldiers, dressed in bandages and war-torn uniforms, marched at the head of their respective regiments.

Whether in the streets, on the rooftops, or looking out from windows, no one missed the manipulative show. Anatole France in his childhood memoir *La Vie en fleur* recalls an encounter in the park with a shy boy from aristocratic family:

3.20 Clément Pruche, *Retour de Crimée*. Reproduced with permission of La Bibliothèque nationale de France.

> Il me parla avec exaltation des victoires de Crimée. Il avait vu, d'une fenêtre de la place Vendôme, passer les troupes revenues d'Orient, et portant leurs habits de campagne usés et troués. Les blessés marchaient à la tête des régiments; les femmes leur jetaient des fleurs; on acclamait les drapeaux et les aigles. Le souvenir seul lui en donnait des battements de coeur.
>
> (He spoke to me with great excitement about the victories in Crimea. He had watched from a window in the Place Vendôme the soldiers returning from the East, wearing their battle uniforms, all worn and torn. The wounded men marched at the head of the regiments; women threw them flowers; people cheered the flags and eagles. Just thinking about it made his heart palpitate.) (52)

George Sand, who had privately supported the war – "Moi je ne me défends pas du chauvinisme, je me bats en imagination contre les

Russes" (I am not afraid to show my patriotism, I am fighting the Russians in my imagination) – was moved by the procession of bedraggled soldiers.[13] Writing to her cousin, René Vallet de Villeneuve, on 2 January 1856, she reported: "Paris a été très ému de la rentrée des troupes et j'ai vu ce spectacle navrant peu fait pour inspirer l'amour de la guerre quoi qu'on en dise. Je crois que je deviendrais folle si j'avais là un fils et si je le voyais revenir sans bras ou sans jambes" (Paris was very moved by the return of the troops. I saw the heartbreaking spectacle, hardly made to inspire love of war, whatever people say. I think I would go mad if I had a son over there and if I saw him returning with no arms or legs) (*Correspondance*, vol. 13, 486).

In his *Histoire de France, période contemporaine,* Louis Grégoire questioned the good taste of the staging that put the injured on display. The sight of mutilated soldiers leading the units provided tangible evidence of the suffering these men had endured and elicited strategically patriotic feelings. Prosper Mérimée noted that the next day there were lineups at the recruiting office for men to enrol.[14] This was Napoleon III's own brand of theatre of war. Ustazade Silvestre de Sacy, writing in his paper *Le Journal des Débats* on 30 December 1855, watched the emotional spectacle bring war and epic to the streets of Paris: "Pour la première fois, la génération présente assistait à une de ces fêtes héroïques et sombres familières à nos pères et qui pour nous paraissaient entrées dans l'histoire et dans l'épopée" (For the first time, this generation got to be present at one of those heroic, sombre events so familiar to our fathers, an event both historic and epic) (1). Well into the twentieth century, some historians were still moved by the drama of this commemoration of military sacrifice: "Mieux vaut bannir ici la notion même de 'propagande' … Le défilé militaire catalyse et déploie une 'éthique héroïque'" (Best to abandon the idea of "propaganda" here … This military parade catalysed and demonstrated a "heroic ethic") (Becker, *La France*, 29).

This was not just another colourful military parade. The troops had been specifically instructed to march not in their parade-ground finery but in their battle-worn campaign uniforms, ragged with wear. The strategically placed amputees, and the ragged uniforms and dented eagles, served as characters, props, and costumes for the grandest show on the boulevard:

> La vue des uniformes usés, les drapeaux criblés de balles, les figures bronzées ou fatiguées des soldats produisaient la plus vive émotion. On remarquait particulièrement … plusieurs généraux blessés, entre autres le général Mellinet, qui porte une profonde cicatrice à la joue droite; le

> général Blanchard, amputé du poignet, ont été tour à tour l'objet d'une douloureuse sympathie.
>
> (The sight of those battle-worn uniforms, the flags full of bullet holes, the tanned and tired faces of the soldiers, moved everyone ... General Mellinet with the deep scar on his right cheek and General Blanchard, amputated at the wrist elicited particular sympathy.) (de Sacy, 1)

The parade proceeded past spectators on the street and theatres on the boulevard. As the carefully choreographed procession moved through the city towards the Place Vendôme and the emperor, the lines separating *theatre* on the boulevard from the *theatres* on the boulevard blurred as the different theatres created sets for the parade just outside their doors.

> Les théâtres du boulevard avaient fait placer devant les estrades qui bordent la chaussée deux décors ... Devant le théâtre de l'Ambigu une Renommée en plâtre tenait à la main une couronne de lauriers. Sur la façade du théâtre des Variétés se trouvait un transparent représentant la Victoire au milieu de couronnes de lauriers et d'armes de toute espèce.
>
> (The boulevard theatres had erected two stage sets in front of the stands lining the street ... In front of the Théâtre de l'Ambigu, a plaster goddess held a crown of laurels. And on the facade of the Théâtre des Variétés there was a transparent panel representing Victory encircled by crowns of laurels and all kinds of arms.) (1)

The journal *Musée des Familles* noted that various theatres had even built their own "arcs de triomphe" (127). In short, while the theatre of war for the French army – in all its guts and glory – was being played out on the Crimean Peninsula, for the citizens of Paris the theatre of war was being staged as show business, a thanksgiving parade rolled into an early New Year's Day celebration: applauded, reported, illustrated, and reviewed much like the visit by Queen Victoria. The Ministry of State quickly commissioned a painting of the event, "Entrée dans Paris des troupes revenant de Crimée, le 29 décembre 1855," by Edmond Guet, which was later displayed at the Salon of 1857. The emperor himself purchased a painting of the "Retour à Paris des troupes de l'armée de Crimée" by Emmanuel Massé, which he lent to that same Salon. The entire production – monuments, decorations, costumes, choreography, paintings – was calculated to stamp the glory of the emperor's first war and his imperial lineage on the national psyche.

One is reminded of the words of Jean Baudrillard, writing in 1991 about another foreign war. He might as well have been talking about the Crimean War when he reflected: "The media promotes the war, the war promotes the media … The spectacular drive of war remains intact" (*The Gulf War Did Not Take Place*, 31, 32). The Rentrée, like the war itself, filled the pages of newspapers and the illustrated press, stirring up patriotic emotion for a distant war that had already cost the French some 90,000 lives. For the vicomte de Beaumont-Vassey the scene was unforgettable; the crowds – as doubtless intended – went wild with enthusiasm. The emperor would not have been displeased, for it was indeed in his interest to elicit "la plus vive émotion," "la plus noble émotion," over and above any critique of this crippling war and the government that had embarked on it. "Ce fut une scène extraordinaire et dont personne, à Paris, ne perdra le souvenir" (It was an extraordinary scene that no one in Paris will ever forget) (Beaumont-Vassy, *Histoire de mon temps*, 218).

While no individual in Paris in December 1855 would, by the vicomte's account, ever forget that scene, like the war it commemorated it quickly vanished from public memory once it was over. More precisely, it vanished from Parisian memory, for it is not at all clear that outside the metropole this event was noticed. Despite predictions by many commentators, the re-entry of the troops that was designed to be *inoubliable* did not in the end secure either popular or national loyalties. That is because cultural memory, when grounded in lived experience rather than durable external objects and rites, is by nature ephemeral. The makeshift Arcs de Triomphe came down as quickly as they were erected. The two commissioned paintings were not enough to preserve the significance of that moment.

After the war, the emperor allowed himself one final hurrah in the streets of Paris to commemorate the war and the taking of Sebastopol. The event gave him the occasion to combine in one spectacle two successes of his empire: the victory of the French army in Crimea and the modernization of the city of Paris by Baron Georges-Eugène Haussmann.

As part of his urban redesign of Paris, Haussmann had envisaged "la croisée de Paris," a network of major arteries to cross through the city so as to give access from its extremes. One of the first boulevards Haussmann undertook was the Boulevard du Centre, designed to open the city's north–south axis. The work began in 1855 contemporaneously with the war. Along its way the boulevard cut through some of the most crowded and insalubrious neighbourhoods in Paris, which in the past had been sites of cholera as well as political unrest. Several days after the taking of Sebastopol in September 1855, the still incomplete boulevard was renamed le Boulevard de Sébastopol in honour of the victory.

Once completed, on 5 April 1858, the new boulevard was inaugurated with great pomp. With the emperor and empress presiding, the ceremony was staged by city architect Victor Baltard, who had also designed Les Halles. The decoration was sumptuous. Hundreds of flagpoles on both sides of the boulevard from the Place du Châtelet to the Gare de l'Est were topped with banners bearing Napoleon's bees and "N"s. Special tickets were made available to the public, and crowds lined the street, which was decorated with flags, banners, and ribbons much like the banners and ribbons that had welcomed Queen Victoria in August 1855 and had welcomed back the soldiers from Crimea in December 1855.

The decorative centrepiece, however, was the enormous gold lamé curtain stretched across the boulevard just before it meets the Boulevard

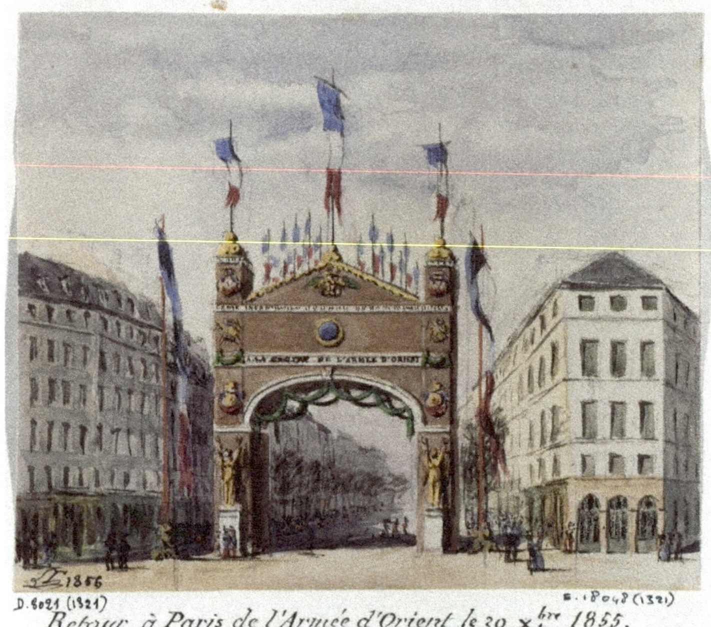

3.21 Léon Leymonnerye (1803–1879), *Arc Vis-à-Vis de la Colonne de Juillet élévé pour le retour à Paris de l'Armée d'Orient le 29 décembre 1855.* An imposing arch was erected on the Place de la Bastille for the dramatic re-entry to Paris of soldiers from Crimea. Photograph courtesy of Musée Carnavalet, Histoire de Paris.

3.22 Pierre Ambroise Richebourg (1810–1875), *Inauguration du Boulevard de Sébastopol, le 5 avril 1858, en présence se l'Empereur Napoléon III et de l'Impératrice Eugénie. 1er, 2ème, 3ème et 4ème Arrondissements, Paris.* Inauguration of the Boulevard de Sépastopol. Note the destroyed building on the far right of the picture. Photograph courtesy of Musée Carnavalet, Histoire de Paris.

Saint-Denis and turns onto the Boulevard de Strasbourg. The curtain was suspended from two tall minarets and decorated with gold stars and green diamonds; above it floated a row of tricolour banners. "As the emperor turned onto the new boulevard, a tricolour flag was raised, giving the signal to draw back the curtain at the Boulevard Saint-Denis to present the long perspective for the first time. The curtain opened in the centre, and the two halves fell back upon the minarets. Described by one viewer as something "out of a magical play," it had an undeniably theatrical quality. It unveiled the new street as if the street itself were a monument. "When the generations who follow traverse our great city," the newspaper *Le Constitutionnel* reported, "in reading the names inscribed on our bridges and on our streets they will remember the glory of our arms from Rivoli to Sebastopol" (Truesdell, *Spectacular Politics*, 92). But if monument it was, the boulevard would become a monument to modern urbanization rather than to the glory of the war whose victory it commemorated.

The illustrated press – including the press in London – was filled with images of the inauguration. In addition to drawings of the event engraved for wide distribution in the press, some papers, like *L'Illustration*, included engravings based on photographs by Pierre Ambroise Richebourg.

But photographs (sometimes) don't lie. At the time of the celebration, buildings and homes along the route had long been expropriated to make way for the new boulevard, but there were no new buildings

3.23 *Inauguration du boulevard de Sébastopol, le 5 avril 1858*. (Based on the photograph by Richebourg.) Reproduced with permission of La Bibliothèque nationale de France.

lining it yet. In Richebourg's photograph a ruined building can be seen on the right, next to one of the ceremonial towers, a reminder of the wreckage that lay behind the glittering display, whether the destruction of neighbourhoods of Paris or the human cost of the victory at Sebastopol.

Two years after the Crimean War, the spectacular drive of the war, directed from the top, seemed, in Baudrillard's words, still intact. But as with the emperor's earlier spectacles, it would not take many years for people to forget this one. As the significance of the Crimean War faded from memory, so too did the significance of the name of the broad boulevard that takes Parisians from the Gare de l'Est to Châtelet. In *The Power of Place: Urban Landscape as Public History* (1997), Dolores Hayden makes the case for "the power of ordinary urban landscapes to nurture citizens' public memory, to encompass shared time in the form of shared territory" (9). As if to defy her premise, the Boulevard de Sébastopol quickly abdicated the role of public memory keeper; its name now recalls above all a busy metro station at the intersection of the Rue Réaumur.

Aleida Assmann tells us that for events to be transformed into long-term collective memory that can be transmitted from generation to generation, they need to be emplotted in an "affectively charged and mobilizing narrative" ("Transformations," 55). However rousing and moving, the seductive narratives embedded in the Parisian spectacles of Napoleon III did not enter collective memory. What they did memorialize was the canniness of the man behind the scenes, who managed to turn a bloody war about church doors, personal ego, and a craving for international respect into patriotic entertainment. The plays, the performances, the palaces, and the parades, however popular, did not find their way into any myths of national identity.

It is a curiosity of the place – or non-place – of the Crimean War in French collective memory that neither mass media (in the form of the press), literary texts, symbolic commemorations, nor the stage fulfilled the role of stable conveyor. Does cultural memory need to circulate in material form to lodge itself in the public imagination? It is with this thought that we now turn to the role and the impact of visual art in transmitting and preserving the cultural memory of that war.

Chapter Four

Crimea: The Visible War

If the Crimean war is *invisible* in French cultural memory, in France in the years both during and after the campaign, it was anything but.

The visual coverage of the war in France was as extensive as it was varied in form and accessibility: large-scale academic paintings, lithographs, photographs, caricatures, panoramas, and more. From major state-sponsored exhibitions to weekly illustrated papers, board games, decks of cards, and household items, images of the war ran the gamut and were available to all classes. There were, for example, at least thirty-two illustrated cotton scarves from Rouen representing scenes from the Crimean War (Bassargette, "Une imagerie educative," 63). The most famous battles, such as the taking of the Malakoff Tower, could be found as easily in epic-sized paintings in the Salon of 1857, such as Adolphe Yvon's 6- by 9-metre *Prise de la Tour Malakoff*, as in a bourgeois home on dessert plates, of which there were many versions and manufacturers. In the words of art historian Pierre-Lin Renié, the Crimean War generated a "deluge," a "revolution" of images of all kinds. Maps, panoramas, portraits of generals, officers, and men of state, caricatures, and battle scenes packed the windows of print dealers ("De l'imprimerie photographique," 25).[1]

The first major occasion for an exhibition of paintings of the war was conceived before the war itself. After the success of the 1851 Great Exhibition in London, with its celebration of commerce and industry and its millions of visitors, Napoleon III was keen to see the British and raise them one. On 8 March 1853, he cancelled a French national exhibition that was planned for 1854, decreed in its place L'Exposition universelle de 1855 (the Universal Exhibition of 1855), and appointed an Imperial Commission to organize it, led by his cousin Prince Napoleon. Little would one have imagined that by the time the exhibition

4.1 Adolphe Yvon (1817–1883), *La Prise de la Tour Malakoff, le 8 septembre 1855.* 1857. CC BY-SA 3.0, via Wikimedia Commons.

opened, France and Britain would be military allies fighting a war on the Crimean Peninsula, and that the exhibition would serve as a patriotic platform to celebrate battles won together – especially where the French had led.

The Universal Exhibition of 1855 attracted attention from all quarters in France – there were at least eighty reviews in publications ranging from *L'Assemblée nationale* to *Le Coiffeur parisien*, including a full set of caricatures by Cham (Amédée Charles Henri, Comte de Noé) in the satirical publication *Le Charivari* ("Promenades à l'Exposition") and more caricatures by Bertall in the *Journal pour rire*. In an effort to be more truly "universal," Prince Napoleon and his commission included alongside the industrial display a vast exhibition of paintings, sculptures, prints, and architecture to highlight accomplishments in the arts as well as in science, technology, and business. (The relatively new medium of photography was featured in the Palais de l'Industrie.) In this way the international prestige of French culture would be reaffirmed. By many accounts, the exhibition of fine arts was the section that attracted the most attention from the public and critics alike. A partial list of reviewers of that exhibition reads like a who's who of mid-century French authors and critics: Charles Baudelaire, Maxime Du Camp, Alexandre Dumas, Théophile Gautier, Edmond and Jules de Goncourt, Nadar, and more. The Palais des Beaux Arts built for the occasion contained works by more than 2,000 artists, more than half of whom were French. Four French artists were honoured with retrospectives: Eugène Delacroix, Alexandre-Gabriel Decamps, Jean-Auguste-Dominique Ingres, and Horace Vernet. Ingres, the academic neoclassicist, was associated with, among other things, paintings of Napoleon I. Vernet, a popular artist with the public, if not the critics, was France's foremost battle painter and was similarly associated with Napoleon I and military greatness. The choice of these two artists was politically expedient, in that wherever he could, Napoleon III sought to legitimize his empire publicly through dynastic association with his uncle. Official memory was articulated with the aid of preexisting war narratives, which provided a national repertoire of usable images, plots, and figures. That repertoire included works of art that underpinned the remembrance of war. In this instance the dominant narrative linked the wartime leadership of Napoleon III to that of Napoleon I.

4.2 "Bombardement de la Tour Malakoff," china plate by J. Viellard. 1857. Author collection. Many sets of commemorative plates representing battles of the Crimean War were produced by different manufacturers.

4.3 "Guerre d'Orient, jeu de loto." Board game. Image courtesy Alain Rabussier.

4.4 "Loterie de la Guerre d'Orient." Reproduced with permission of La Bibliothèque nationale de France. This board game illustrates the popular, widely distributed Épinal images produced by the house of Pellerin.

4.5 "Camp français devant Sébastopol no. 14." 1855. From the house of Pellerin, Épinal. Collection of the Musée de l'image – Ville d'Épinal/cliché H. Rouyer.

Napoleon III, though not a great lover of art himself, was acutely sensitive to the added value that art brought to his political agenda.[2] In at least one of the Ingres paintings on display the link from the great Napoleon to the one Victor Hugo had disparaged as "le petit" was not to be missed.[3] Opposite the famous painting of the *Apotheosis of Homer* (1827), which had been commissioned for a ceiling in the Louvre, hung the *Apotheosis of Napoleon I*, which Napoleon III had himself commissioned from Ingres just days before announcing the Universal Exhibition. It was a monumental work designed to adorn the ceiling of the Salon de l'Empereur in the Paris Hôtel de Ville.

In the allegorical painting, Napoleon I is taken by chariot to the Temple of Glory and Immortality while Fame crowns him and Victory leads

4.6 "Drôleries d'Orient." Reproduced with permission of La Bibliothèque nationale de France.

4.7 "Guerre de Crimée." Tapestry. Inventory number 95.72.84, Collection of the Musée d'art et d'industrie de la ville de Saint-Etienne – photo SARA.

4.8 "Victoire de l'Alma, remportée sur les russes par les armées alliées, le 20 septembre 1854." Collection Musée des Traditions et Arts Normands-Château de Martainville, inv 2001.1.49 © Véronique Hénon. One of 32 commemorative handkerchiefs by Lamy Godard Brothers.

4.9 "Etablissement orthopédique fondé à l'occasion de la prise de Sébastopol." Handkerchief by F. Daniel et Cie. Ville de Paris/Bibliothèque Forney.

4.10 Jean-Auguste-Dominique Ingres (1780–1867), *l'Apothéose de Napoléon I* (1853). © RMN-Grand Palais/Art Resource, NY.

him. The original painting was destroyed in the fire at the Hôtel de Ville during the Commune in 1871, but there remain preparatory drawings at the Musée Carnavalet and a watercolour at the Louvre that together give an accurate idea of the composition. Most telling, perhaps, is the inscription on the armrest of the throne: "in nepote redivivus" (he lives again through his nephew). In 1855, when the painting was first exhibited at the Universal Exhibition and the siege of Sebastopol still seemed endless, victory and glory were very much on the emperor's mind. But so was apotheosis. Outside the context of the Universal Exhibition, in 1854, in a gesture of imperial gall, Napoleon III commissioned his own apotheosis from Guillaume-Alphonse Cabasson, in which he is surrounded by Greek gods and goddesses and his uncle proudly salutes him from heaven.[4]

Horace Vernet's paintings at the Universal Exhibition fed the propaganda machine of the Second Empire even more directly than Ingres's. Where Ingres's painting of the *Apotheosis of Napoleon I* asserted Napoleon III's imperial credentials, Vernet's paintings of two Napoleonic battles, *Montimirail: L'empereur Napoléon I, 1814* (1822) and *Hanau: L'empereur Napoléon Ier, 1813* (1824), quietly declared the transmission of military genius from Napoleon I to his nephew, who at that very moment was waging war against his uncle's old enemy, Russia. The message was not lost on an enthusiastic French public: Napoleon's appeal, as the critic Claude Vignon noted in her review of the Exhibition, "s'attache à la passion collective qui est toujours vivante en France: au patriotisme" (is linked to France's still fervent collective passion: patriotism) (Vignon, *Exposition universelle*, 220).[5]

While Vernet's battle paintings referenced the Crimean War indirectly, there was no shortage of explicit images of the war in the French section of the exhibition. In France, large-scale battle painting, a category of history painting meant to demonstrate moral virtue, had always figured prominently at Salon exhibitions. More than ten paintings representing the Crimean War hung in the most popular room of the French gallery at the Universal Exhibition of 1855, inspiring one critic to comment that passing from the French gallery to the British was like going from war to peace (Pointon, "From the Midst of Warfare," 236).

Isidore Pils, who was awarded a medal for his painting *Tranchée devant Sébastopol* (*A Trench at Sebastopol*), sidestepped some of the more familiar conventions of battle painting to characterize the distinctive nature of this war, a war defined more by the disquiet of siege than by action. This was a battle painting without a battle.

Commenting on this painting in his review, Théophile Gautier applauded Pils's approach:

> M. Pils a exposé cette année *Une tranchée devant Sébastopol, une Embuscade de Zouaves,* dans un style tout différent de ce qu'on est habitué à voir. Les

4.11 Isidore Pils (1815–1875), *Tranchée devant Sébastopol* (1855). Musée des Beaux-Arts Bordeaux/F. Deval.

> zouaves, vêtus de leur caban à capuchon, ont des physionomies fermes et mélancoliques, des attitudes simples où se laissent lire l'ennui et la fatigue.
>
> (This year M. Pils exhibited *A Trench near Sebastopol, a Zouave Ambush,* a painting done in a style quite different from what we are used to seeing. The faces of the Zouave soldiers, dressed in their hooded pea coats, are firm and melancholy. Their bodies convey boredom and fatigue. One reads in their simple attitudes of boredom and fatigue.) (Gautier, *Les Beaux arts en Europe,* vol. 2, 23)

Pils set his painting – and the viewer – in a trench, a "non-lieu" where bored, exhausted soldiers spent long days and cold, muddy nights waiting for action. This was a war of nerves as much as of weapons, and the jury, it would seem, appreciated Pils's representation of a new war in a new way.

The painting earned the artist two large state commissions, *Le Débarquement des troupes en Crimée* and *La Bataille de l'Alma*. Pils, a past winner of the Prix de Rome (1838), was the son of a soldier who had fought in the Grande Armée during the First Empire. By honouring him the state was further reaffirming its place in the lineage of the First Empire and its glories. But Pils did not privilege military leaders or moments of great Napoleonic drama. Nor did he travel to Crimea, as some artists did.

Instead, he spent time at a military training camp and worked largely from press reports and illustrated newspaper reportage. This approach may have contributed to his non-episode paintings as well. In the epic-size *Battle of Alma* that he would go on to paint (6 by 9 metres), he presents soldiers straining to cross the river and get into position for battle rather than clashing with the enemy. Pils's *Battle of Alma,* which would not be completed and exhibited until 1861, eventually earned him the epithet "le peintre d'Alma" (Vottero, "Autour d'Isidore Pils," 198). But already at the Universal Exhibition of 1855 there were no fewer than four paintings of the Battle of Alma on display, representing a battle that had taken place just eight months before the exhibition opened. It was the first major battle of the Crimean War and a decisive victory for France.

Topical and patriotic as they were, the four paintings of the Battle of Alma at the exhibition (by J. Beaume, J.L.H. Bellengé, G. Doré, and E. Lami) were not especially favoured by the critics. In his review, Julien de la Rochenoire found in Bellengé's painting "beaucoup de travail pour un bien peu résultat" (a lot of work for not much result) and complained that Lami hadn't understood the battle much better (Rochenoire, *Le Salon de 1855*, 84–5). Independent of the quality of the paintings, this genre of battle history painting, once the most respected of artistic genres in the academic hierarchy, was losing steam. In the "Salon of 1846," reflecting on the battle paintings of Horace Vernet, whose work he never liked, Baudelaire had complained: "Je hais cet art improvisé au roulement du tambour" (I hate this art that is improvised to the beat of a drumroll) (*OC*, vol. 2, 469). In 1855 the Goncourt brothers lamented that now that religious painting was no longer in vogue, all that was left to nineteenth-century painters was battle painting, a genre valued for documentary accuracy, not art or imagination: "une illustration de la tactique, la mise en scène panoramique d'un rapport militaire, elle est descendue au trompe-l'œil des boutons d'un régiment ou du dessous de la botte d'un general" (An illustration of tactics, the panoramic display of a military report, it has been reduced to optical illusions of a regiment's buttons or the underside of a general's boot) (Goncourt, *La Peinture*, 16). Various critics would make similar arguments about a tired genre that served the interests of political propaganda more than art. The comte de Nieuwerkerke, Director of Fine Arts under Napoleon III, could not have been more off target when he declared that history painting alone would conserve the image of contemporary individuals in action and "la physionomie de l'époque dont elle retrace les événements" (the physiognomy of the epoch whose events it retraces).[6] There was, in general, a "déjà-vu" character to the exhibition that undermined the endurance of its paintings in cultural memory.

4.12 Isidore Pils, *La Bataille d'Alma. 1861.* © RMN-Grand Palais/Art Resource, NY.

It is telling, then, that if any paintings did achieve endurance during the Universal Exhibition of 1855, it was not pictures of the Crimean War hanging in its exhibit halls but rather those on display in a separate pavilion outside the exhibition. Gustave Courbet had seen his monumental canvas *L'Atelier du peintre, allégorie réelle déterminant une phase de sept années de ma vie artistique (The Painter's Studio: A Real Allegory Summing Up Seven Years of My Artistic and Moral Life)* rejected by the jury of the Universal Exhibition, and he retaliated by mounting his own exhibition, where he showed that painting along with another forty in his "Pavilion of Realism," brazenly set up by him within sight of the official exhibition. The scale of that painting and its mysterious representation of the artist's personal, aesthetic, and intellectual worlds challenged the impersonal grandeur of the large-scale history paintings that were traditionally favoured by academic juries. In his appeal to a new form of Realist expression and subject matter Courbet upended the official conventions and tastes that were on display in the battle paintings across the road. In the end it was *The Painter's Studio* that entered the Musée d'Orsay in Paris and the canon of cultural memory, while the paintings of the Battle of Alma were put to rest deep in the archives.

Of those battle paintings at the Universal Exhibition, one stood out for reviewers, and that was Gustave Doré's *Bataille de l'Alma, attaque de la colonne du Général Bosquet,* in which the artist represents the confusion and collective combat of soldiers. The case of Doré is a particularly interesting one because of the way he used different genres and media to represent the war for different consumer publics.

Known at the time for his 1854 illustrations of the works of Rabelais, Doré was viewed by many members of the jury as an illustrator, not an artist.[7] Others came to his defence. The critic Edmond About called in Michelet, for whom the people, not the leaders, were the heroes:

> Tous les peintres d'histoire installent du premier plan un général avec son état-major … Pour vous, vous avez eu l'idée originale et généreuse de faire une bataille de soldats. C'est dans le même esprit que M. Michelet a écrit l'histoire de la France, reléguant les princes au fond du tableau, de donnant la place d'honneur au héros véritable, le peuple.
>
> (All history painters put a general and his staff in the foreground … You, on the other hand, have had the original and generous idea of showing us a battle of soldiers. It was in this same spirit that M. Michelet wrote his history of France, relegating the princes to the back of the painting and giving honour of place to the real heroes, the people.) (About, *Voyage à travers l'exposition,* 193–4)

Others agreed, and Doré was commissioned to do a painting of the Battle of Inkermann.

This was not the first time Doré had tackled the subject of the Crimean War. Though his name was, and still is, linked to illustrations of great works of literature – Balzac, Cervantes, Dante, Rabelais, Shakespeare, and others – in the mid-1850s he was heavily invested in the Crimean War. In 1854 he produced a biting book of anti-Russian caricatures in response to the war that had just started. A graphic novel *avant la lettre,* the idiosyncratic *Histoire pittoresque, dramatique et caricaturale de la sainte Russie* is composed of 500 sequential woodcut drawings of various sizes interspersed with accompanying captions that caricature Russia's history as a succession of barbarian rulers. As the violent history of Russia unfolds for the reader, it eventually catches up with current events, the cruel ambition of the tsar, and the Crimean War. In the final pages Doré tries to assure the French public of imminent victory with minimal harm to themselves and minimal suffering to the Russian people, victims too of barbaric tyranny. As of April 1856, however, following the signing of the Treaty of Paris, all sales of *Histoire de la sainte Russie* were outlawed.

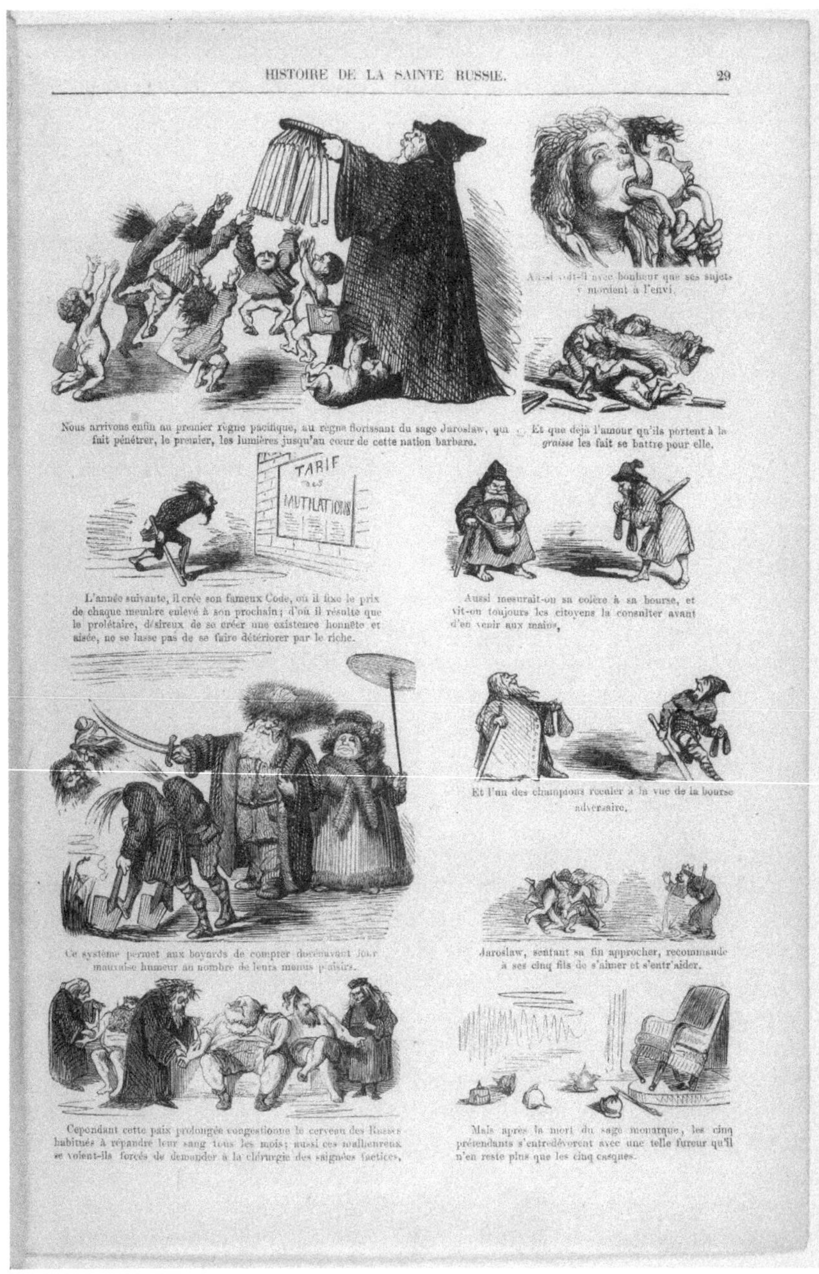

HISTOIRE DE LA SAINTE RUSSIE. 29

Nous arrivons enfin au premier règne pacifique, au règne florissant du sage Jaroslaw, qui fait pénétrer, le premier, les lumières jusqu'au cœur de cette nation barbare.

Aussi voit-il avec bonheur que ses sujets y mordent à l'envi.

Et que déjà l'amour qu'ils portent à la *graisse* les fait se battre pour elle.

L'année suivante, il crée son fameux Code, où il fixe le prix de chaque membre enlevé à son prochain; d'où il résulte que le prolétaire, désireux de se créer une existence honnête et aisée, ne se lasse pas de se faire détériorer par le riche.

Aussi mesurait-on sa colère à sa bourse, et vit-on toujours les citoyens la consulter avant d'en venir aux mains,

Et l'un des champions reculer à la vue de la bourse adversaire.

Ce système permet aux boyards de compter dorénavant leur mauvaise humeur au nombre de leurs menus plaisirs.

Jaroslaw, sentant sa fin approcher, recommande à ses cinq fils de s'aimer et s'entr'aider.

Cependant cette paix prolongée congestionne le cerveau des Russes habitués à répandre leur sang tous les mois; aussi ces malheureux se voient-ils forcés de demander à la chirurgie des saignées factices,

Mais après la mort du sage monarque, les cinq prétendants s'entredévorent avec une telle fureur qu'il n'en reste plus que les cinq casques.

4.13 Gustave Doré (1832–1883), *Histoire de la Sainte Russie*. 1854. Reproduced with permission of La Bibliothèque nationale de France.

Doré's caricatures did not have the impact he had hoped for; the same year, however, two other albums of satirical caricatures of Russians in the Crimean War were published to great acclaim by the well-established artist and caricaturist Honoré Daumier. These caricatures satirizing the "Russian bear" engaged directly with the contemporary Russian enemy in Crimea. Daumier's lithographs first appeared in the "Actualités" section of the satirical journal *Le Charivari* and were quickly gathered together in 1854 in two albums, *Les Cosaques pour Rire: album de quarante caricatures* and, in conjunction with the caricaturist Cham (Charles Amédée de Noé), *Chargeons les Russes: album de quarante caricatures*. Given the nature of political caricatures, whatever their immediate success the different albums did not produce the kind of lasting visual trace that would memorialize the war.

Doré's own representations of the Crimean War did not stop at *Histoire de la sainte Russie*. In 1854 he joined in a project with Charles Philipon, legendary founder of *La Caricature* and *Le Charivari*, to produce

4.14 Honoré Daumier, "Un Ours contrarié." *Le Charivari*, 28 August 1854. National Gallery of Art, CC0, via Wikimedia Commons.

4.15 Gustave Doré, "Chasseurs d'Afrique in a reconnoitring excursion headed by General d'Alloville charging the Cossacks," "Arrival of General Ulrich in the bay of Kamiesk." *Musée français-anglais,* March 1855. Reproduced with permission of La Bibliothèque nationale de France.

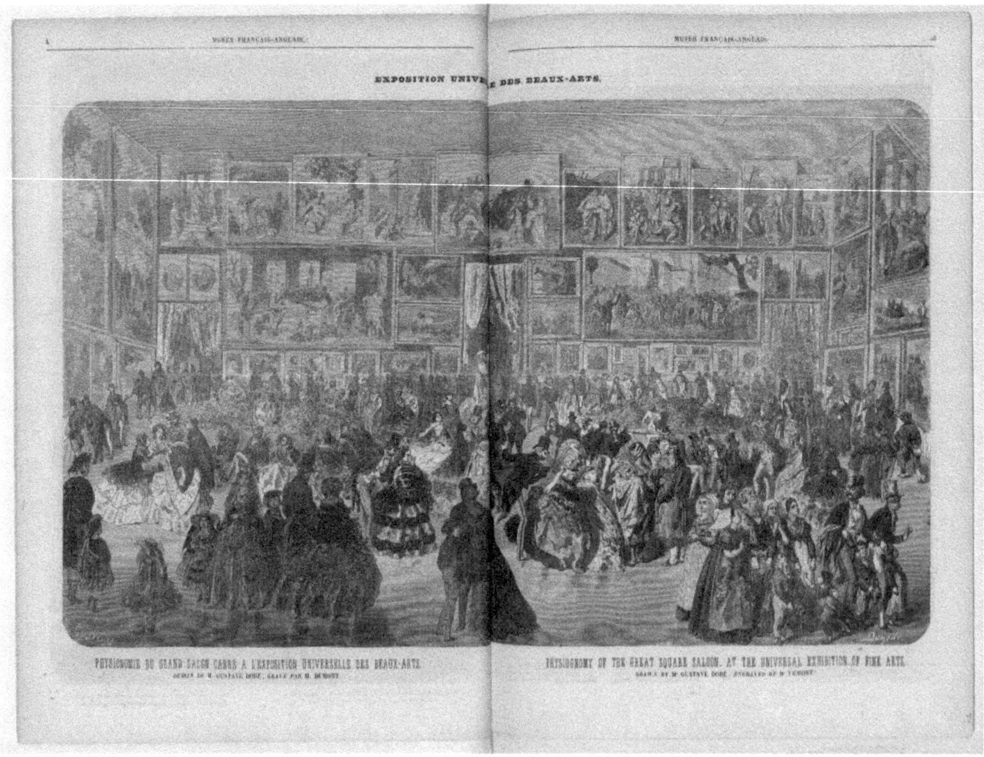

4.16 Gustave Doré, "Physiognomy of the Great Square Saloon at the Universal Exhibition of Fine Arts." *Musée français-anglais,* June 1855. Reproduced with permission of La Bibliothèque nationale de France.

4.17 Gustave Doré, "The Battle of Tchernaya," *Illustrated London News*, 29 September 1855. Author collection.

illustrations for a new publication that would be offered to subscribers of *Le Journal pour rire*, for which he also drew caricatures. In a gesture intended to complement the military alliance of France and Britain, Philipon created the monthly *Musée français-anglais*, which was launched on both sides of the Channel in January 1855. Unlike the *Journal pour rire*, this eight-page "journal of monthly illustrations" was not meant to be comic. It included etchings of topical events for a cross-channel readership. There were always illustrations – sometimes a centrefold – devoted to "La Guerre d'Orient," most often based on drawings by Doré. Doré's war images were frequently featured on the front cover as well.

The significance of Doré's work on the Crimean War lies less in the specific images he produced than in the different visual genres he used simultaneously to represent a topic that was on the minds – and in the eyes – of a broad French public. From the academic dignity of large-scale history paintings to popular caricatures and newspaper illustrations, these works were available to a large cross-section of the public throughout France, made possible by the unprecedented proliferation of old and new modes of visual representation that coincided with the Crimean War.

More than any other medium, it was, in fact, the illustrated press, much like *Le Musée français-anglais,* whose images communicated the news of the war to a general public that did not attend Salons. In his editorial for the first issue of *L'Univers illustré* (22 May 1858), Théophile Gautier declared: "Notre siècle n'a toujours pas le temps de lire, mais il a toujours le temps de voir; où l'article demande une demi-heure, le dessin ne demande qu'une minute" (Our century does not always have the time to read, but it always has time to look; where an article may take half an hour to read, a drawing requires only a minute) (in Bacot, *La Presse illustrée,* 80). The Crimean War represented the meeting of a new kind of war with a new kind of medium that, much like film and television in the twentieth century, encouraged and created a public taste for current events. In Britain the war generated an insatiable appetite for news: "the painful excitement for information, beggars all description," wrote one government official (Knightley, *The First Casualty,* 2). The illustrated press in particular was able to translate the war into sellable news. In France it was the weekly *L'Illustration,* founded in 1843, that led the way. An instant success, it attracted tens of thousands of loyal readers with its high-quality prints, diversity of news items, contributions from a network of correspondents, and insistence on images. Like other weeklies it was available for purchase by the issue or by subscription. In 1854, the year France entered the war, *L'Illustration* had more than 14,000 subscribers; by 1855, that number had risen to 24,000 (Hornstein, *Episodes,* 245). *L'Illustration* had a pool of artists on the ground in Crimea to draw from, including members of the military. The war sold so well that in the summer of 1855 (coinciding with the Universal Exhibition in Paris), Jean-Baptiste Alexandre Paulin, editor-in-chief of *L'Illustration,* was exasperated at the lack of impressive battles as the siege dragged on: "Histoire de la semaine, *L'Illustration,* 18 août 1855. Les nouvelles de Crimée sont plus nulles que jamais" (Story of the week, *L'Illustration,* 18 August 1855. News from Crimea remains as boring as ever) (249). It was the immediacy of the images and the telegraphed stories of the week they illustrated that attracted readers. And the images were plentiful and ubiquitous. Unlike the formal paintings hanging at exhibitions and Salons, these weekly illustrations, and the publications they appeared in, provided a sense of immediacy and promised more news to come.

Illustrations in the press were created mainly from drawings and sometimes from photographs, which at the time required an engraver's skills before they could be published. From the outset, *L'Illustration* ascribed an informational role to its images that was consistent with its practice of getting reliable reports from special correspondents dispatched to the field. Constantin Guys, the French artist celebrated by Charles Baudelaire as the "Painter of Modern Life," worked as a Special Visual Correspondent in Crimea, where he made drawings for the *Illustrated London News*. *L'Illustration* for its part sent the painter Jean-Baptiste Henri Durand-Brager to Crimea as its own Special Artist. Durand-Brager assured the readers that he would introduce them to the everyday life of the soldier in his tent, in the trenches, on the field of battle, or in the ambulance: "Je ne négligerai rien, je ne reculerai devant aucune espèce de peine, pour mettre sous les yeux de vous lecteur la physionomie de cette vaillante armée" (I will neglect nothing, I will not recoil from painful scenes, in order to present you, reader, with the face of this valiant army) (*L'Illustration,* 5 May 1855; quoted in Puiseux, *Les Figures de la guerre*, 68).

The weekly made sure to promote Durand-Brager's military credentials: he had previously worked as an official draughtsman on French naval expeditions. This legitimized the authenticity of his drawings for the reading public. By offering the unprecedented immediacy of visual reportage, journals such as the *Illustrated London News* and *L'Illustration* positioned themselves as indispensable news sources, all the while stressing, as in the eyewitness drawings by Guys and Durand-Brager, the unadorned rendering of "facts."[8]

There was also the new medium of photography, which started signalling factuality both for the artist and for the public. The Universal Exhibition of 1855 offered the first international exhibition of photography. There, in the English photography section of the Palais de l'Industrie, the Crimean War photographs by the British photographer Roger Fenton – "father of war photography" – were on display and attracted keen attention.[9] In his 1856 *Esquisses photographiques à propos de l'Exposition Universelle et de la guerre d'Orient*, Ernest Lacan devoted sixteen detailed pages to Fenton's remarkable photographs. The Crimean War was, in fact, the first major war to be photographed.[10] Fenton had been sponsored by the

Episodes de la campagne de Crimée.

Expédition de Crimée. Attaque du village du Lazaret.

Bien de bien saillant ne s'est passé depuis mon dernier envoi, soit à l'armée de siége, soit à l'armée d'observation. Le temps est devenu un peu plus maniable ; on aperçoit quelquefois le soleil, et le soldat s'en trouve bien. Les pluies continuelles ont cessé, et le froid ne se presse pas d'arriver, ce dont on doit lui savoir gré. Nos batteries se taisent toujours, quoique tout soit prêt ou à peu près, sauf quelques nouveaux travaux et une nouvelle batterie, que le génie a commencés depuis une huitaine de jours du côté de la Quarantaine, pour tourner le Lazaret, de manière à l'enfermer dans les lignes françaises, ainsi que la petite église, ou plutôt l'ermitage de Saint-Vladimir, et le fort Génois ; ce travail a facilité un coup de main assez intéressant à enregistrer : quelques chasseurs à pied de garde avancée se sont rués, dans la nuit du 21 au 22 décembre, vers une heure du matin, sur un poste russe, qui s'est enfui ; ils l'ont poursuivi, et, soutenus par quelques hommes de la légion étrangère, ils en ont mis en fuite un second, sont arrivés jusqu'au petit village situé au-dessous de la batterie en terre de la Quarantaine, l'ont attaqué, et, après une courte fusillade, s'en sont emparé.

Attaque de la tour [illegible] par une division anglaise.

Attaque de [illegible] par les Russes. — D'après les dessins de M. Durand-Brager.

4.18 Henri Durand-Brager (1814–1879), "Episodes de la Campagne de Crimée." (Texte et dessins) *l'Illustration,* 27 January 1855. Author collection.

English publisher Thomas Agnew and Sons to travel to Crimea and document the war. The British government endorsed his mission, hoping that his photographs would reassure a public increasingly agitated by William Russell's critical reports in *The Times* about the dismal conditions faced by soldiers at the front. Fenton spent three and a half months in Crimea and produced 360 photographs. For technical as well as strategic reasons he photographed no combat scenes or wounded and dead soldiers; his album provided instead an eyewitness record of daily life, the landscape of the war, and pictures of British, French, and Turkish officers and men. Like the drawings in the illustrated press, Fenton's images were at opposite poles to the grand history paintings that hung elsewhere at the Exhibition; they focused on scenes of daily life at the front with no grandiose heroics. Such images were all the more pertinent given that the nature of this drawn-out siege was low on moments of glory.

4.19 "M. Durand-Brager, correspondent de L'Illustration dessinant en Crimée." *L'Illustration*, 9 February 1856 (dessin de J. Worms, gravure de B.H. Cie). Author collection.

Some of Fenton's pictures were published as wood engravings in the *Illustrated London News*. In September 1855 they were presented in a large exhibition organized by Agnew in London and in other British cities (Stein, "Roger Fenton's Killing Fields," 184). They did not, however, achieve the commercial success he had hoped for in Britain or in France.

Meanwhile, in Paris images of the war were everywhere, including in the windows of Goupil et Cie, which produced all kinds of reproductions for sale: lithographs and engraved, etched, and photographic copies of paintings, as well as photographs. As Pierre-Lin Renié notes, "la guerre de Crimée précipite la révolution des images. Cartes, panoramas, portraits de généraux, d'officiers, d'hommes d'État, caricatures et scènes de batailles envahissent les vitrines des marchands d'estampes" (the Crimean War precipitated a revolution in images. Maps, panoramas, portraits of generals, officers and men of state, caricatures and battle scenes took over merchants' window displays) (Renié, "De l'imprimerie photographique," 5). In a letter to her husband, Jean-Charles Langlois, who was documenting scenes in Crimea, Mme Langlois advised him not to bother photographing any more "charming views" of Sebastopol: "lorsque je m'informais chez MM. Rittner et Goupil … ils me disaient qu'ils étaient inondés de vues de ce pays" (When I spoke to Mister Rittner and Mister Goupil … they told me they were flooded with views of the place) (Robichon and Rouille, *Jean-Charles Langlois,* 265). Thus, for instance, in the *Feuilleton du Journal de la librairie,* 21 July 1855, a full-page ad from Goupil et Cie announces: "La Campagne de Crimée, série de 24 planches, dessinées et lithographiées par E. Guérard d'après des documents officiels" (The Crimean Campaign, a series of 24 plates, drawings and lithographs by E. Guérard, based on official documents). Among the titles: "En avant les Zouaves (bataille d'Alma, attaque de droite du général Bosquet)" (Onward Zouaves: The Battle of Alma, attacked from the right by General Bosquet) and "Devant Sébastopol, nuit du 23 au 24 mars. Le général Monet détruit les ouvrages russes en avant de la tour Malakoff" (In front of Sebastopol, night of 23–24 March. General Monet destroys the Russian installations near the Malakoff Tower) (383). On the previous page there is an ad for "Sébastopol et ses environs, vue dessinée à vol d'oiseau et lithographiée par MM Ang, Cicéri et Benoit … Prix: imprimé en couleur sur paper ... en feuille – 6 fr; monté sur toile et verni – 10fr; sur toile et plié dans un étui – 10 fr." ("Sebastopol and surroundings, bird's eye view, drawn and lithographed by Messrs. Ang, Cicéri and Benoit … Price: printed in colour on sheet paper – 6 francs; on canvas and rolled in a tube – 10 francs") (382). By comparison, Fenton's photographs sold for the equivalent of 20 francs.

There was another reason why Fenton's photo reportage may not have sold well. Whereas paintings and newspaper illustrations could represent battles and warfare, for technical reasons Fenton's photographs – like the photographs of all others – were restricted to scenes before and after combat and would have disappointed customers expecting more "genuine" pictures of the war that corresponded to the familiar tropes of action.[11] Like little Adrien in *La Colonne,* the public expected battles in their war pictures. For the mid-nineteenth-century public for

4.20 Roger Fenton, "View of Balaklava from the top of Guard's Hill. Harbor with tent encampments in the foreground, ships in the harbor and, on a hill in the background, ruins of the old Genoese castle." 1855. Library of Congress, LC-USZC4–9353.

whom this was still a new medium, it was not camera exposures but newspaper illustrations based on drawings "pris sur le vif" and quickly executed that communicated "authenticity." Durand-Brager's Crimean pictures in *L'Illustration*, like Constantin Guys's in the *Illustrated London News*, were stirring because they were made on the spot "in a rapid, breathless sketching idiom … destined for immediate publication in a press apparatus offering … assurance of the factual accuracy of anything transmitted through it" (Keller, *The Ultimate Spectacle*, 71).

Such images in the illustrated press were stirring, but they did not correspond to the hegemonic narrative the emperor had been seeking to convey. After the war and the signing of the Treaty of Paris that brought

4.21 Roger Fenton, "Zouaves and Soldiers on the Line," 1855. Library of Congress, LC-USZC4–9249.

a formal end to the conflict (30 March 1856), Napoleon III was keen to "recruit" fixed images of the war that would memorialize it in the grandest possible light, especially given how long it had dragged on and the heavy loss of life. His ambition required official paintings that would scream imperial triumph and national glory. To produce this institutionalized top-down memory, he turned to the Musée Historique de Versailles, which Louis-Philippe had inaugurated in 1837 to transmit the history of France through paintings of great military achievements. An entire wing of the building was devoted to the Galerie des Batailles, which featured, among others, early paintings by Horace Vernet, some of which had been shown at the Universal Exhibition of 1855. This would be the place to commemorate France's most recent victory in war. The Superintendent of Fine Arts, the comte de Nieuwerkerke, set to work on a Salle de Crimée, organized around large-scale paintings representing four heroic moments of the war: the Landing of the Troops, the Battle of Alma, the Battle of Inkermann, and the Taking of the Malakoff, the Russian stronghold protecting Sebastopol. These would be connected by a secondary sequence of paintings of other scenes and battles to provide a complete series of the glorious events, including paintings of the Sisters of Charity tending to the wounded on the field of battle.[12] A former exhibition space in the museum, the Salle du Maroc, which could accommodate paintings six metres in height, seemed the perfect venue.

Three paintings from the Universal Exhibition of 1855 were selected for the Salle de Crimée, with the bulk of the paintings remaining to be commissioned. Thirty-three of them would be exhibited first at the Salon of 1857, including Doré's winning *Bataille d'Inkermann*, which was selected as one of the major battle pictures for the Salle de Crimée.

4.22 La Salle de Crimée in the Château de Versailles. Postcard. © RMN-Grand Palais/Art Resource, NY. Pils's *Bataille de l'Alma* is visible at the far end.

Isidore Pils and Adolphe Yvon were commissioned to produce the other three major battle paintings, with Pils charged with *Le Débarquement des troupes en Crimée* and *La Bataille de l'Alma* and Yvon *La Prise de Malakoff*. The latter painting was of particular political significance, for this was the occasion to shape the story of the recently concluded war with an ending that could only be interpreted as a French victory. Yvon's monumental *Prise de Malakoff* (6 by 9 metres), conceived as the centrepiece of the Salle de Crimée, does not in fact contain a single British soldier or officer. It shows only a few Russians, recognizable by their brown uniforms, while the colourful French uniforms of the Zouave regiment dominate the rest of the canvas. To the victors – in this instance the French, alone, without their allies – the glory.[13]

Beset by problems, however, the Salle de Crimée fell short of de Nieuwerkerke's ambitious plans in 1856. Because of the drawn-out commissioning process, late delivery of one of the major commissioned

4.23 Cham (Amédée de Noé) (1818–1879), "Polissons d'enfants! Nous ne vous mènerons plus jamais à l'Exposition voir les belles batailles de M. Yvon, puisqu'elles vous font ce effet-là," *Salon de 1857 illustré par Cham.* Reproduced with permission of La Bibliothèque nationale de France.

paintings, and shortage of space, the Salle de Crimée, intended for posterity, existed only briefly and remained incomplete. Today many of the Second Empire paintings hang in four small rooms in the museum, covered much of the time by temporary exhibition walls. In the most literal sense, the paintings migrated from the museum, where the state displayed what it had selected to define its cultural identity, to the peripheral space of forgetting and passive memory, the space of remembered experience that no longer circulates. Those state-sponsored paintings of the Crimean War that were meant to give permanence to the history of a great military achievement in the most canonical of settings, the Musée historique de Versailles, are now rolled up in the archives, hidden away. As Maxime Du Camp predicted in 1861: "Tout cela ira tranquillement prendre sa place dans les docks du musée de Versailles, et personne ne s'en occupera plus" (All of this will quietly find its place in the docks of the museum at Versailles and no one will care about it anymore) (*Le Salon de 1861*, 25).

In the absence of a completed Salle de Crimée ordered by the emperor, the biennial Salon of 1857, coming as it did on the heels of the peace treaty, was left to establish the official visual narrative of French triumph in the Crimean War. The message could not have been more blatant: it was "an undisguised reflection of the Government view of the utility of art," in Patricia Mainardi's words (*Universal Expositions*, 293). The Salon d'Honneur of the Salon of 1857, the first room one entered, traditionally assembled what were considered the best paintings in the exhibition. That year, however, it instead featured portraits of the emperor and empress and paintings of the Crimean War. In the introduction to his review of the Salon, Jules Verne sized up the room:

> À la place d'honneur, entouré des portraits des nouveaux maréchaux de France, figure un grand tableau de Ch. Muller, représentant *La Réception de la Reine d'Angleterre par l'Empereur et l'Impératrice*. Nous citerons sans ordre … *Le Congrès de Paris*, de Dubuffe [sic]; les *Batailles de l'Alma* et *La Prise de Sébastopol*, de Bellangé; un tableau d'Horace Vernet, représentant le Prince Napoléon à la bataille de l'Alma; un admirable *Débarquement des troupes en Crimée*, par Pils.
>
> (Occupying the place of honour and surrounded by portraits of the new maréchals of France, there is a large painting by Charles Muller that represents the *Emperor and the Empress Receiving the Queen of England*. Then there are … the *Congress of Paris* by Dubuffe; the *Battle of Alma* and the *Taking of Sebastopol* by Bellangé; a painting by Horace Vernet representing Prince Napoleon at the Battle of Alma; and the admirable *Landing of the Troops in Crimea* by Pils.) (*Salon de 1857*, 52)

At the Salon of 1857, two full rooms – sixty-six paintings, engravings, and drawings, as well as Yvon's monumental *Prise de Malakoff* and an extended panorama made up of twenty-one paintings of the "Siege of Sebastopol" by Durand-Brager – were dedicated to the Crimean War. If all the busts, portraits, and military genre scenes are included, there were more than 100 works. The sheer number of paintings of the Crimean War at the Salon of 1857 spoke to an overt celebration of military strength.

As if to underscore the importance of the war and the authenticity of the images on the wall, the exhibit focused as much on the history of the events represented as on their visual interpretation. Many works had narrative titles, for example, Jean-Louis-Hippolyte Bellangé's *Prise des embuscades russes devant le bastion central (Sébastopol) dans la nuit du 2 mai, 1855. Mort du colonel Viennot de la légion étrangère.* (The Defeat of Russian Ambushes in Front of the Central Bastion, Sebastopol, the Night of 2 May 1855. Death of Colonel Viennot of the Foreign Legion). Some were accompanied by official military reports in the Salon booklet; Clément Pruche's *Bataille de Tchernaia, au port de Traktir*, for example, came with an excerpt of the official military report by the commander-in-chief,

General Pélissier. Still others came with brief reports excerpted from newspapers. Thus Antoine-Valentin Jumel's *Prise de Sébastopol* was accompanied by an article from *Le Moniteur universel.* That battle painting would be purchased by the emperor himself.

Battle scenes so dominated the Salon that in the satirical guidebook he produced, *Le Salon de 1857 illustré,* the caricaturist Cham (Amédée de Noé) poked fun at the sheer number of Crimean War paintings. In one drawing a bourgeois mother and father are frantically trying to stop their two young sons from scrapping. Both parents have their arms in the air, and the mother is threatening the boys never to take them again to see Mr. Yvon's "lovely battle paintings," since they always fight when they see them.

Other caricatures in the album refer to the popularity of Crimean War pictures featuring Zouave soldiers with their distinctive North African uniforms. In one drawing a woman complains that her portraitist insisted she be dressed as a Zouave because "ce sont les seuls portraits qu'on regardera à l'Exposition de cette année" (they are the only portraits anyone will look at in the Exhibition this year). In another, the colonel of a Zouave regiment surveys a wall full of portraits to see if all his soldiers are present, and so on.

4.24 Cham, "– Ah! mon Dieu! Caroline, tu fais peindre ton portrait habillée en zouave? – Que veux-tu, ma chère, le peintre n'a pas voulu me faire autrement, ce sont les seuls portraits que l'on regardera à l'Exposition de cette année à ce qu'il dit." *Salon de 1857 illustré par Cham.* Reproduced with permission of La Bibliothèque nationale de France.

Edmond About, a critic fiercely committed to the primacy of history painting, devoted an entire chapter of his review of the Salon, *Nos Artistes au Salon de 1857*, to the paintings of the war, prefacing his remarks about the various artists and paintings with a declaration about the insufficiency of language to translate this heroic epic. For him, the poetry of this war, as Charles Baudelaire later maintained, could only be expressed visually: "L'épopée héroïque, que l'esprit moderne a chassée de la poésie, n'a plus de refuge que dans la peinture. Je plaindrais le pauvre diable qui entreprendrait de rédiger en vingt-quatre chants l'Iliade de Sébastopol; mais il est encore permis à nos peintres de s'élever jusqu'au sublime" (The heroic epic, banished from poetry by the spirit of modernity, finds its place only in painting. I pity the poor chap who tries to produce an Iliad of Sebastopol in twenty-four cantos; our painters, however, are still permitted to strive for the sublime) (*Nos Artistes au Salon de 1857*, 330).

About, however, found little that was sublime in the works of the artists on display. Of Horace Vernet, he simply noted two good portraits and one bad battle (*Bataille de l'Alma, 20 septembre 1855*). He had more to say about the paintings commissioned from Isidore Pils and Adolphe Yvon but was not overwhelmed by either man's efforts. Yvon's painting in particular was crammed with episodic details and portraits that did not add up to a coherent vision and that lacked the grandeur expected of large-scale battle paintings. The paintings lacked the poetry this epic needed. "Le *Débarquement* de M. Pils, et *La Prise de Malakoff*, de M. Yvon sont à égale distance de l'épopée. Ces deux ouvrages n'ont pas leur équivalent en poésie. L'un participe de la comédie, l'autre du mélodrame; mais tous les deux sont peints en prose" (*The Landing* by M. Pils and the *Taking of Malakoff* by M. Yvon fall equally short of an epic. These two works have no poetry. One suggests comedy, the other, melodrama; but both of them are painted in prose) (340).

Maxime Du Camp's review, *Le Salon de 1857*, did not mention any of the paintings representing the Crimean War. The history painting he admired, not because of the subject matter, but because of its greatness, was Millet's *Des Glaneuses* (*The Gleaners*), a scene of peasant labour and rural poverty.[14] "Et les tableaux de bataille, me dira-t-on? Je n'en vois guère qu'un seul qui mérite qu'on s'y arrête. C'est un *Bivouac en 1812* par M. Devilly" (And the battle paintings? you ask. I only see one that is worth any attention. It's a *Bivouac in 1812* by M. Devilly) (*Le Salon de 1857*, 49). Du Camp's silence was clear; he was looking for art, not military propaganda. For him the time of great history paintings had passed.

The critic who seemed most enthusiastic about the Crimean paintings at the Salon was the relatively unknown Jules Verne, whose *Salon de 1857*, published in seven articles in the prestigious *Revue des Beaux arts,* was his first venture as an art critic. Verne's observations reflect an amateur response to the Salon's 2,700 paintings. What stands out in his *Salon* is precisely the attention he pays to the paintings of the Crimean War:

> Ainsi, par exemple, la guerre de Crimée aura certainement les honneurs du Salon; ses principaux événements s'y trouvent développés sous toutes les formes possibles; il n'est pas un épisode qui n'y soit reproduit à satiété; Sébastopol y est pris très souvent d'assaut; Malakoff et le Bastion Central y sont à chaque instant ruinés par les bombes et les obus des armées alliées; les zouaves et les highlanders y fraternisent au bivouac non moins que dans la mêlée.
>
> (Thus, for example, the Crimean War will certainly garner the honours at the Salon; the principal events of the war are presented in every possible way; there is not a single episode that is not fully reproduced; lots of assaults on Sebastopol; lots of pictures of Malakoff and the Central Bastion destroyed by the bombs and shells of the allied armies; Zouaves and Highlanders stand side by side in the bivouac just as they did in the melee.) (*Salon de 1857*, 233)

Three of the seven articles in Verne's *Salon* contain long passages on the Crimean paintings, especially Yvon's *Prise de Malakoff (Taking of the Malakoff)*, which he describes in great detail and for which he predicts a place of honour in the Musée de Versailles. While other critics deplored it, the painting's impact and its success did in fact extend beyond the Salon and the museum. As late as 1876 in an article on battle painting in the *Revue des Deux Mondes*, Henri Houssaye declared that everyone knew Yvon's painting, either in the original or from all the reproductions ("La Peinture de batailles," 874). It circulated in France more than any other battle painting, having been made available in three different photomechanical reproductions soon after it was shown at the Salon of 1857. These included a Salon installation view by Pierre-Ambroise Richebourg, a reproductive photograph by Robert Jefferson Bingham that was sold in two different formats, and, finally, a photogravure by Charles Nègre, based on Bingham's photograph (Hornstein, *Picturing War*, 161–2). Additionally, a woodblock engraving of Bingham's photograph of the painting appeared on 1 October 1857 in *Musée des Familles*, which boasted that "ce bulletin vivant de Malakoff se répandra jusque dans les ateliers et les chaumières" (this live report from Malakoff will hang everywhere, from artists' studios to thatched cottages) (Musée des

Familles, "Le Tableau de M. Yvon," 11). Yvon's *Taking of the Malakoff* circulated widely in this new age of mass distribution. But mass distribution did not guarantee mass recollection.

For artists, the line dividing popular illustrations and reproductions on the one hand, and official academic battle paintings on the other, was, as in the case of Gustave Doré, supple. Durand-Brager, who had provided drawings for *l'Illustration*, also submitted a panoramic series of twenty-one paintings of the Siege of Sebastopol to the Salon of 1857. Like Yvon's *Malakoff*, this series was destined for the Salle de Crimée. Durand-Brager had returned to Crimea in 1856 with a young photographer to document the sites of the siege before they all disappeared or were transformed.[15] Photography, in this instance, was not an artistic end in itself, as was the case for Fenton. Rather, it was a documentary resource for recreating the complex spatial dimensions of the siege. Two large canvases based on these photographs anchored the series, providing a broad topographical overview of the port of Sebastopol and the French fortifications along the coast; these were accompanied by nineteen smaller paintings representing various locations of strategic importance. The panoramic series of twenty-one paintings was a great success at the Salon of 1857 and was reproduced for sale.

As for the legacy of the Salon of 1857, the Crimean works that Verne championed and that had dominated the Salon d'Honneur soon retreated into real and symbolic storage; instead it was Millet's *Des Glaneuses* and Courbet's *Demoiselles des bords de la Seine* that entered the canon. Not to be outdone by the Crimean War, Courbet's large painting earned a caricature by Cham in his *Salon de 1857 illustré*.

It is fitting that the modern realism of Courbet's painting should have, in the end, gained lasting triumph at a Salon saturated with battle paintings. At the Salon of 1850–1851 Courbet had challenged the "noble" conventions of history painting with his monumental genre painting of a "banal" scene of daily life in the Franche-Comté, *The Burial at Ornans*. The complete title of painting refers to it as "historic": *Tableau de figures humaines, historique d'un enterrement à Ornans*. These ordinary lives were part of Courbet's new, social history painting based on the real. It was the historic battle paintings of the Crimean War that were destined for burial.

Three years after the war officially ended, and two years after the Salon of 1857 that had celebrated it, the Salon of 1859 displayed its own share of military paintings, but by now there were fewer paintings of the Crimean War. In his highly personal review of that Salon, in which he famously denounced photography, Charles Baudelaire offered his reflections on military art and on the inadequacies of battle paintings,

4.25 Henri Durand-Brager, *Siège de Sébastopol: Vue de Kamiesch*. Photograph. © RMN-Grand Palais/Art Resource, NY.

whose value, as other critics had said, was tactical rather than aesthetic. He did, however, single out one small Crimean War painting for praise: *Guerre de Crimée, Fourrageurs (The Crimean War, Foragers)* by François Tabar, a military painting that depicts soldiers returning from gathering fodder, their uniforms unbuttoned, their red pants against the grass like poppies in a field. "C'est une idylle traversée par la guerre" (This is an idyll swept through by war). The collision of the worlds of "fourrageurs" and "guerre" created the poetry and emotion of the simple episode that Baudelaire so admired. The soldiers collecting fodder for their horses might soon be cannon fodder themselves.

That same year Baudelaire focused on more images from the Crimean War when he devoted "Les Annales de la guerre," the sixth section of his essay "Le Peintre de la vie moderne," to Constantin Guys's war drawings. If scenes of fashionable women in the streets of Paris connote the modernity we associate with Guys, for Baudelaire so did the scenes from the battlefields of the Crimea, albeit in a different way This distinctly modern war, a war of telegraphs, photographs, rapid communications,

4.26 Gustave Courbet (1819–1877), *Demoiselles des bords de la Seine,* 1856–57. Wikimedia Commons.

4.27 Cham, "Femme du monde prise subitement de la colique à la campagne (par M. Courbet). Le peintre a voulu prouver qu'il pouvait peindre la femme comme il faut tout aussi bien que la femme commune." *Salon de 1857 illustré par Cham.* Reproduced with permission of La Bibliothèque nationale de France. Parody of Courbet's painting of the young ladies by the Seine.

and rapid-fire long-range rifles, could only be adequately expressed by an art of modernity that captured, as Baudelaire asserted, "le transitoire, le fugitif, le contingent" (the transient, the fleeting, the contingent). For this purpose the drawing or the sketch was clearly better suited than the grand battle painting. The energy in Guys's art was a product of "rapid-fire" speed of execution, "sur le vif" (on the spot).

Guys had honed his skills as a draughtsman on the battlefields of the Crimea: pencil in hand, he dashed off sketches that had to be sent posthaste to London for reproduction in the *Illustrated London Times*. The truth, in this instance, was not in the details of topography or the buttons on the uniform but in the eye of the artist seizing a moment in time. It is not by chance that the first drawing Baudelaire pauses to discuss is one of General Canrobert in greatcoat and high boots, his arm in a sling, smoking a cigar and looking at the "hazy sinister horizon" after the Battle of Inkermann. Baudelaire was particularly taken by Guys's note in English below the drawing for the engraver: "Canrobert on the battle field of Inkermann, *Taken on the spot*" (Baudelaire, OC, vol. 2; my emphasis).

4.28 Constantin Guys, "Canrobert on the battle field of Inkermann. Taken on the spot." Sketch, 1854. Photograph courtesy of author.

Guys's images, published in a British weekly, were not, as we have noted, familiar to the French public. For them it was artists like Durand-Brager, Vernet, Yvon, and Pils, whose official paintings were reproduced in photographs, etchings, decorative plates, and press illustrations, or else in widely available colourful "images d'Épinal," that represented the war.[16] There was, in addition, the work of Jean-Charles Langlois, who translated the official story of the Crimean War into one of the most popular and spectacular art forms of the time, the panorama. Presenting visually realistic images of the nation's history in a public form, the panorama offered perspectives through which "new individual and national identities could take shape through the consumption of a version of the past" (Samuels, *The Spectacular Past*, 19).

4.29 Constantin Guys, "General Canrobert after the Battle of Inkerman [*sic*]." *Illustrated London News*, 13 January 1855. Author collection.

Imported into France from England in the early nineteenth century, the panorama was a new mass medium that operated at the intersection of art, entertainment, and popular education. It was designed to give spectators the illusion that they were at the centre of a represented scene, be it a distant land or a distant battle. In his *Souvenirs littéraires*, Maxime Du Camp recalls the overwhelming effect Langlois's panoramas had on him as a child:

> Je me rappelle encore l'émotion dont je fus saisi, lorsque, étant petit enfant, on me conduisit … dans une vaste rotonde où je vis pour la première fois un panorama de Langlois, qui était celui de la bataille de Navarin. C'était extraordinaire d'animation, de fougue et d'emportement … Le colonel Langlois faisait vraiment oeuvre de magicien et créait la réalité.
>
> (I can still recall the overwhelming feelings when I was taken for the first time to a vast rotunda, to see a panorama by Langlois. It was the Battle

> of Navarino. It was incredible in its animation, its passion, its energy … Colonel Langlois was a true magician, he created reality.) (*Souvenirs littéraires,* vol. 1, 357)

Structurally the panorama was made up of a cylindrical painting, a large rotunda designed to exhibit it, a viewing platform at the centre, and a hidden source of light under the roof. Spectators climbed a dark staircase to reach the platform, which placed them at a height, angle, and distance calculated to maximize the three-dimensional illusion of a scene in the round. In many ways a predecessor of film and virtual reality, the panorama was a carefully controlled experience that lent itself easily to political propaganda. For Walter Benjamin, panorama rotundas were the dream houses of French society.[17] In 1810, Napoleon visited the panorama of the Battle of Wagram by Pierre Prévost; he was so impressed and flattered that he commissioned the building of seven rotundas on the Champs Elysées to feature the principal battles of the revolution and empire. His idea was that the canvases should then "tour" France and the major cities of the empire for propaganda purposes (Comment, *The Painted Panorama,* 45.)[18] In Britain, scenes from the Napoleonic Wars would become a panoramic staple, especially the wildly popular "View from the Battle of Waterloo."

Emperor Napoleon III, like his uncle, recognized the appeal of the panorama, and in October 1855, one month after the French took the bastion at Malakoff, he sponsored Jean-Charles Langlois to travel to Crimea to produce a panorama of the taking of Sebastopol.

Given Langlois's distinguished military credentials, his direct link to Napoleon I, his training as an artist under Théodore Géricault and Horace Vernet, his early Salon successes, and his subsequent mastery of the genre of the panorama, one would have been hard-pressed to find a more strategically apt and imperially pleasing candidate for the task of objectifying the drama of the Crimean War. Langlois had served as an officer in Napoleon's army and had been wounded at the Battle of Waterloo. While pursuing his military career and rising through the ranks to become colonel, he also gained increasing recognition as a military artist. Under Louis-Philippe several of his paintings ended up in the historical museum at Versailles. But even as he continued to exhibit battle paintings at the Salons, Langlois became increasingly drawn to the popular art form of the panorama.

In 1831 Langlois presented his first panorama, a scene from the naval battle of Navarino (1827), fought during the Greek war of independence. There followed panoramas of many more battles, in particular Napoleonic battles, including the Battle of Moskova and the Fire of

Moscow in 1812, as well as the Battle of Eylau from Napoleon's first Russian campaign. All of these panoramas were great successes.

For *La Prise de Sebastopol*, rather than making studies by hand, he took along a photographer, Léon Méhédin, to document the field of battle. Langlois's visit coincided with Adolphe Yvon's state-sponsored trip to make studies for *La Prise de Malakoff*. The presence of the younger painter, who had no war experience, irritated Langlois but also gave him occasion to reflect on the limits of battle painting itself with its pretension to represent war in its totality, something that only a panorama could do.

Langlois and his assistant Méhédin spent several months photographing contiguous views, moving in a 360-degree circle from a central point on the Malakoff bastion. (Fourteen of the photographs are now in the collection of the Musée d'Orsay.) From that vantage point the spectator would see the city and port of Sebastopol in their state of ruin as well as the fortifications and trenches. Langlois decided to represent the events occurring between 2 p.m. and 3:30 p.m. on 8 September 1855, when the allies launched their assault against the Malakoff tower. This time frame, Langlois explained, represented the war's climax, the point at which the crucial Battle of Sebastopol was decided (Samuels, *The Spectacular Past*, 29). Viewers would be rewarded with the sensation of witnessing history in the making. On his return to Paris, Langlois set to work painting his panorama with a team of artists while he awaited the completion of "La Rotonde," which the city was building on the Champs Élysées for the express purpose of displaying his panorama. The impressive building – current site of the Théâtre du Rond Point – with its columns, portico, and cupola, served as a temple of illusion. When the municipal council of Paris questioned the cost, Eugène Delacroix came to the defence of Langlois and the genre: "Le spectacle de nos grandes actions représenté par la peinture dans des proportions et avec une illusion qu'aucun tableau ne peut atteindre, est une chose belle et par le spectacle et par les sentiments qu'il peut inspirer" (The painted spectacle of our great actions is represented in proportions and with a degree of illusion that no painting can achieve. This is beautiful both as a spectacle and for the feelings it can inspire) (14 April 1858, *Journal*, vol. 3, 325). The rotunda was completed in 1860 and featured in the 25 August issue of *L'Illustration*, shortly before the opening.

French spectators of the mid-century were familiar with panoramas, but nothing prepared them for the illusionistic effect of Langlois's *Prise de Sébastopol*.

Théophile Gautier's review in the *Moniteur universel* was enthusiastic. To add to the fullness and realism of the scene, Langlois provided

4.30 Jean-Charles Langlois (1789–1870) and Léon Méhédin (1828–1905), *La Tour Malakoff*. © RMN-Grand Palais/Art Resource, NY.

4.31 Jean-Charles Langlois and Léon Méhédin, *Panorama de Sébastopol pris de la Tour Malakoff*. Two of the fourteen photographs taken in Sebastopol by Jean-Charles Langlois and Léon Méhédin for the construction of their panorama. © RMN-Grand Palais/Art Resource, NY.

a thirty-eight-page booklet with descriptions of the different points of view and extracts from the reports of the French and Russian generals. Additionally, he scattered objects from the siege on the platform – sandbags, rocks, helmets, and the like. Gautier found the panoramic installation admirable both for its artistic integrity and for its strategic truthfulness:

> Le spectateur est supposé placé sur la tour même de Malakoff au moment où l'attaque héroïque l'emporte sur la résistance désespérée. Un cercle de décombres vous entoure: fascines, sacs de terre, poutres, pierres, cadavres, pièces démontées, casques, schakos, débris de toutes sortes … Vous êtes au centre même du carnage, dans le cratère de destruction … Ce fracas peint sur la toile, où l'on entend par les yeux, et on se croirait devenu sourd au milieu de ces explosions, de ces cannonades, de cet immense hurrah!
>
> (The spectator is made to feel like he is on the Malakoff Tower itself at the very moment when the heroic attack overwhelms the desperate resistance of the Russians. You are surrounded by all sorts of rubble, bundles of wood, bags of earth, wooden beams, rocks, cadavers, broken parts, helmets, shakos, all kinds of debris … You are in the very centre of the carnage, in the crater of destruction … Those crashing sounds painted on canvas? You hear them with your eyes, it feels like you have gone deaf in the midst of these explosions, the cannon fire and the cheers.) ("Panorama," 47)

The panorama reached out to a broad, heterogeneous public. Walter Benjamin would later comment that in panoramas, "we perceive that wars, too, are subject to fashion … The impecunious come and look around to see if somewhere there is not a used battlefield they can make their own without going to great expense" (Benjamin, *The Arcades Project*, 528). Four hundred thousand spectators viewed the *La Prise de Sebastopol* at the Rotonde during the four and a half years it was on display. When Jules Michelet went to see it with friends in November 1860, the line to get in was so long that they left (Michelet, *Journal*, 557). Langlois's panorama also served as an educational tool for the masses. Ticket prices were kept low, with significant discounts for students and members of the military. On Sundays and holidays tickets were reduced from 2 francs to 50 centimes to make the panorama accessible to workers. The war and its final battle were made available for all to see.

Exciting and educational as the experience of the panorama was, it was also an entertainment with a limited run. Gautier ended his article on a melancholy note:

> Bientôt la nature aura effacé les stigmates de la guerre et le panorama de M. Langlois, commencé quelques heures après la victoire, conservera seul le souvenir physique du théâtre de tant d'exploits. Dans un temps donné, la toile où est représentée la prise de Sébastopol sera blanchie pour faire place à un autre grand fait d'armes.

> (Nature will soon cover over the stigmata of war and M. Langlois's panorama, begun a few hours after the victory, will remain the only material memory of the scene of so many daring acts. Sooner or later the canvas representing the taking of Sebastopol will be washed over to make room for another great feat of arms.) ("Panorama," 47)

Gautier is reflecting here on the inevitable disappearance of this war from memory. Before long, he notes, the canvas of the panorama of Sebastopol will be erased to make room for new battles. And indeed, he was right. In 1865 the *Prise de Sébastopol* was taken down to make room for Langlois's new panorama, *Le Bataille de Solférino* (1859), a battle in the Italian war for independence in which the French army under Napoleon III joined forces against the Austrians with the Sardinian army under Victor Emmanuel II. Yet another tribute to Napoleon III's military success, this would be the last of Langlois's panoramas. As for the panorama of Sebastopol, no one knows what happened to it. After Paris it went to Brussels, and then all trace of it was lost. Like the Salle de Crimée, it vanished from sight and from memory.

If I have insisted on the proliferation of images surrounding the Crimean War, it is because they illustrate so well the enigma at the heart of this book: how did a war that was materially so visible become invisible in French collective memory? Let us recall that at the very time the Salon of 1857 was saturated with paintings of the war, Alfred de Vigny was already lamenting that no one remembered this war, whose terrible human losses were like a "haircut" for the French.

Every society sets up images of its past to steer emotions and motivate people to act. But an abundance of images and resources does not guarantee that people will retain them. For all the mnemonic energy invested in them, cultural messages addressed to posterity can get lost in the mail. Individuals and nations are perfectly capable of ignoring and forgetting the best-told stories, the biggest paintings, the most unforgettable spectacles. The crucial issue in the history of memory,

Alan Confino states, is not how a past is represented, but why it was received or rejected (Confino 2010, 81). In the gleanings that follow, we address this question as well as the specific question that has been looming. Why and how was this war, the Crimean War, erased from French memory?

Chapter Five

À la recherche de la guerre oubliée: Crimea, the Forgotten War

The history of memory is not how a past is represented but why it was received or rejected.

Alan Confino "Memory and the History of Mentalities"

On 16 January 1852, just two years before Britain and France declared war on Russia, while sitting at his desk, ruminating over the embryonic novel that would become *Madame Bovary*, Gustave Flaubert declared in a letter to Louise Colet that he would like, above all, to write "un livre sur rien," a book about nothing. Writing on the Crimean War in French cultural memory has often felt like I was myself writing a book about nothing, that is, about something that isn't there. I have spent (too) many years examining a hole in the donut that is "my" decade. For all the imprints, vernacular or official, that this war stamped on French culture, there remains a void. There were, as we have seen, heartfelt patriotic poems and officially commissioned epics as well as stories and novels that made reference to the war. There were endless press reports in the ever-expanding print media that thrived on news from the war, with action on the front rubbing shoulders with widely circulated illustrations. There were ritual spectacles and parades in the streets of Paris that celebrated new alliances and heroic accomplishments and whipped up popular enthusiasm: unforgettable moments that were soon forgotten, just like the dozens of popular songs and plays and equestrian extravaganzas viewed by French citizens in Paris and beyond. There were bridges built and streets, squares, and boulevards renamed, not just in Paris but across France. Thousands of images circulated, running the gamut from political cartoons and *images d'Épinal* to photographs – a new medium – and enormous academic paintings hanging in sites of great cultural prestige: the kind of cultural artefacts that feed a society's self-image and identity. Yet this war left virtually no impression on the French collective imagination, and that invisibility is all the more startling when we recall the lasting impact the war had on British culture and national mythology.

In this chapter we tackle the big question that has been hovering throughout this book: *why* did this war not enter French collective memory? Which raises another: given the material props and media surrounding it, *how* did it fall off the radar? In the absence of any one "aha!," I offer in this chapter a set of hypotheses that address the historical and representational contexts that determined perceptions of this war and that played a part in its disappearance:

Hypothesis 1: Historical confusion – How do you remember a war you can't explain?

> – Mais pourquoi leur disputions-nous la possession de cette clef? Quel besoin en avions-nous? (– But why were we fighting for the possession of a key? What did we need it for?)
>
> Luc Descaves, *La Colonne*

> [Crimea was] the most ruinous, most cruel, and least justifiable of all modern campaigns.
>
> William Russell, *The Times* (London)

Trevor Royle, the British historian, once wrote that "the Crimean War is either one of history's bad jokes or one of the compulsive subjects of historical writing … Only a handful of wars throughout history have seen as much uncertainty and confusion as to its sense of purpose than this one" (*Crimea*, ix). While the compulsion to write about this war is hardly evident in France, especially when compared to Britain, the confusion surrounding this costly "bad joke" is nonpareil.

To begin with, the French pretext for the war was puzzling. It is safe to say that the origin of the war in a conflict over church keys in the Holy Land was of limited concern except, perhaps, for the Catholic hierarchy, clerics in Bethlehem and Jerusalem, and Napoleon III, who was looking to reinforce support from his Catholic base. In his seven-volume history of the Second Empire, Pierre de la Gorce observes that outside a small group of politicians and journalists, very few French citizens even realized there was a dispute over the Holy Places. This was so true that according to some, the French government could have retreated on that issue without fear of public condemnation (Case, *French Opinion*, 49). Victor Hugo thought the dispute "laughable."

While the ubiquitous press coverage and illustrations flowing home from the war made it relatively clear *where* the French army had gone and *whom* they were fighting, for most French citizens *why* they were there was much harder to pin down. Alexis de Tocqueville, who appreciated the geopolitical implications of the war, declared that it "was carried on for purposes in which the mass of the people of France take no interest" (in Senior, *Correspondence*, 141). "Pas grand enthousiasme," Pierre Rain recalled. "La Crimée était bien loin et touchait vraiment peu de nos intérêts" (No great enthusiasm. Crimea was far away and really touched few of our interests) ("Les Relations," 631). Even after the dramatic French capture of Sebastopol, Tocqueville confessed to his friend Nassau Senior, "I myself, who understand the object for which all this blood is shed [to stop Russia expansionism] and who approve that object do not feel the interest which such great events ought to excite; for I do not expect a result equal to the sacrifice" (in Senior, *Correspondence*, 141, 167). On the occasion of the fiftieth anniversary of the taking of Sebastopol, an anonymous author in *L'Illustration* noted sadly that "la guerre de Crimée n'avait été, d'un bout à l'autre, comme l'écrivait, le 24 août 1854, le Général Bosquet, qu'une aventure" (the Crimean war was, from start to finish, as General Bosquet wrote on 24 August 1854, just an adventure) ("Un Cinquantenaire militaire, Sébastopol, 1855–1905"). How was one to remember an "adventure," a war whose stakes and outcome were, for most French citizens, so unclear?

It was not just the nature of this war that was bewildering; so was the nature of the enemy. Looking back in 1857, Toqueville admitted that few even among the higher classes understood it. A country neighbour asked him: "Que diable veut cette guerre? ... si c'était contre les Anglais – mais avec les Anglais, et pour le Grand Turc, qu'est-ce que cela peut signifier?" (What the devil is this war about? ... If it were against the English – but *with* the English and *for* the Grand Turk, what can that possibly mean?) (in Senior, *Correspondence*, 233). Like Tocqueville's country neighbour, Joseph Massot-Reynier, the *procureur* in Toulouse, spoke for most French citizens when he reported confusion over the origins of the war and the parties involved. The masses, he explained, "are even a little astonished under the present circumstances to see us allied to the English whom they do not distinguish much from the Russians when we speak of the enemy" (in Case, *French Opinion*, 20). Many of the people supporting Napoleon

III did so out of devotion to the Napoleonic legend, and for a significant number the idea of an alliance with the English, their long-standing enemy, was far more scandalous than the threat of Russian expansion into Ottoman territory. Thus, in Edmond About's novel, *L'Homme à l'oreille cassée* (1862), the narrator struggles to describe the Crimean War to a disbelieving veteran of the Napoleonic Wars:

> Que de raisonnements il fallut pour lui faire comprendre la campagne de Crimée, où les Anglais avaient combattu à nos côtés! … Je comprends, disait-il, qu'on tape sur les Russes: ils m'ont fait manger mon meilleur cheval: mais les Anglais sont mille fois pires! Si ce jeune homme (l'empereur Napoléon III) ne le sait pas, je le lui dirai.
>
> (You can't imagine how hard it was to make him understand the Crimean campaign where the English had fought alongside us … I understand wanting to get back at the Russians: they made me eat my best horse: but the English are a thousand times worse! If that young man (Emperor Napoleon III) doesn't know that, I'll tell him.) (About, *L'Homme à l'oreille cassée*, 109)

Scepticism about the alliance was apparent even beyond France. A *New York Times* journalist commented in July 1855: "England has for centuries been to her an omni-present enemy, ready to foil her designs and check her progress, and therefore, the pretence that the parchment alliance between Victoria and Napoleon is a veritable alliance between the French and English people has always been regarded in this country as a tale too idle to cram down the throats of reflecting men" ("How Stands the Alliance between Britain and France now?").

The confusion extended beyond observations among the metropole's "reflecting men" all the way to the battlefield. Letters and memoirs written by those sent to Crimea recount how during moments of truce to recover the bodies of the wounded and dead, French and Russian soldiers mingled before returning to battle as deadly adversaries. It is during just such a moment in Tolstoy's *Sebastopol Sketches*, against a field of disfigured corpses, that a French officer offers his cigar holder to a Russian officer who has admired it and begs him to do him the kindness of accepting it as a souvenir. As recounted in French memoirs, Russian officers, many of them fluent in French, confided to their French counterparts that if it were their choice they wouldn't be fighting each other, but the English. Letters by French officers and soldiers are filled with admiration and empathy for the Russians and mockery – sometimes contempt – for their English allies. It is not an accident that the title of General Herbé's Crimean War memoir is *Français et Russes en Crimée*. He tells the story of one French captain who fell wounded next to a wounded Russian officer: "Ils se seraient promis de se donner réciproquement de leurs nouvelles, en déposant leur carte à l'endroit même où ils étaient tombés" (They promised each other to stay in touch, each leaving his calling card on the spot where they fell) (168). In his *Lettres de Crimée*, Charles Bocher describes similar unexpected friendships. He himself made plans to meet with a Russian officer in Paris after the war. He concludes: "Il n'y a aucune animosité entre les deux armées ennemies, et, quoi qu'on en dise, on y désire également la paix. Nous sommes toujours en froid avec les Anglais" (There is no animosity between the two enemy armies and whatever people say, they each want peace. The English still leave us cold) (127).

Many French, including military officers, believed that the ill-prepared and selfish British had dragged them into this war to protect their own commercial interests. In 1878 Flaubert was still indignant: "Sans doute par l'effet de mon vieux sang normand, depuis la guerre d'Orient, je suis indigné contre l'Angleterre ... Car enfin, que veut-elle? Qui l'attaque?" (Doubtless it is because of my old Norman blood, but ever since the Crimean War, I am furious with England ... In the end, what does she want? Who is attacking her?) (letter to Madame Roger des Genettes, 12 January 1878, *Correspondence*, vol. 4). The outcome of the war had immediate consequences for both Russians and British in the form of significant and far-reaching military and social reforms. By comparison, aside from commemorative dinner plates, in the everyday lives of Frenchmen and women there was no perceptible gain. The short-lived neutralization of the Black Sea arising from the Treaty of Paris would hardly summon feelings of national pride. The war had an impact on Europe, but not particularly on France.

The English, by comparison, saw the alliance with France as an act of reconciliation. In letters to his family, Major Ranken, a Canadian recruit to the British army, described the French soldiers aboard the ship to Crimea from Marseille with ethnographic curiosity and smug approval: "The Chasseurs de Vincennes slept like sheep on deck; but sang, and made themselves merry with their hardships. Some of them are very fine, handsome fellows, with the soft blue eyes and dark eyelashes so popular among sentimental young ladies; and I am quite sure, as their manners are really good, that, if well washed and dressed, they would cut, respectable figures in an English ball-room" (*Canada and the Crimea*, 170).

A poem on "The Alliance of England and France" by another patriotic Canadian ends with an evocation of brotherly love:

Hark! "La belle France" gives the cry,
"En avant!" and instantly,
Through the plain is heard a shout,
Every vale and hill rings out,
Echoing back proud Britain's cry
"Forward, forward!" win or die;
Thus are linked as brethren true,
Those who fought at Waterloo!

(Hayward, *The Battles of Crimea*, 9)

To a French ear that final "Waterloo" connoted anything but "brethren true," for memories of the humiliating defeat by the English in 1815 were still very much alive, overshadowing even the story of the catastrophic retreat of Napoleon's army from Moscow in 1812. In his letters from Sebastopol, a particularly bitter Charles Bocher was uncompromising:

> Nous avons plus de sympathie pour nos ennemis que pour nos alliés … Nous ne nous entendons pas ici avec les Anglais … les Anglais, qui ont le plus encouragé cette aventureuse entreprise de Crimée, à laquelle ils sont les seuls intéressés, se sont faits si petits, si faibles, lorsqu'il a fallu agir vigoureusement dans ces derniers temps, qu'ils ont presque complétement disparu des attaques de Sébastopol
>
> (We have more sympathy for our enemies than for our allies … We don't get along with the English here … The English, who are the ones who really pushed for this adventurous undertaking in Crimea in which they alone have interests, are so useless, so weak that when in recent times we needed to act forcefully, they all but disappeared from the attacks on Sebastopol.) (Bocher, *Lettres*, 75, 79, 85)

Given the confusion surrounding allies and enemies and the nature and objectives of this war, Vigny's observation in 1857 that people didn't think about it anymore is, perhaps, less startling than one might expect. The French had won the war, but what did they have to show for it? The losses were personal and painful for the families and towns that gave up their young; for France as a whole, these deaths seemed as inexplicable as the war that claimed them.

How would one remember a war in which the *where* was clear but not the *who*, the *why*, and the *thus*?

Hypothesis 2: Napoleon III's war – All power, no glory

Les piloris infâmes
Ont besoin d'être ornés parfois d'un empereur.
(Shameful pillories
Sometimes need to be adorned with an emperor.)

Victor Hugo, "Non," *Les Châtiments*

From the start of his empire, from the start of his career, Louis-Napoléon lived in the shadow of his larger-than-life uncle, Napoleon Bonaparte. Biographer Alan Strauss-Schom calls Louis-Napoléon the *Shadow Emperor*; for Victor Hugo, he was "Napoléon le Petit." Karl Marx called him a "grotesque mediocrity" playing "a hero's part" (*The Eighteenth Brumaire*). He found support in the provinces, but for the educated Parisian elite he was an unscrupulous despot. Two weeks after the *coup d'état* in December 1851, an incensed Toqueville commented to Senior: "We cannot bear that the fate of France should depend on the selfishness, or the vanity, or the fears, or the caprice of one man … and of a set of military ruffians and of infamous civilians … But these are not the feelings of the multitude … He must do something to distract public attention; he must give us a substitute for the political excitement which has amused us during the last forty years. Great social improvements are uncertain, difficult, and slow; *but glory may be obtained in a week*" (in Senior, *Correspondence*, 7, 8; my emphasis).

In early 1854 the ongoing tensions between the Catholic and Orthodox churches in the Holy Land, the tsar's ambition, and the vulnerability of the Ottoman Empire presented the new emperor with just such an opportunity. Russia was the one country the French could fight to restore national pride. In the words of Pierre Rain, "on sent que cette entreprise, pour l'empereur, est un geste de puissance, d'autorité, de revanche (for the emperor this undertaking is a gesture of power, authority, and revenge) ("Les Relations," 631). France would defeat the "colossus of the north" and reclaim the power and prominence it had lost in 1815. While sending the troops off to Crimea, Napoleon III never forgot to remind his soldiers of their Napoleonic predecessors and the victories of the Grande Armée. In this, his first war, the new emperor would assume the laurels of the great Napoleon and deliver the glory. Prosper Mérimée, an intimate of the court, in a letter to Madame de Montijo, mother of Empress Eugénie, in March 1855, offered his reflections on the rewards the emperor stood to gain in this war:

> Si la paix se faisait maintenant, l'empereur en aurait la gloire … Sauf l'argent dépensé, à quoi personne ne pensera dans deux ans, et les gens tués, à qui on pensera encore moins, nous aurions gagné beaucoup: 1. La dissolution de la Sainte Alliance; 2. La constatation de nos forces militaires, maritimes et financières; 3. L'acceptation de l'empereur parmi les vieilles familles couronnées et la reconnaissance de l'influence qu'il doit exercer en Europe. Il me semble que tous ces avantages-là sont grands.
>
> (If we were to achieve peace now, the emperor would get all the glory … Aside from the money spent, which no one will think about in two years, and the people killed, whom they will think about even less, we will have gained a lot: 1. The dissolution of the Holy Alliance [the coalition of countries established after the defeat of Napoleon in 1815]; 2. Respect for our military, maritime, and financial strength; 3. Acceptance of the emperor among the old crowned families and recognition of the influence he must exert in Europe. It seems to me that all these are great advantages.) (*Correspondence*, vol. 2, 451–2)

Early on, however, it was clear to his critics that the power Louis-Napoléon had violently seized would earn him few laurels. Even the judicious Nassau Senior, in his article "On the State of the Continent," accused the emperor of "unscrupulous oppression, of ignorance of the feelings of the people, of being an idle administrator, of being unacquainted with business himself, and not employing those who understand it, of being impatient of contradiction, of refusing advice and punishing censure." But, he later acknowledged, there were domestic gains for which the emperor could hope: "If Louis-Napoleon pleases the vanity of France by military glory, and rewards her exertions by a triumphant peace … if he takes advantage of the popularity which a successful

5.1 Horace Vernet, *La Prise de la Tour Malakoff*, 1858. © musée Rolin, Autun.

war, an honourable peace, and internal prosperity must confer on him … he may pass the remainder of his agitated life in the tranquil exercise of limited, but great and secure power, the ally of England, and the benefactor of France) (*Correspondence*, 105, 119).

For Napoleon III, in other words, the war was an exercise in public relations. With the allied victory in the Crimea, with General MacMahon's triumphant stand at Malakoff, with the Treaty of Paris, Louis-Napoléon did indeed please the vanity of France, which brought him, and the nation, their brief moment of glory.

> Le premier, Mac-Mahon, a bondi dans la place:
> Une immense clameur s'élève dans l'espace,
> Et le drapeau français par les balles criblé,
> Flotte sur Malakoff noblement mutilé. […]
>
> France, bondis d'orgueil, ton héroïque armée,
> Aux yeux du monde entier grandit ta renommée,
> Avec calme et comptant sur tes fils aguerris,
> Attends le dernier mot du Congrès de Paris.
>
> (MacMahon, the first, sprang into place
> A huge clamour was heard all around
> And the French flag pierced through with bullet holes
> Flew over Malakoff with its noble wounds. […]
>
> Rise up with pride, France, your heroic army
> Has redoubled your fame in the eyes of the world,
> Count calmly on your warrior sons
> And await the final word from the Congress of Paris.)
>
> (Jonquet, "La Guerre d'Orient")

Early accounts of the war sold briskly, proudly touting France's triumph. With its patriotic declarations, Jules Ladimir's *Histoire complète de la Guerre d'Orient* went through fourteen editions in 1856. "Cet immense résultat a fait tomber cette croyance que la Russie était invincible chez elle; et que l'on remarque combien est éclatante cette preuve de la supériorité, de l'intelligence, de la combinaison et de la science sur la pure force physique" (This remarkable victory shattered the belief that Russia was invincible on her own territory. One cannot miss the stunning proof of the superiority of intelligence, association and science over pure physical force) (4). This said, the Crimean War would fade from subsequent history textbooks; Victor Dury's illustrated *Histoire de France,* for instance, a classic that appeared in 1858, went through twenty editions by 1913 without a single image of the Crimean War (Geslot, *La Guerre de Crimée*).[1]

Despite all the parades and paintings he commissioned to transmit its national significance, Crimea would not be the war for which Louis-Napoléon or the Second Empire would be remembered. For the success of such political and cultural formats of memory, Aleida Assmann reminds us, ultimately depends on "the stability and continuity of the political infra-structure," and the political infrastructure of the Second Empire was shaky ("Transformations," 56). The empire that Louis-Napoléon had begun with a bold military *coup d'état* collapsed eighteen years later in crushing military defeat in the Franco-Prussian War of 1870, which literally fractured the country. To the extent that the Crimean War was Napoleon III's war, whatever glory and prestige he might gave bought in Crimea and at Sebastopol would be fatally, irreversibly, erased by the devastating humiliation of the Franco-Prussian War and another siege, this time of Paris. Whereas the victory in Crimea was forgotten, the defeat in the Franco-Prussian War gave rise to "one of the greatest waves of commemorative activity the nation had seen" (Varley, *Under the Shadow of Defeat,* 1). For his successors in the Third Republic, the shameful defeat emblematized the shameful career of an emperor whose legacy needed to be obliterated while the sacrifices of the nation were told. After the defeat of 1870, as Pierre Nora amply demonstrates, historians of the Third Republic rejected the residue of the empire to synthesize the narrative of France and the Republic (*Lieux de mémoire,* vol. 1).

In a supreme act of hubris, the emperor, determined to bolster France's prominence as a great power in Europe and his own declining popularity, had declared war on Prussia on 19 July 1870. On 1 September the Armée de Châlons, accompanied by Napoleon III and led by General MacMahon, the man who had raised the flag on the Malakoff fort, was encircled and bombarded at Sedan by the Prussian army. On 2 September the emperor surrendered and more than 100,000 French soldiers were taken prisoner, as was the emperor himself. He was forced to leave France the next day; after being confined in Wilhelmshöhe Castle, he eventually went into exile in England, where he died. What Waterloo had been to his uncle, Sedan was to him. The victory in one unnecessary war – Crimea – was utterly eclipsed by the defeat in another that was traumatic and truly unforgettable. As the Republican newspaper *Le Siècle* subsequently declared: "Which Frenchman, even after many centuries, will forget the name Sedan, more fateful than even the names Poitiers, Agincourt, and Waterloo?" (quoted in Varley, "Under the Shadow of Defeat," 323). The taking of Sebastopol had been memorialized as a moment of French imperial triumph in Charles Langlois's monumental panorama on the Rond Point of the Champs Elysées; an even more monumental panorama of the Battle of Sedan, considered the most expensive picture of its time and viewed by millions, would declare in Berlin's Alexanderplatz a moment of Prussian imperial triumph.[2]

Thus, when considered at all, the Crimean War that won glory for Napoleon III would be linked to the Franco-Prussian War, the debacle that wiped out the empire. In Lyon, a statue erected to Louis-Napoléon with much pomp during the Second Empire was torn down in 1870 at the news of defeat and made into cannonballs (Cohen, "Symbols of Power," 493). Secular Republicans blamed the defeat on a corrupt Second Empire, an empire too closely tied to the Church. As Maurice Agulhon explained: "In Paris it was of great importance to the political élite that the Empire … should maintain a distance between its own political position and clerico-legitimism." Outside of Paris, in most departments, the Empire was seen primarily as "a great victory for the Catholic Church," an "alliance between the throne and the altar" (Agulhon, *Marianne into Battle,* 133). Accordingly, conservative Catholics who had supported the emperor blamed the collapse on France's moral decline. In the eyes of the Church, "cataclysmic events such as wars … were not the product of shifting political and social forces but God's punishment for national infidelity" (Varley, *Under the Shadow of Defeat,* 42). Nowhere is this more evident than in the 1878 play about the Crimean War, *Le Conscrit ou le Retour de Crimée.* If the French triumphed in the Crimea, the play declares, it was because they were acting in the name of the Church. And if they lost the war in 1870, it was because they had lost their faith to impious ideas "par malheur trop tolérées de l'autorité!" (far too tolerated by the state!). In a bluntly transparent message, the sergeant recruiting young men to go to Crimea tells them of a prophecy he heard from a saintly man in 1846: "Que notre belle patrie serait envahie par une nation étrangère et que cette nation serait la Prusse! … si cela devait arriver … c'est que la main de Dieu se sera appesantie sur elle! […] La France est la fille aînée de l'Église et ses enfants ne se montreront pas ingrats!" (Our beautiful homeland will be invaded by a foreign nation and that nation will be Prussia … My friends, it that were to happen … it is because God's hand will have weighed down on her … France is the eldest daughter of the Church and her children must not be ungrateful) (Doin, *Le Conscrit,* 7–8). For Ernest Doin and the Catholic voices he represented, the Crimean War was indeed a latter-day Crusade; no monument to the victory in Crimea would be more fitting than Notre Dame de France, whose statue, made from Russian canons, dominated the rural valleys of the Auvergne.

Unlike the Crimean War, which is evoked in Doin's play, the Franco-Prussian War and its consequences did affect the collective identity of French citizens on their own land. It also got far more than a few sentences from Émile Zola. In 1892 he devoted the nineteenth novel in his Rougon-Macquart series, *La Débacle*, to that war, the battle at Sedan, the Paris Commune, and Napoleon III's ignominious demise. It is, in fact, the only novel in the series that focuses on the phenomenon of war, and it sold 100,000 copies in the first four weeks (Carroll, *The Politics of Imperial Memory*, 2). *La Débacle* represents the historical conclusion to a series that covers the entire span of the Second Empire. In *La Curée* (1871), the Crimean War warranted only a few sentences. Although he had lived through the Crimean War as a young man, and even referred to it in his *Contes à Ninon*, after 1870 for the republican Zola there was no room for stories, even critical ones, of imperial victories or victors on the Black Sea, whose ephemeral glory and political gains were already long lost. As he notes in the preface to the series, in the midst of his writing, the fateful fall of the emperor that he had imagined, without daring to hope, provided him with "le dénouement terrible et nécessaire de mon œuvre … le tableau d'un règne mort, d'une étrange époque de folie et de honte" (the terrible, necessary dénouement to my work ... the tableau of a dead régime, a strange period of madness and shame). For Zola, the Napoleonic myth that Napoleon III had cultivated and exploited fed a hollow patriotism that had led the country into a war it could not win. The emperor's military adventure – like his imperial reign – was corrupt, condemned and erased.

Hypothesis 3: Mediations of memory

The past cannot be "remembered"; it has to be memorized.

Aleida Assmann, "Transformations between History and Memory"

For things worth remembering to be constituted as memory, Ann Rigney tells us, they must be translated into transmissible cultural forms so that information is structured in a meaningful way ("Remaking Memory," 13). "Institutions and larger social groups, such as nations, do not 'have' a memory – they 'make' one for themselves with the aid of memorial signs such as symbols, texts, images, rites, ceremonies, places, and monuments [that have to be] grafted into the hearts and minds of individuals." And it is with such a memory, Aleida Assmann explains, that these groups and institutions construct an identity (A. Assmann, "Transformations," 55).

For the British, France's allies in the Crimean War, the different media serving memorization were highly effective and affective. Symbols like the Victoria Cross, the dramatic and poetic Charge of the Light Brigade, narratives and images of quintessentially (virile) male and (nurturing) female heroism – the Thin Red Line, the Lady with the Lamp (Florence Nightingale) – practices such as Crimean War re-enactments, and monuments such as the Crimean War memorial on Waterloo Place have charged deep collective memory and contributed to a national story.[3] The British story of the Crimean War is one of duty and self-sacrifice, that is certain, but it is also the story of the post-war transformation of everyday lives by practices that emerged in direct response to the impact of new forms of journalism.

It is hard to overstate the role that Britain's free press played in mediating and mobilizing public opinion during the Crimean War. William Russell's front-line reports that exposed military negligence brought down a government.[4] During the Crimean War, more readers than ever before wrote to *The Times* and other newspapers with observations and opinions about the campaign. The coverage also provoked a shift in public sympathy towards the common soldier and away from aristocratic officers who had long been cast as heroes. Hence the anonymous guardsmen on the Crimean War Memorial in London. Because no awards were available to acknowledge the heroic actions of the ordinary British serviceman, in 1856 Queen Victoria saw to the creation of a new medal, the Victoria Cross, which she backdated to 1854 and which was ordained "with a view to place all persons on a perfectly equal footing in relation to eligibility for the Decoration, that neither rank, nor long service, nor wounds, nor any other circumstance or condition whatsoever, save the merit of conspicuous bravery shall be held to establish a sufficient claim to the honour."[5]

On the French side there was no episode of equivalent drama and daring to match the Charge of the Light Brigade.[6] No memorable heroes, male or female. No national monuments. No transformative effects of press coverage. The extraordinary skill and daring of the colourful Zouave soldiers at the Battle of Alma was highly praised by all, but no single gripping narrative was "emplotted" to dramatize their bravery. The closest thing to a memorable dramatic moment would be MacMahon's declaration atop the Malakoff redoubt, "J'y suis, j'y reste," but that is hardly a mobilizing story, apocryphal or not. In France, the Crimean War lived on as military *histoire* but not in *histoires*.

There was no emblematic narrative of heroism, nor was there a shameful man-made scandal equivalent to the blundering and class privilege in the British senior ranks that stirred the nation. In Britain, the Crimean War produced simultaneous narratives of heroism and scandal, what Rachel Bates, quoting a poem by Robert Monckton Milnes, has called "a tangled web of pride and shame." Having assumed that the campaign would be quick and easy, the British were ill prepared for the brutal winter of 1854–55. British officers were well sheltered and well fed while their men were dying of cold, malnutrition, and disease. "Lord Cardigan ... slept onboard his private yacht, enjoyed French cuisine, and entertained a stream of visitors from Britain." The Saxon Minister to London recorded that "several English officers who went through that rigorous winter, have since told me with a smile that they first learned of the [army's] suffering from the newspapers" (Figes, *Crimea,* 283). Front-line reports were full of devastating accounts. In his letters to his parents at the start of the campaign, French Captain Jean-Jules Herbé questioned the very suitability of British officers for war. He admired their brand-new elegant uniforms and the beauty of their horses but worried about their great weakness: "c'est qu'ils sont habitués à trop de confort" (they are too accustomed to comfort) (*Français et Russes,* 30).

The French army was, by comparison, highly efficient, and command was not based on hierarchies of class. French military academies produced an order of professional military officers, technically more advanced, tactically superior, and socially far closer to their men than the aristocratic officers of the British army. In addition, the French, many of whose officers and soldiers had served in Algeria, had learned how to supply an army on the march efficiently. The Zouave soldiers trained in Algeria were masters of the fast attack and expert at fighting on difficult terrain, as they proved at the Battle of Alma. The terrible figure of 75,000 men dead from illness was shocking and tragic to be sure, but those deaths were not represented as *scandalous.*

This, of course, does not mean there were no scandals to report on the French side. The scandal was that there was no room for public reporting of scandal. As Astrid Erll notes: "Whatever we know about the world, we know through media and in dependence on media" (*Memory in Culture,* 114). The independence of the British press made it possible for journalists like Russell to describe the frightful conditions of the common soldiery, whereas the French press was heavily censored and subject to an officially enforced ignorance that enabled unofficial forgetting. In Britain, cultural memory of the war was shaped by the newspapers, which provided not just official dispatches but a forum for personal letters from soldiers at the front, which were printed alongside them. Editorials and articles surrounded letters to the editor from civilians weighing in on the Crimean campaign. *The Times* itself, Stephanie Markovits notes, became a protagonist in the war (*The Crimean War*, 15).

The reporting of the war in France could not have been more different. As Napoleon III would later declare to Émile de Girardin in 1863: "La liberté de la presse, jamais!" (Freedom of the press, never!) (Kalifa et al., *La Civilisation de journal*, 232). Throughout the Crimean War, French reports were subjected to systematic censorship at the hands of the Ministry of War, a difference in policy much noted at the time (Royle, *Crimea*, 333). There was no room for public debate; by decree, the emperor reserved the right to prohibit papers from getting involved in foreign affairs. At the same time, warnings were issued to newspapers that dared to write that the freedom of the press was not "pleine et entière" (absolute) in France (Vincent, "Lois," 79–80). In England, journalism played a central – perhaps *the* central – role in embedding the Crimean War in the national imagination, whereas in France, strict state controls aggressively limited the press and whatever narratives it might have communicated to a general public.

There was, as we have seen, no shortage of popular journalistic illustrations to communicate the visual actuality of the war in France, but the images were limited for the most part to caricatures satirizing the enemy and topographical and chronological information. Accordingly, while there were many illustrations of military types, settings, and events, the harsh conditions of the terrible winter of 1855 were not represented, nor was the scourge of cholera. The impact of journalistic illustrations was, moreover, short lived.

If French state censorship limited narratives about the Crimean War in print, in the realm of painting, I would argue, it was French state *sponsorship* that ironically limited the narratives of the war. There it was outmoded official state commissions that dominated, epic in size and intended to impart the sweeping narrative the emperor sought to convey. Napoleon III privileged such images in an effort to "touch the masses" (Yon, "Les Mises en scène," 130). His project to create the never completed "Salle de Crimée" at the national Musée historique de Versailles illustrated the limits of top-down curation of national memory. Like the lasting impact it sought to ensure, the project was doomed from the start. The paintings destined for that gallery were made up of submissions from state-supported exhibitions and Salons and drew on the tradition of academic history painting, a tired genre that celebrated the noble deaths of soldiers in the service of the nation, a genre very much at the opposite end of the spectrum from journalistic illustrations of military reality. As with literary representations of the war, there was no stable visual idiom in place to translate the modern nature of this unheroic war, which was short on grand battles and mired much of the time in stagnant trenches. In any event, this was not a reality the state wanted to commemorate or transmit. The Salle de Crimée, conceived as an act of political memory, failed as an initiative of cultural memory. It lasted only briefly, remained incomplete, and disappeared, taking with it the paintings of the Crimean War it was meant to display for all to see and remember.

Hypothesis 4: The invisible enemy. Lessons from an epidemic.

> Le vrai combat, le combat meurtrier, le combat dont on ne revient guère, n'a pas lieu à la tranchée ou à l'assaut, il a lieu à l'hôpital (The real combat, the deadly combat, the combat from which one rarely returns, doesn't take place in a trench or in an assault, but in the hospital.)
>
> J.C. Chenu, *Rapport*

The image of war that the nineteenth century inherited was framed in grandeur and glory. Memory cultures until the Second World War, Anne Rigney tells us, strongly emphasized triumphs and victories and the heroic individuals judged responsible for them ("Remaking Memory," 244). We have referred on several occasions to the Charge of the Light Brigade, one of the most infamous episodes in British military history. The event was defined by incompetent, irresponsible leadership and scandalous loss of life, yet the charge itself has since become a point of national pride, and the poem dedicated to it continues to be emblematic of British heroism and valour. "Collective remembering," James Wertsch and Henry Roediger comment, "is willing to change information (even facts) in order to be loyal to a narrative" ("Collective Memory," 324). In *The Times*, William Russell represented the horsemen with "a halo of flashing steel above their heads" (14 November 1854, in *Despatches*). Tennyson's poem was promoted as a form of uplifting therapy for sick and wounded soldiers in 1855 (Bates, "Negotiating," 505). In 2004, on the 150th anniversary of the charge, more than 200 British ex-soldiers and enthusiasts led by Prince Philip gathered near Balaclava to mark the army's most famous blunder. The headline in *The Telegraph* blared: "Heroism of the Light Brigade still shines."

However romanced, the virile glory-in-battle trope was no less entrenched in France, greatly heightened by the mythical status of

Napoleon Bonaparte himself, whose remains had been ceremoniously returned to France in 1840. Ulrich Keller makes the point that when wars were still celebrated as "a chivalrous exercise of virtue," the aesthetic attraction of colourful flags and galloping horses served as an apologia of military force ("Images of War," 2007). The French public relished images of military greatness and relived them in the grand equestrian spectacles of the Crimean War that they enjoyed at the Hippodrome in 1855. Maxime Du Camp explains:

> Or, la gloire est essentiellement nationale en France; le soldat joue au milieu de nous un rôle considérable; ... Nous prenons feu facilement, nous en appelons volontiers au brutal argument du canon; l'uniforme nous séduit, la fanfare nous exalte, nous aimons les monarchies à cheval et brandissant l'épée.
>
> (Now glory is essentially a national feature in France; soldiers play an important role for us.... We are quick to take up arms, we defer willingly to the brutal language of the cannon; we are seduced by uniforms, we are thrilled by fanfares, we love monarchies on horseback, brandishing swords.) (*"Orient et Italie,"* 293)

The Crimean War was, as we have noted, the first – the only – major war the French won in the nineteenth century, an occasion for the kind of national glory Du Camp speaks of that could thrill the masses. Yet in terms of the losses and the nature of the losses the French suffered, no war could have been more categorically inglorious. The Crimean War may be seen as a bridge between the romantic ideal of the heroic still prevalent in the Napoleonic era and the gruesome reality of endless waiting in trenches, a reality that culminated in the collective trauma of the First World War.

In the introduction to his 1858 book about the war, the French inspector of military health facilities, Lucien Baudens, speaks of two images of war – the first composed of brilliant and glorious feats of arms, the second of bleak suffering. Everyone, he writes, is familiar with the first. As for the second, people have only the vaguest notion. Baudens was a military doctor; the second image was the one he saw in the Crimea. It was also the war he succumbed to before his book was published. But vague notions and bleak images do not make for legends. Maxime Du Camp is eloquent about the sombre costs of glory:

> Quand les drapeaux sont repliés, que les canons sont muets, que la victoire a refermé ses ailes, que les vainqueurs ont ceint leurs fronts du lau-

> rier triomphal… quand le bruit s'est éteint et que la fumée s'est envolée, lorsqu'on a enfin oublié les dangereux enivrements du combat, il est bon de descendre courageusement jusqu'au cœur même de la réalité, de compter les plaies, de sonder les blessures, de ranimer les morts pour les interroger, et de voir, en un mot, ce que coûte la gloire.
>
> When the flags have all been folded and the cannons are silent, when victory has closed her wings and the victors have donned their crown of laurels … when the noise is over and the smoke has lifted, when people have finally forgotten the dangerous intoxication of combat, it is important to descend bravely into the very heart of reality, to count the wounds, to probe the injuries, to revive the dead in order to question them and to see, in a word, what glory costs.) ("*Orient et Italie*," 293)

The Crimean War that was a military victory on the national scale, was catastrophic on the human scale. Of 310,000 Frenchmen sent to Crimea, 95,000 perished, that is, almost one in three.[7] Of these, 10,000 died in battle and 10,000 in hospital of injuries; 75,000 died of illness, primarily epidemics of cholera, typhus, and scurvy. That is almost one man in four. Was the death of a man by disease any less "manly" or heroic than that of those who died in battle?

In his speech of 24 February 1855, Hugo quoted from recent correspondence he had received on the battles and casualties in the Crimea. The progress of the war was conveyed in a medical as opposed to military bulletin:

> Les pleurésies, les fluxions de poitrine, les rhumatismes, et les pulmonies ont paru parmi nous, et quoique la diarrhée et la dyssenterie soient moins intenses, les cas de scorbut augmentent considérablement. Hier, 7 janvier, le 63e régiment n'avait que sept hommes sous les armes. Le 40e n'en avait que trente. Une forte compagnie du 90e a été réduite à 14 hommes par les épreuves de la semaine dernière.
>
> (Pleurisy, chest fluxions, rheumatism, pulmonary disease are spreading through our troops and even though cases of diarrhoea and dysentery have gone down, cases of scurvy have increased considerably. Yesterday, 7 January, the 63rd regiment had only seven men healthy enough to fight. The 40th had only thirty and the mighty company of the 90th was reduced to fourteen.) ("Sixième anniversaire de 1848")

Flaubert's friend and colleague, Maxime Du Camp, declared that the real enemy in the Crimean War was not the Russian army but the cholera epidemic, which had defeated the leaders of the allied forces themselves, General Saint-Arnaud and Lord Raglan. The truth is that before the French troops ever faced a single Russian bullet in Crimea, 10,000 of them had died of cholera there. Alexander William Kinglake recalls the staggering suffering of the French, who ironically had brought cholera with them on the troop ships from Marseille:[8]

> In the day's march, and sometimes within the space of only a few hours, hundreds of men dropped down in the sudden agonies of cholera; and out of one battalion alone, it was said that, besides those already dead, no less than 500 sufferers were carried alive in the wagons. On the 8th of August [1854] it was computed, by an officer of their Staff, that out of the three French divisions which marched into the Dobrudja, no less than 10,000 lay dead or struck down by sickness. (Kinglake, *The Invasion*, 391)

The Advocate for Peace similarly reported on the horrific French losses. In the first months of the war even the heroic Zouaves, "the most perfect soldiers in the world," were not spared:

> A division of Zouaves ... returned the day before yesterday ... According to their own account they lost 3000 men in three days ... For the first two days ... all went well; after that they began to drop down dead suddenly, and to die off an hour or two by the hundred; in fact, one battalion of 1200 left 600 behind them ... Those that have come back are hollow-cheeked and miserable looking fellows, and are dying here in shoals. In fact without exaggeration, the French bury their dead in fifties. ("Some Sketches from the Present War," 185–6)

The British too were struck by cholera, though not at the same time or with the same intensity as the French. Their numbers were, of course, much smaller. They subsequently suffered from many other illnesses. Some froze to death during the winter of 1855 for lack of winter uniforms, starved for lack of adequate rations, or died of infection for want of medical hygiene, and many such stories were told in the press. Yet the image the British retained of Crimea is still dominated by the romantic vision of 600 brave soldiers on horseback riding into enemy fire and a brave and fiercely assertive nurse who went to Crimea to tend to the wounded. The dash and daring of masculine strength and female determination in the face of insurmountable odds trumped the reality of dehydrated men on dirty floors in ill-equipped hospitals.

Pictures of feverish young soldiers dying hollow-eyed in pools of vomit did not in mid-nineteenth-century France signify war and warriors. In 1869, in his book on contemporary war, Paul Leroy-Beaulieu looked back on the military victims of illness in Crimea with empathy and dread:

> Ces 75,000 victimes du choléra, du typhus, de la pourriture d'hôpital, durent subir toutes les lenteurs, toutes les souffrances, tous les désespoirs d'une mort dont rien ne tempérait l'horreur. Nous tenons à faire cette distinction entre les malades et les blessés; on ne comprend bien toutes les calamités de la guerre, que quand on s'est rendu un compte exact des souffrances de ces multitudes obscures, lentement, inutilement consumées par les maladies.
>
> (These 75,000 victims of cholera, of typhus, of hospital rot, had to endure slow and painful suffering, the terrible despair of a death of unrelieved horror. We need to distinguish between the sick and the wounded; you cannot grasp all the calamities of war until you have taken a full account of the suffering of these obscure multitudes, slowly, uselessly consumed by illness.) (*Les Guerres contemporaines*, 16)

The antimilitarist Lucien Descaves similarly underscored the grim realities of this war in his novel *La Colonne*. Here is a veteran's description of what fighting soldiers attacked by cholera looked like: "En quelques minutes … les hommes frappés portaient tout à coup les mains à leur ventre, puis à leur tête, tournaient sur eux-mêmes et tombaient. On les relevait tout noirs, grimaçants, les yeux sortis des orbites, l'écume à la bouche, avec des poignées de cheveux entre leurs doigts crispés" (In just a few minutes … the men stricken by cholera suddenly grabbed their stomachs, then their heads, their body went into contortions and they fell down. We picked them up, all black, grimacing, their eyes bulging out of the sockets, frothing at the mouth, with handfuls of hair between their cramped fingers) (219). Like the 600 members of the Light Brigade who charged at Balaclava, French soldiers attacked by disease ended up in the "jaws of Death," "the mouth of hell," but victorious or not, theirs were not "memorable" war deaths.

Generals were not spared. "Le choléra sévit cruellement dans l'armée," wrote Charles Bocher. "Il y a peu de jours nous avons eu encore un général mort: c'est le dixième depuis le commencement des hostilités. Tous les jours j'assiste à un enterrement" (Cholera is brutally overtaking the army. A few days ago another general died, the tenth since the start of hostilities. Every day I attend a funeral) (*Lettres de Crimée*, 118).

Moved by the official report of Dr. J.C. Chenu on the medical conditions and services during the Crimean War, Maxime Du Camp concluded: "Bien souvent celui qui sauve les armées, ce n'est pas le général, c'est le médecin" (All too often the man who saves armies is not the general but the doctor). On the battlefield, in ambulances, and in the hospital, it was the doctor who wrestled with an invisible but tenacious enemy far more formidable than cannon barrels and precision rifles, with an adversary who killed shamelessly, far from the intoxicating madness of combat. Against that vicious enemy, "les navires cuirassés sont surperflus" (battleships are superfluous) (*Orient et Italie*, 308). What further appalled Du Camp was that when the wartime doctors, who put their lives at risk to save the lives of soldiers, died of illness – as so many did – their deaths were not considered consequences of war and their wives were thus not entitled to the same benefits allotted to wives of fallen soldiers (298). Just as battling illness did not count as fighting a "real" war, the treatment of illness did not count as "real" defence of the troops.

Despite the epidemics, on the French side there were, to be sure, battles won and forts taken. On 8 September 1855, the French seized the Malakoff redoubt protecting Sebastopol; the Russians, unable to maintain their defence, abandoned the city. After a year-long siege, this was a great military victory. But once again, illness in the form of typhus soon overshadowed the military triumph, swooping down on the French army "like a vulture attacks a cadaver" (329). Between October 1855 and July 1856 when the French left the Crimean Peninsula, 12,963 men died: 242 from wounds, 12,721 from illness. The 242 injured in battle might well be remembered as war heroes honoured for their sacrifice. But what of those 12,721? They included thirty-one French doctors who died of typhus. They too, like the soldiers they cared for, were remembered not as wartime heroes but as victims. Their story was laid to rest in medical reports and church registries, not novels, not paintings, not poems.[9]

Could it be that the Crimean War was forgotten in France *because* 75,000 men died of illness, not battle?

These figures and the circumstances surrounding them have, since 2020, taken on new meaning. As I write these words we are living through the second year of an epidemic that has now taken millions, not thousands, of lives and that has come to us with its own set of military metaphors. We are told that we are *at war* with an invisible enemy, an illness, a virus. Those who have succumbed to the illness are *brave warriors* who have *lost the battle* despite the *heroic efforts* of the people on *the front lines*. We are told not to expect civilization to return to normal with a V-Day-like emotional catharsis. Commenting on the eve of Memorial Day 2020 on the singularly martial language that has been used when discussing the coronavirus, Micki McElya asks: "if we are all warriors, why aren't the currently more than 86,000 American pandemic dead treated as patriots and honoured for their sacrifices?" ("Almost 90,000 dead"). (Those numbers have now exceeded one million in the United States.) In failing to "read for illness," we end up affirming how military conflict has come to define history. We remember and revere the virile, not the viral: the men with guns, not the deathly ill.

In Canada, 11 November (Armistice Day in Britain) is known as Remembrance Day, a day when we pause to remember the moment when the First World War officially ended. What we do not routinely remember is the influenza pandemic of 1918–20 that killed as many as 100 million people, including far more soldiers than had been slaughtered in that monumental war. The Spanish flu is remembered, Laura Spinney declares, not as a historical disaster, but as "millions of discrete, private tragedies." Nina Burleigh is more direct: the 1919 pandemic, she says, "fell into a collective memory hole" (Burleigh, "Why Do We Forget Pandemics?"). Bluntly put, to die of a rampantly spreading disease is "rotten luck," something for all of us to forget.

Reflecting on how one narrates an epidemic, Frederick Kauffman posed this question in the *New York Times*: "What will the Covid plot be? … It's possible … that the cultural works of our time will redact it from our collective memory … Has narrative at long last deserted us?" ("How Covid Breaks All the Rules"). Those who lived through the epidemics of the Crimean War one century ago possessed even fewer narrative templates to shape the plot.

There was, instead, the long-standing tradition of battle narratives that predates even Homer. Jules Ladimir's reflections in 1856 on the French losses during the war exemplify the glory that was awarded exclusively to those who died in battle: "ceux qui pleurent sur des parents tombés au champ de bataille ont du moins la satisfaction de savoir que ces hommes sont morts de la mort des héros et que leur mémoire vivra longtemps dans le souvenir de la patrie reconnaissante" (Those who weep for family members fallen on the field of battle at least have the satisfaction of knowing that these men died the death of heroes and that their memory will live long in the memory of their grateful homeland) ("*Histoire complète*," 4). For those whose family members had not died on the field of battle there would be, it seems, no such satisfaction, no memory of heroic feats to cherish. In Jonathan Freedland's words, "the bereaved cannot console themselves that the dead made a sacrifice for some higher cause, or even that they were victims of an epic moral event, because they did not and were not" (in Burleigh, "Why Do We Forget?").

For a long time, I was convinced that the Crimean War had not been suppressed from French memory – there was no scandal, no trauma. Rather, it had been forgotten. I have since revised my opinion. It took a pandemic to help me see that behind the forgotten military victory there lay a medical defeat that was indeed traumatic, one that redefined the nature of war and sabotaged myths of military valour.

Hypothesis 5: Collective forgetting

> People do not so much "forget" or deny something as that they are incapable of registering it as meaningful because it does not fit any available frame ...or seem connected to received narratives. Rigney, "Remaking Memory"

War may be the most significant event that nations commemorate to link narratives of the past with the present and to articulate national identity. Yet as we have seen, a war can also be thought "insignificant."

In *Collective Memory of Political Events,* James Pennebaker identifies art and literature as vital to keeping collective memories alive. Nevertheless, he notes, in the end the events that will be retained are those that represent significant long-term institutional changes and that affect the lives of a large segment of the population. If both art and literature failed to retain or transmit the cultural memory of the Crimean War, could it be because – though the events of that war changed the lives of many people in France, including Napoleon III himself – it did not change the lives of the general population? For all its importance on a European scale, and for all the impact it had in Britain and Russia, the Crimean War did not trigger sweeping changes in France. Put in the cynical terms of Hippolyte de Villemessant, founder of *Le Figaro*: "To my readers, an attic fire in the Latin Quarter is more important than a revolution in Madrid" (quoted in Benjamin, "The Storyteller," 87–8). But one might ask – what if the revolutionary fighters in Madrid *came* from the Latin Quarter?

Maurice Halbwachs, the French sociologist who coined the term collective memory, claimed that "social frameworks" shape what people remember by filtering narratives according to their collective significance: only those things are transferred that are deemed relevant to the collectives within which people position themselves. Anne Rigney explains: "People do not so much 'forget' or deny something as that they are incapable of registering it as meaningful because it does not fit any available frame or seem connected to received narratives" ("Remaking Memory," 12).

Surprisingly, perhaps, winning a war versus losing one has no effect on collective memory (Pennebaker and Banasik, 4). The fact that the French lost in 1870 did not make the Franco-Prussian War any the less memorable, *au contraire*. In his famous lecture of 1882, "Qu'est-ce qu'une nation?" (What Is a Nation?), Ernest Renan made that clear: "En fait de souvenirs nationaux, les deuils valent mieux que les triomphes" (Where national memories are concerned, grief is of more value than triumphs). Within the frameworks of French national identity in the second half of the nineteenth century, victory in Crimea meant nothing, defeat at Sedan meant everything. And whereas in that same lecture Renan proposed that "l'oubli ... [est] un facteur essentiel de la création d'une nation" (forgetting ... is an essential factor in the creation of a nation), forgetting the Crimean War served no meaningful purpose in the creation of the French national narrative. It was neither actively erased as a *lieu d'oubli* nor memorialized as a *lieu de mémoire*.

The cultural props that are used in disseminating narratives about the past and that create "realms of memory" – images, texts, celebrations, performances – are many, and the relationship between collective memory and material forms such as monuments can be especially powerful. Their relative fixedness creates a sense of stability and belonging for the collective. The scarcity of such monuments to the war in France is, then, telling. And it is with this awareness in mind that we return to where we started this exploration of cultural memories of the Crimean War, with the story of two monuments.

If collective memories are sustained by monuments, then the Crimean War Memorial in central London, made from Russian cannons seized at Sebastopol, has for a century and a half declared that war a defining moment in British national identity. Lest the message be lost, hundreds more cannons, with plaques mounted, were scattered throughout the British Empire. By comparison, the absence of any national monument to the Crimean War in France, let alone la Francophonie, has positioned it, in Jan Assmann's words, "outside the horizon of the relevant" for French national identity. When we look at the equivalent French monument made from Russian cannons after the war, the colossal Madonna perched on a volcanic spur in "la France profonde," we read a very different story of national identity. And it was a durable story that, unlike the victory in Crimea, did speak to a large segment of the population in 1860: the story of Notre Dame and her eldest daughter, France, "fille aînée de l'église." A daughter and a nation, we recall, for whom the pretext for this war was an ecclesiastic showdown in the Holy Land. Although

Catholicism, Annette Becker argues, was particularly suited to "the elevation of war into a sacred experience," the absence of any reference to the war around that monumental Madonna speaks clearly to the triumph of the Church, not the army (Varley, *Under the Shadow of Defeat,* 10). French national grandeur, as the abbé Mullois declared in his *Histoire populaire de la Guerre d'Orient* (1856), was built on principles of religion, devotion, and patriotism, in that order. In his detailed *Histoire du siège et de la prise de Sébastopol* (1856), Just-Jean-Étienne Roy put the religious origins of the war in explicitly political terms: the question of the Holy Sites was not just a matter of local quarrel. It was a reminder that in the glorious tradition of France, the laws of politics and faith were one for believers and non-believers alike:

> Ainsi, il y a là tout à la fois une question de foi religieuse et une question d'influence politique, et c'est ce qu'ont compris tous les gouvernements qui se sont succédés en France, aussi bien ceux qui s'honoraient du titre de très-chrétiens que ceux qui manifestaient la plus profonde indifférence en matière de religion.
>
> (Thus we can see that it is simultaneously a question of religious faith and a question of political influence. That's what the succession of governments in France have all understood, both those who were declared themselves proudly Christian and those who demonstrated the most profound indifference to religion.) (43–4)

After the Second Empire collapsed, along with most of the premises and priorities it had endorsed, the twinned laws of faith and politics were derisively and decisively attacked by the Third Republic. Following the Franco-Prussian War, as Antoine Prost reflects in his contribution to Pierre Nora's *Lieux de mémoire,* war memorials to the dead became "le lieu privilégié ... d'un culte républicain, *d'une religion civile ... qui n'a ni dieu ni prêtre.*" (the privileged site ... of a republican cult, *a civic religion ... without God or priest*) ("Les Monuments aux morts," 221; my emphasis). To the extent that the costly war in Crimea originated in an ecclesiastic conflict – led, moreover, by a disgraced emperor who was currying Catholic favour – it was destined to be actively forgotten by a resolutely anticlerical Republican regime that privileged the secular links between nation building and memory constructs. The very links, that is, that are at the heart of the first volume of *Les Lieux de mémoire,* "La République." Here is Aleida Assmann commenting on that volume and on the Third Republic:

> The birth of the nation ushered in a new era of secularisation that changed dramatically the structure of cultural memory. Until then, *religion and genealogy* had occupied the central areas of cultural memory. The modern nation-state, on the contrary, was to define itself primarily through a new concept of identity based on *language, territory, history and the arts.* (A. Assmann, "Theories of Cultural Memory," 83, My emphasis)

French citizens during the last third of the nineteenth century inherited a national identity that was defined in opposition to French identity as imagined by the Second Empire. While the cultural memory of large swathes of the French population continued to be shaped locally by "religion and genealogy," the Third Republic formally declared the Church's influence antithetical to its principles and proclaimed national identity in uncompromisingly secular terms. And in December 1905 – almost fifty-four years to the day after Louis-Napoléon's *coup d'état* – the attack culminated in a law declaring the separation of church and state.

That, however, is the beginning of another story.

The war that France fought over three years and won, a war during which she regained her prestige on the European stage but lost 95,000 men, was metaphorically buried, like many of those men, on a peninsula far from home on the Black Sea. How and why that happened, how we remember what we have forgotten, is the story of this book.

Notes

Chapter 1

1 On the controversial nature of monuments and memorials, see, for instance, Solnit, "The Monument Wars."
2 See Cabourg, "En Crimée"; and Barluet, "À Sébastopol."
3 Here, for instance, is a partial list of streets and squares commemorating the victory at Sebastopol. (Although the correct name of the city is Sevastopol, for the purposes of consistency, I retain the French spelling throughout.)

    Boulevard de Sébastopol, Rennes
    Avenue Sébastopol, Metz
    Rue Sébastopol, Courbevoie
    Rue Sébastopol, Strasbourg
    Rue Sébastopol, Béziers (Languedoc)
    Rue Sébastopol, Toulouse
    Rue Sébastopol, Choisy-le-Roi
    Rue Sébastopol, Brest
    Rue Sébastopol, Bègles (Gironde)
    Rue Sébastopol, Marcq-en-Baroeul (Pas-de-Calais)
    Rue Sébastopol, La Queue-en-Brie (Val-de-Marne)
    Rue de Sébastopol, Tours
    Rue de Sébastopol, Nouméa (Nouvelle-Calédonie)
    Rue de Sébastopol, Reims
    Rue de Sébastopol, Montréal
    Place Sébastopol, Marseille
    Impasse Sébastopol, Brioude (Auvergne)

  See also "Carte interactive: La guerre de Crimée dans les rues de Paris et de sa banlieue," *Le Parisien*, 27 February 2015.
4 Henri Gaubert in *Les Mots historiques qui n'ont pas été prononcés* quotes the general when asked about the famous statement. "Je ne crois pas avoir

donné à ma pensée cette forme lapidaire … Je ne fais jamais de mots." (I don't believe I expressed myself in such a succinct way… I am never pithy) (236).

5 Following the deadly storm on the Black Sea on 14 November 1854 that destroyed at least thirty-seven British and French ships along with the winter supplies they carried, Urbain Le Verrier, director of the Observatoire de Paris, convinced Napoleon III in 1855 to create a telegraphic storm warning system, which later developed into an international meteorological service across Europe.

6 "Our whole medical system is shamefully bad … Here the French are greatly our superiors. Their medical arrangements are extremely good, their surgeons more numerous, and they have also the help of the 'Sisters of Charity,' who have accompanied the expedition in incredible numbers. These devoted women are excellent nurses, and perform for the sick and wounded all the offices which could be rendered in the most complete hospitals. We have nothing." William Russell. *The London Times*, 13 October 1854, 8 (see Russell, *Despatches*). Edward Wrench, a surgeon during the Crimean War, detailed the inadequate conditions under which British soldiers and doctors were operating. He compared the poor medical provisions on the British side with the superior preparation of the French: "The English army being, however, unprovided with ambulance train, was dependent for the removal of their sick on the loan of the French mule litters, a mode of carrying the sick which they had invented in their recent Algerian campaigns." Wrench, "The Lessons of the Crimean War," 206.

7 British National Archives, Kew, *Foreign Office and predecessor: Political and Other Departments: General Correspondence before 1906, Ottoman Empire*, FO78/1129/91. Quoted in "The End of the Crimean War," *Weapons and Warfare*, https://weaponsandwarfare.com/2019/09/29/end-of-the-crimean-war-1855.

8 Katharyne Mitchell comments: "The production of public memory often relies on both official and vernacular cultural expressions in this way, with the vernacular element tied more to the local, often city scale, and the 'official' or state element tied to the national scale" ("Monuments," 444.) In the case of the Crimean War, French monuments to public memory are overwhelmingly local.

9 Thouvenel makes it clear that French concerns about holy sites were not of a strictly religious nature. "Si le territoire sacré, objet de tant de convoitises … se séparait enfin du reste de l'empire turc, tout porte à croire que nous serions devancés en Palestine par les Russes, qui n'y cessent de gagner du terrain et qui font, dans ce but, des sacrifices considérables" (If this holy territory, coveted by so many … were to

finally separate from the Turkish empire, it seems very likely that we would be outstripped by the Russians who keep gaining territory and, to this end, have made considerable sacrifices" (Thouvenel viii). On the role of General Aupick in negotiations with the Turkish sultan, see Thouvenel, 3–6.

10 Paul Berman draws comparisons between Vladimir Putin's aggressive nationalism in 2022 with its overtones of religious mission and Nicholas I's nationalist defence of Orthodoxy: "Putin has given to his own reading of the royal and religious past a nationalist interpretation, such that Orthodoxy's struggle against Catholicism emerges as a national struggle of the Russians, who, in his interpretation, include the Ukrainians, against the Poles." Berman, "The Intellectual Catastrophe."

11 Tensions between Orthodox and Catholic Christians over holy sites did not end with the Crimean War. In September 2004, during the Orthodox Holy Cross celebrations at the Church of the Holy Sepulchre, Greek and Russian Orthodox monks fought with Catholics over the impropriety of a door to a Franciscan section of the church being left open while the Orthodox processed past it (Bowman 388).

12 Saint-Arnaud served in Algeria between 1837 and 1851 as a captain in the French Foreign Legion. There, he distinguished himself by his brutality and was promoted to general. Louis-Napoléon brought him back to France as Minister of War. He then oversaw the operations of the military *coup d'état* that put Louis-Napoléon on the throne as emperor. He was subsequently promoted to *maréchal* before heading the campaign in Crimea, where he became a national hero after leading the French troops to victory at the Battle of Alma. Few knew at the time that he was suffering from stomach cancer. His death from cholera shortly after the victory at Alma aboard a ship en route to France turned him into an icon of patriotic dedication. See Maspéro, *L'Honneur de Saint-Arnaud*.

13 Tsar Nicholas had addressed Napoléon III as "Sire et bon ami" rather than the "Monsieur mon frère" called for by protocol in correspondence between sovereigns (see Anceau 211). Clearly sensitive to being shunned in this manner, the emperor commented, "One picks one's friends, but not one's family." By contrast, following the diplomatic tradition, Queen Victoria did not hesitate to address him as "mon frère."

14 A small contingent of 20,000 troops from Sardinia also joined the alliance. The major theatre of war was the Crimea, but a secondary campaign was fought in the Baltic.

15 In most sieges, the advantage lies with the attackers. This was not the case at Sebastopol, where the proximity to Russia allowed the city's defenders to bring in a constant supply of reinforcements. Except in the final stages of the siege, the Russians always had more soldiers and cannons than the

allies. Moreover, unlike the Russian forces, the allies were ill prepared for the harsh winter conditions they had to endure, which included the Great Storm of 14 November 1854, in which thirty-seven allied ships were lost or wrecked. As Tsar Nicholas had quipped, the allies would not be able to stand up to his four generals: November, December, January, and February.

16 On British representations of the war, see Markovitz, *The Crimean War in the British Imagination*; Lalumia, *Realism and Politics in Victorian Art of the Crimean War*; Dereli, *A War in Action: A Study of the Literature of the Crimean War Period*; and Berridge, "Off the Chart: The Crimean War in British Public Consciousness."

17 Tennyson's poem became a staple in the school curriculum of the English-speaking world beyond Britain. It is featured in the 1936 short comedy film "Two Too Young," an instalment of the popular American series *Our Gang*. The central episode features young Alfalfa reciting "The Charge of the Light Brigade" while firecrackers planted by mischievous classmates go off in the pockets of his pants.

18 Other examples of popular historical fiction set during the war include *Flashman at the Charge* (1973), part of the Flashman series by George MacDonald Fraser, and *The Scarlet Thief* (2013), by Paul Fraser Collard in the popular Jack Lark series.

19 "The acceleration in media communication thanks to telegraphy played a central role in the British public response to the war. At the start of the campaign in the Crimea the fastest news could get to London in five days. By the winter of 1854 ... news could be communicated in two days; and by the end of April 1855, when the British laid an underwater cable between Balaklava and Varna, it could get to London in a few hours." Figes, *Crimea*, 305.

20 The legacy of serfdom was inextricably tied up with the war. The defeat underscored the limits faced by a serf-holding agrarian society that refused to modernize and industrialize. See Kozelsky, *Crimea in War and Transformation*.

21 On the impact of the Crimean War on Russian national identity, see Maiarova, *From the Shadow of Empire*, esp. chapter 1, "A Shifting Vision of the Nation."

22 "Crimean Military Park Opens," https://www.rferl.org/a/crimean-military-park-opens-with-historical-boom/30825557.html.

23 See, for instance, the translated title of the 2015 book by Sergey Gorbachev, *From the Third Defence to the Russian Spring: On the Anniversary of the Return of Sevastopol and Crimea to the Russian Federation* (*Ot tretyey oborony k Russkoy Vesne. K godovshchine vozvrashchenya Sevastopolya i Kryma v sostav Rossii* (Simferopol: Salta, 2015).

24 Cf. Jean Giraudoux's 1935 play "La Guerre de Troie n'aura pas lieu" (The Trojan War Will Not Take Place).

25 See "Crimean war memorial," http://www.geograph.org.uk/photo/3432234. Many of the Russian cannons gifted to towns in Britain were melted down during the Second World War. See, for instance, Bartlett and Payne, "Britain's Crimean War Trophy Guns."
26 The French Ministry of the Army used to have a site dedicated to the military prestige of the popular chocolate confection.
27 Capitalizing on the recent French victory, in 1856 Alexandre Chauvelot, a canny entrepreneur, decided to publicize his latest subdivision, "La Nouvelle Californie," by creating a Crimean War theme park, the centrepiece of which was a model of the tower from the Malakoff fort. In 1860 he got authorization from Napoleon III to change the name of the locale from Californie to Malakoff. The tower was destroyed in 1870 during the Franco-Prussian War and was never replaced. "À l'origine de Malakoff," https://www.malakoff.fr/125/a-propos-de-malakoff/histoire/a-l-origine-de-malakoff.htm.
28 A section of Place de l'Alma was renamed Place Diana in 2018.
29 De Croze, *Nos Zouaves en Crimée*. The fearlessness of the Zouaves at Alma became legendary. From his position high atop 50 metre cliffs across the river from where the French arrived, the Russian General Menshikov had judged it unnecessary to defend his position with artillery. A regiment of Zouaves, most of them North Africans, were at the head of the French division. "Leaving their kitbags on the riverbank, they swam across the river and quickly climbed the cliffs under heavy cover of the trees. The Russians were amazed by the agility of the Zouaves … Once they had reached the plateau, the Zouaves hid behind rocks and bushes to pick off the defending forces of the Moscow Regiment one by one until reinforcements could arrive" (Figes, *Crimea*, 209).
30 In 1875, then-President Patrice de MacMahon uttered "Que d'eau, que d'eau" as he looked on at the terrible flooding in Toulouse. The story goes that the prefect of the *département* then turned to him and said, "Et encore, Monsieur le Président, vous n'en voyez que le dessus … !"
31 Ça vaut mieux que d'attraper la scarlatine
Ça vaut mieux que d'avaler de la mort aux rats
Ça vaut mieux que de sucer de la naphtaline
Ça vaut mieux que de faire le zouave au Pont de l'Alma
Ray Ventura et ses collégiens, "Ça vaut mieux que d'attraper la scarlatine."

Chapter 2

1 The Grassot in question is the same comic actor referred to at the start who likened the slow service at the café to the siege of Sébastopol.

2 Gustave Courbet, the Realist painter and president of the Commune's Art Commission, considered the column a monument to an imperial ideology of war and conquest, devoid of aesthetic value. He endorsed its destruction and was subsequently imprisoned, released, and sentenced to pay for its reconstruction. Unable to pay, he went into exile in Switzerland, where he died in 1877.

3 These include the scandalous *Sous-Offs* (1889), which led to Descaves being charged with offending the army and public morality. That novel turned him into a bestselling author. The historical point of reference in *La Colonne* is in fact not the Crimean War but the Commune, the revolutionary moment that preoccupied the pro-Communard Descaves all his life.

4 I am grateful to Catherine Nesci for bringing this article to my attention.

5 Vigny came from a long line of military officers and was himself, until 1827, a lieutenant in the French army. His book *Servitude et grandeur militaires* (1835) reflects upon the loss of grandeur and principles of honour and valour in war.

6 Book review by H. Dartois in *Études religieuses, philosophiques, historiques et littéraires, revue mensuelle. Partie bibliographique,* vol. 56 (Paris: Retaux-Bray, 1891), 419.

7 See also his poem "La Guerre d'Orient" (Crémazie, *Œuvres,* vol. 1., 276–80).

8 The memorable return from the Crimea is discussed in detail in chapter 3, "Spectacles of War."

9 Dumas was sufficiently incensed by the outburst at the Académie Française that he inscribed the copy of the poem he sent to the emperor as follows: "La lecture de ce poëme faite à l'Académie française par M. Alfred de Vigny, a été interrompu quatorze fois par les Membres hostiles au gouvernement – Il croit devoir en informer l'Empereur" (The reading of this poem by Mr. Alfred de Vigny at the Académie Française was interrupted fourteen times by members hostile to the government. – The author thought it his duty to inform the Emperor).

10 The forty members of the Académie Française, who occupy their seats for life, are known as "les immortels."

11 William Simpson, known as "Crimean Simpson," was the Special Artist for *The Times.* His eyewitness accounts of the conditions faced by soldiers in the trenches suggest that Hugo's statement was more than rhetorical: "One regiment … arrived in the Crimea over one thousand strong, and one day in the winter it had not above twenty men fit for duty. When the rain came, trenches became mud … In this the men had to do duty for twenty-four hours at a time … Before midnight the rain would change to snow; and before morning, it would be a hard frost. The men must have

been first wet through and then frozen into icicles ... The wonder is that any one was able to survive" (*Autobiography*, 25).

Hugo's allusion to the deadly winter suffering recalls the harrowing crossing of the Berezina River by Napoleon's army during the retreat from Moscow in November 1812. The river's name quickly entered collective memory as a synonym for disaster. The battle at Berezina was represented in several early works by Balzac, most notably in his short story "Adieu" (1830).

12 Mais le canon n' était pas nécessaire pour nous décimer. L'hiver s'en chargeait avec son état-major de maladies: choléra, scorbut, dysenterie, bronchites, congélations, ophtalmies, le diable et son train, quoi! ... nous couchions par terre, dans vingt centimètres de neige ... En réalité, nous couchions au milieu d'un cimetière, et nous étions tués autant par les morts qui nous empoisonnaient, que par les vivants qui nous fusillaient. (But they didn't really need cannons to decimate us. The winter took care of that with its staff of illness: cholera, scurvy, dysentery, bronchitis, frostbite, snow blindness, the devil and his team! ... We slept on the ground in twenty centimetres of snow ... The truth is, we were sleeping in the middle of a cemetery and we were killed as much by the cadavers that poisoned us as by the living who were shooting us.)

(Descaves 226–7)

13 On Jacques Aupick's career in Constantinople, see Pichois, *Le Vrai visage du général Aupick*; and Goldfrank, *The Origins of the Crimean War*, 78–81.

In his *Souvenirs littéraires*, Maxime Du Camp recounts the dinner he and Flaubert had as guests of the general at the palace of the French delegation in Constantinople while visiting the Middle East. When the general asked if he had any news of literary events since he left Paris, Du Camp mentioned a letter he had just received from Louis de Cormerin, who made note of a poet he met at the home of Théophile Gautier, a certain Baudelaire, "qui fera parler de lui" (whom people will talk about). As soon as he pronounced the name Baudelaire, Mme Aupick lowered her head and the general gave him a dirty look. A guest at the table touched Du Camp's foot to warn him he was on slippery territory (*Oeuvres*, vol. 2, 76–7).

14 Baudelaire, *The Flowers of Evil*, trans. William Aggeler (Fresno: Academy Library Guild, 1954).

15 The *Illustrated London News*, considered the first illustrated weekly of its kind, began publication in 1842. In 1843 the equivalent French weekly, *L'Illustration, journal universel*, began publication. Like the *Illustrated London News*, between 1854 and 1856 *L'Illustration* was filled with reports, maps, and illustrations of the war. On coverage of the Crimean War in *L'Illustration*, see Bacot, *La Presse illustrée au XIXe siècle*, 69–76.

16 See Duflo, *Constantin Guys*, 108.
17 See Baudelaire's letter to Arsène Houssaye in 1860 describing his article of the artist: "C'est l'analyse du talent d'un homme *inconnu* et *plein de génie*, dont je possède une centaine de dessins" (It's the analysis of the talents of a unknown man, a man of genius. I have about a hundred of his drawings).
18 Writing in May 1861 to Auguste Laucassade, director of *La Revue européenne*, Baudelaire invites him to look at his collection of Guys drawings: "Si vous voulez vérifier mes assertions relativement à M. G., venez un de ces jours feuilleter mon album, et quand je repêcherai celui que j'ai communiqué au ministère d'État, je pourrai vous montrer des multitudes de scènes de la guerre de Crimée dessinées sur les lieux et en face des événements" (If you want to verify some of my assertions about M. G., come over one of the these days to go through my album, and when I get back the one I sent to the Minister of State, I'll show you dozens of Crimean War scenes drawn on site in the midst of the action). See Duflo, *Constantin Guys*, 108.
19 The epithets are from "Le Peintre de la vie moderne" (OC, vol. 2, 694).

Chapter 3

1 See, for example, Jules Leconte, "Souvenir de 1855":

J'entends ces mots: "La Reine d'Angleterre
Pour quelques jours doit venir à Paris."

En un clin-d'oeil, l'immense Capitale
Voit centupler ses ardents visiteurs […]

(I hear these words: "The Queen of England
Is coming to Paris for a few days."

In the blink of an eye, the immense Capital
Sees its enthusiastic visitors multiply a hundred fold […])

2 Albert Vandam recalls that several days after the performance, he ran into Dumas on the Chaussée d'Antin. "'Well you ought to be pleased,' I said; 'it appears that not only has the Queen asked to see your piece, which she had seen in London, but that she enjoyed it even much better the second than the first time.' 'C'est comme son auteur,' he replied: 'plus on le connaît, plus on l'aime'" ("Just like the play's author; the more you know him, the more you like him"). *An Englishman in Paris*, 164.
3 Amateurs of the Crimean War continue to stage annual re-enactments of major battles on the sites where they took place: A British paper, *The Daily Mash*, reported on 5 March 2014:

Battle re-enactors volunteer for Crimean War
Men fascinated by military history and dressing up fancy are eager to recreate Britain's victory in the 1853 conflict by taking on the Russian army.
Bank manager Roy Hobbs said: "We're incredibly excited about fighting the Russians with nothing but our replica smoothbore muskets. …
"We'll hire a minibus to take us from Sevastopol airport to the battlefield, then march slowly in a line towards the enemy positions full of tense Russian soldiers armed with AK-47s while shouting 'Death to the Tsar!'
"Once we've defeated them like we did in 1856 we'll probably all go to the pub. They say war is hell, but in my experience it's also a really good day out."

Partizan Press has produced a series of books dedicated to the different uniforms and weapons of the Crimean War as well as a *Guide to War Gaming the Crimean War*. There are few French participants at these re-enactments.

4 In London, Crimean equestrian extravaganzas were produced at Astley's amphitheatre, a circus arena: "If London was to see in the flesh, living and moving, the Crimean battles presented to them in stills by the newspapers, Astley's was the place for it." Responding to the demand, William Cooke, manager of Astley's, announced in September 1854 the imminent production of *The Siege of Silistria* would be based on the French play that had been playing at the Paris Hippodrome. As a result of various misadventures, including the mistaken announcement of the fall of Sebastopol, various versions of the play, increasingly unlike the French production, were created and deferred. See Bratton. "Theatre of War."

5 Eugène Grangé and Pierre-Étienne Piestre dit Eugène Cormon, *Théâtre des zouaves, tableau militaire mêlé de couplets* (Paris: Morris, 1856) (produced in Paris, Théâtre des Variétés, 1 September 1855).

6 Daniel Loizillon, *Les Zouaves en Crimée. Vaudeville en un acte* (Constantine: Arcadie Imprimeur, 1854).

7 See for instance, Coti, "Le Vol d'aigle" in his volume of verse, *La Guerre d'Orient*:

En avant, vrais lions, fantastiques zouaves!
Gravissez ces rochers […] [que]
La chèvre seule peut atteindre à leur sommet:
Grimpez comme la chèvre et bondissez en masse
Sur le Russe effrayé de votre insigne audace.

(Forward, fantastic zouaves, true lions!
Scale these rocks …
Whose summit the goat alone can reach:
Climb like the goat and pounce
On the frightened Russian, startled by your daring.) (7–8)

8 The association of Zouaverie with military aplomb and entertainment was so strong that in 1860, Zouave regiments – wearing versions of the French uniform – were created in the United States. That same year, theatrical companies claiming to be presenting genuine French Zouave soldiers who had fought in the Crimea started touring. They called themselves simply "The Zouaves" and played theatres from New York to New Orleans, offering an eclectic program than included restaging key battles of the Crimean War, along with "Vaudevilles, Opera Bouffes, Operettas, and Military Drill." Newspapers announced performances by the Zouaves, who amidst the dreariness of a long and arduous campaign in the Crimea could find time to indulge in theatricals when everyone else almost was thinking of home and its comforts. See Wasserman, "Transcultural Cross Dressing," 12.

9 For a detailed account of the ingenious construction and operation of the Théâtre des Zouaves and its audience, see Bapst, *Le Maréchal Canrobert*, 425–6.

10 Although the British as a whole took pleasure in the Zouave theatre, there was at least one exception. In the 24 May 1855 entry in her journal, a rather grumpy Frances Duberly, who had accompanied her officer husband to Crimea, complained about mockery of English soldiers: "I have been much amused today by hearing of the theatre which the Zouaves have established at the front, and where they perform, greatly to their own satisfaction, 'Les Anglais pour rire.' That is hardly fair tho'– for they caricature the English soldier … who struts with his head stuck up in the air." In a chilling juxtaposition, right after her reflection on the Zouave play, Mrs. Duberly continues: "This morning brought us news. Twelve hundred French were killed and wounded besides many officers. One company went in 100 men, and came back 3" (Duberly 177–8).

11 "Chant pour la rentrée des troupes à Paris"

(Air de "L'Honneur du Drapeau")
Pourquoi ces chants et ces cris d'allégresse
Et tout Paris accouru sur nos pas?
C'est pour fêter dans une sainte ivresse
Notre victoire et nos combats. […]
Et si bientôt la voix de la patrie
Vient nous crier: volez au champ d'honneur.
Nous répondrons à cette voix chérie:
Vive à jamais la France et l'Empereur
(Paris, 29 décembre 1855)

([To the tune of "Honour to the flag"]
Why this singing and cries of joy
And all of Paris following our steps?
It's to celebrate in saintly jubilation

Our victory and our battles. […]
And should our homeland call upon us
To rush off to the fields of honour,
We will reply to that dearest call:
Long live France and the Emperor!
[Paris, 29 December 1855])

In Guffroy, *Les Fastes de l'armée française*.

12 The bronze for the reliefs on the Vendôme column was melted from Russian cannons captured by Napoleon Bonaparte at Austerlitz. See Matsuda, "Idols of the Emperor," 74.

13 Letter to Alphonse and Laure Fleury, 10 October 1854 (Sand, *Correspondance*, vol. 12, 589).

14 In a letter dated 1 January 1856, Prosper Mérimée described the scene:

> [Les régiments] sont entrés à Paris en tenue de campagne, avec leurs vieilles capotes déchirées, leurs drapeaux en loques et leurs blessés marchant en avant avec les vivandières. Il y eut une nuée de larmes … On me dit que, le lendemain, il y avait foule dans les bureaux de la guerre pour s'enrôler … Si vous aviez vu les haillons de ces soldats de Crimée, vous auriez dit, comme tout le monde, qu'il n'y a rien de plus beau.
>
> ([The regiments] entered Paris in battle dress with torn coats, their flags in shreds, and the wounded marching at the head with the canteen women. There was not a dry eye … I heard that the next day crowds lined up at the recruiting office to enrol. If you had seen the rags of these soldiers from Crimea, you would have said, like everyone else, that there is nothing more beautiful) (*Lettres*, 1879).

Chapter 4

1 On the diversity of ceramic and faience dishes commemorating the war, see Beaux-Laffon, "Guerre de Crimée et faïence fine."

2 Napoleon III was never considered an art lover by his contemporaries. Maxime Du Camp offers this description of the Emperor's visit to the Salon of 1853: "[Il] parcourut les salles au pas accéléré, sans dire un mot, sans faire une observation, passant devant les meilleurs toiles avec une indifférence qu'il ne cherchait pas à dissimuler. On voyait qu'il accomplissait une des mille corvées que lui imposait son rôle de souverain." (He rushed through the rooms at a hurried pace, saying nothing, noticing nothing, passing by the best paintings with an indifference he did not try to hide. You could see that he was just filling

one of the thousand obligations that were thrust upon him in his role as sovereign). In Granger, *L'Empereur et les arts, la liste civile de Napoléon III* (Paris: École des Chartes, 2005), 119.

3 In 1852, in response to the *coup d'état* that brought Napoleon III to power, Hugo published the political pamphlet, *Napoléon le petit,* from his exile in Brussels.

4 Though much smaller than the original *Apotheosis of Napoleon I,* Cabasson's *Apotheosis of Napoleon III* has a large cast of allegorical characters. Napoleon III stands in his chariot, France holds both his hand and the *tricolore.* Victory poses the crown of laurels over his head while holding out an olive branch. Above him in the sky, Napoleon I, accompanied by military officers, salutes his nephew, while on the left Hercules and Athena, the goddess of wisdom, lead his horses. In most apotheoses, the deification of a mortal emperor (in ancient Rome, for instance) takes place after his death; here, by contrast, Napoleon III is being glorified before his death and even before the end of the war in the Crimea, where, presumably, Hercules, Athena, Napoleon I, and Victory will lead him to military triumph.

5 Vernet was overwhelmingly favoured by the general public and overwhelmingly disfavoured by critics. Edmond About wryly notes: "Hors de Paris, on ne connaît ni M. Ingres, ni M. Delacroix … ; M. Horace Vernet est admiré jusque dans l'Ardèche" (Outside of Paris, no one knows Ingres, Delacroix …; but Horace Vernet is admired throughout the Ardèche). About, *Nos Artistes,* 135.

6 *Rapport du Directeur de la Division des Beaux-Arts.*

7 A draughtsman, caricaturist, illustrator, watercolourist, painter, and sculptor, Doré worked in all the main genres and formats of his era, but he felt overlooked by critics as a serious artist.

8 Twenty-four thousand French subscribers would have seen the images of the war on the pages of *L'Illustration.* Thousands more would have seen them around the world in inexpensive periodicals that purchased illustrations from *l'Illustration.* These reached a transnational audience in Britain, the Netherlands, Germany, Russia, and the United States. More British people saw Durand-Brager's war images from *L'Illustration* (reproduced in *Cassell's Illustrated Family Paper*) than saw the images by Constantin Guys in the *Illustrated London Times.* See Smits, *The European Illustrated Press,* 1–5.

9 On Fenton's Crimean photographs, see Gordon, *Shadows of War.* Fenton is well-known for his iconic war photograph, "The Valley of the Shadow of Death," which he made near the site of the Charge of the Light Brigade. The photograph, which famously exists in two versions, raises questions about the objectivity and authenticity of photography. On the history of this photograph, see Susan Sontag, *Regarding the Pain of Others* (New York: Picador, 2004); and Morris, *Believing Is Seeing.*

10 The earliest photographs of the war on display at the Universal Exhibition were taken by Karl Bapst de Szathmany, a painter and amateur photographer from Bucharest. The photographs no longer exist but were described in detail by Ernest Lacan in his *Esquisses photographiques, à propos de l'Exposition universelle.*
11 On the relationship between photography and the conventions of war illustration during the Crimean War, see Gervais, "Witness to War."
12 The series by Eugène Appert was purchased by the state in 1855 for the Galeries historiques de Versailles.
13 For a complete list of the works in the Salle de Crimée and how they were hung, see Thoma, "Panorama of War."
14 Millet's painting of three women gleaning sparse remains after the harvest depicts a scene of back-breaking rural poverty. Visually it speaks to the inability of the lower working classes to rise above their station. The painting was viewed with suspicion by a bourgeois Parisian public, who read in it the threat of social radicalism.
15 On Durand-Brager and his photographer, Pierre Lassimonne, see Hornstein, *Picturing War in France*, 2017.
16 On the *images d'Épinal* and popular games associated with the Crimean War, see Jean-François Figeac, "The Crimean War in French Popular Opinion," 74.
17 Benjamin, *The Arcades Project*, 527–36.
18 The military setbacks that were to ensue prevented the realization of Napoleon's project.

Chapter 5

1 On illustrations of the Crimean War in French schoolbooks of the second half of the nineteenth century, see Geslot, "La Guerre de Crimée."
2 The defeat of France represented an important moment in the birth of the German empire. One of the most renowned German painters of his time, Anton von Werner, commemorated the defeat and its aftermath in a number of paintings, most notably *The Capitulation of Sedan*, *The Proclamation of the German Empire at Versailles*, and *The Meeting of Bismarck and Napoleon III*. At 1725 square metres, his panorama *The Battle of Sedan* was considered one of the largest and most costly images at the time of its opening in 1883. On the artistic and political significance of this work, see "The Panorama of Sedan, Obedience through Presence" in Grau, *Virtual Art*, 90–139.
3 The Thin Red Line refers to an episode in the Battle of Balaclava during which 500 Sutherland Highlanders fired at the Russian cavalry. The event was praised in the British press and became emblematic of the qualities of the British soldier. William Russell of *The Times* wrote that he could see nothing between the charging Russians and the British regiment's base

of operations at Balaklava but the "thin red streak tipped with a line of steel." The phrase Thin Red Line became a symbol of British composure in battle and has become an expression for any thinly spread military unit holding firm against attack.

4 Though certainly the most famous, Russell was not the only British war correspondent in the Crimea. Representatives of several other journals and newspapers filed reports for domestic consumption.

5 On the Victoria Cross, see Kriegel, *The Crimean War and Its Afterlife*, 89–122.

6 During the Franco-Prussian War the French experienced their own legendary episode of military daring at the Battle of Reichshoffen, 6 August 1870. In a counter attack that ultimately allowed the remaining French army to retreat, 700 French Cuirassiers led a heroic but ill-advised charge against Prussian troops and were killed at close range when they were ambushed. Within days the Charge of the Cuirassiers of Reichshoffen became as celebrated in France as the Charge of the Light Brigade in England, moving quickly from a news report in the press to the widely recited poem, "Les Cuirassiers de Reichshoffen," by Émile Bergerat.

7 Dr. Jean-Charles Chenu, in his 1865 official report on the health and health services of the French army in the Crimea, gives the exact figures of 95,615 men out of a total of 309,368. This is proportionally much higher than the death tolls in the British army. For information on the epidemic disasters of the Crimean War, see the doctoral dissertation of Lemaire, *La Guerre de Crimée: Chronique et analyse d'un désastre sanitaire.*

8 The cholera was transported by troopship out of Marseille, the only record of cholera spreading from west to east in the Mediterranean. See Rebecca Seaman, "Cholera: Dread Disease," 89.

9 The memory of many army deaths lies buried in registries of local communes. From June 1855 to March 1856, for instance, the small town of Benfeld (Bas-Rhin) received news of the deaths of eight men between the ages of twenty and twenty-eight. The causes of death correspond to the general numbers: two from cholera, two from typhus, one from scurvy, one from scurvy and typhoid fever, one from frozen hands and feet, and one from a fractured skull in battle. The list of names puts a face to the tragic losses. The Antoni family lost both sons, one to cholera, the other to typhus. Joseph Kieffer was an army nurse.

REISSENGER Florent, du choléra
EHRHARD Charles, fracture du crâne devant l'ennemi.
ANTONI Martin, choléra
JONNARD Auguste, de scorbut et fièvre typhoïde.
SCHLEGER Louis, congélation des pieds et des mains.
ANTONI Jean, typhus.
KIEFFER Joseph, typhus
HILDT Charles, scorbut.

(Bernard, "Des décès à l'Armée d'Orient.")

Bibliography

Primary Sources

About, Edmond. *L'Homme à l'oreille cassée*. Paris: Hachette, 1862.
– *Le Mari imprévu*. Paris: Hachette, 1870.
– *Maître Pierre*. Paris: Hachette, 1858.
– *Nos Artistes au Salon de 1857*. Paris: Hachette, 1858.
– *Voyage à travers l'exposition des beaux-arts*. Paris: Hachette, 1855.

Arnault, Pierre-Célestin. *La Crimée, grande pantomime militaire en 2 actes, avec intermèdes équestres, représentant le débarquement des troupes à Vieux-Fort et la bataille de l'Alma*. Paris: Aubusson et Kugelmann, 1855.

Asseline, Alfred. "La Librairie et les libraires." *Le Mousquetaire*, no. 231, 13 July 1854, 1–2.

Auger, Charles. *Siège de Sébastopol: Historique du service de l'artillerie, 1854–1856*. 2 vols. Paris: Veuve Berger-Levraul et fils, 1859.

Baudelaire, Charles. *OEuvres complètes*, edited by Claude Pichois. 2 vols. Paris: Gallimard, 1976.
– *The Flowers of Evil*, trans. William Aggeler. Fresno: Academy Library Guild, 1954.

Baudens, Lucien. *La Guerre de Crimée. Les campements, les abris, les ambulances, les hôpitaux, etc*. Paris; Michel Lévy, 1858.

Bazancourt, Le Baron de. *L'Expédition de Crimée jusqu'à la prise de Sébastopol*. Paris: Amyot, 1856.

Beaumont-Vassy, Edouard Ferdinand de la Bonninière, Vicomte de. *Histoire de mon temps: Deuxième série; Présidence décennale; Second empire*. 2 vols. Paris: Amyot, 1864.

Bédarrides, Jean-Paul. *Journal humoristique du siège de Sébastopol par un artilleur*. 2 vols. Paris: Librairie centrale, 1868.

Bibliographie de la France, ou Journal général de l'imprimerie et de la librairie. Tome 5. Paris: Pillet aîné, 1854. (BF)

Bocher, Charles. *Lettres de Crimée, souvenirs de guerre*. Paris: Calmann Lévy, 1877.

Bourseul, E.-Ch. *Comment finira la guerre. Exposé de la question d'Orient dégagé de tous les faux bruits et envisagé sous son véritable jour au point de vue politique et au point de vue militaire*. Paris: Blot, 1854.

Caillebotte-la-Vente, A. *Réveries et Essais poétiques, précédés d'une chanson sur la Guerre d'Orient*. Manche: Chez les librairies du département, 1854.

Castellane, Boniface de. *Journal du maréchal de Castellane, 1804–1862*. Paris: Plon, 1897.

Catalogue de l'Histoire de France, vol. 4, *1848–1856*. Bibliothèque impériale, Département des Imprimés. Paris: Firmin Didot, 1857. (CHF)

Cham (Amédée de Noé). *Le Salon de 1857 illustré*. Paris: Librairie nouvelle Charivari, 1857.

Chantaume. *Lettres d'un Zouave. Expédition de Crimée*, edited by Général du de Mortemart. Paris: Firmin Didot, 1856.

Charavay, Étienne. *Revue des documents historiques. Suite de pièces curieuses et inédites*. Vol. 8. Paris: Lemerre, 1881.

Chenu, Jean-Charles. *Rapport au Conseil de santé des armées sur les résultats du service médico-chirurgical aux ambulances de Crimée et aux hôpitaux militaires français en Turquie, pendant la campagne d'Orient en 1854–1855–1856*. Paris: V. Masson, 1865.

Cler, Jean-Joseph-Gustave. *Souvenirs d'un officier du 2e de zouaves*. Paris: Michel Lévy, 1859.

La Comète et le croissant. Présages et prophéties relatifs à la question d'Orient; par un astrologue contemporain. Paris: Librairie Nouvelle, 1854.

Conegliano, Charles-Adrien-Gustave Duchesne, duc de. *Le Second Empire, la maison de l'Emprereur*. Paris: Calmann-Lévy, 1897.

Cormon et Grangé. *Le Théâtre des Zouaves*. Paris: Michel Lévy, 1855.

Crémazie, Octave. *OEuvres*, vol. 1: *Poésies*. Ottawa: Éditions de l'université d'Ottawa, 1972.

– *Oeuvres*, vol. 2: *Prose*. Ottawa: Editions de l'université d'Ottawa, 1976.

"Crimean War. Chapter 1. Loss of Life in Different Ways." *Advocate of Peace*, vol 1, no. 7 (July 1869): 106–7.

Crimée 1854–1856. Premiers reportages de guerre. Paris: Musée de l'armée, 1994.

Damas, Le R.P. de. *Souvenirs religieux et militaires de la Crimée*. Paris: Jacques Lecoffre, 1857.

Daudet, Alphonse. "L'Agonie de la Sémillante." In *Lettres de mon Moulin*, 107–20. Paris: Charpentier, 1895.

De Croze, Firmin. *Nos Zouaves en Crimée*. Limoges: Marc Barbou, n.d. (1897?).

De la Conduite de la Guerre d'Orient. Mémoire adressé au gouvernement de S.M. l'Empereur Napoléon III par in Officier général. Brussels: A. Bluff, 1855.

Delacroix, Eugène. Le *Journal d'Eugène Delacroix*. 3 vols. Paris: Plon, 1895.

Délécluze, Etienne-Jean. *Les Beaux arts dans les deux mondes en 1855*. Paris: Charpentier, 1856.

Delord, Taxile, Clément Carraguel, and Louis Huart. *Messieurs les Cosaques: relation charivarique, comique, et surtout véridique des hauts faits des Russes en Orient*. Paris: Lecou, 1855.

De Sacy, Ustazade Silvestre. *Le Journal des débats politiques et littéraires,* 30 December 1855.
Descaves, Lucien. *La Colonne*. Paris: Stock, 1901.
Des Essarts, Alfred. *Portraits biographiques et critiques des hommes de la Guerre d'Orient*. Paris: Garnier, 1855.
Deslys, Charles. *Un Zouave*. Brussels: Alphonse Lebègue, 1855.
Disdéri, André-Adolphe-Eugène. *Palais de Versailles. Vues d'intérieur prises à l'occasion de la visite de S. M. la reine Victoria par Disdéri, photographe des palais de l'Industrie et des Beaux-Arts*. Texte par A. Caron de Lalande. Paris: Imprimerie de l'Empereur, 1857. http://expositions.bnf.fr/napol/grand/018.htm.
Doin, Ernest. *Le Conscrit ou le Retour de Crimée*. Montréal: Beauchemin & Valois, 1878.
Duban, Charles. *Souvenirs militaires d'un officier français, 1848–1896*. Paris: Plon, 1896.
Du Camp, Maxime. *Orient et Italie: souvenirs de voyage et delectures*. Paris: Didier et cie, 1868.
– *Le Salon de 1857*. Paris: Librairie Nouvelle, 1857.
– *Le Salon de 1861*. Paris: Librairie Nouvelle, 1861.
– *Souvenirs littéraires*. Paris: Hachette, 1905.
Dumas, Alexandre. *Bric-à-brac*. Paris: Michel Lévy, 1861.
Du Pays, A.J. "Panorama de la prise de Sébastopol, aux Champs Élysees." *L'Illustration*, 25 August 1860, 115.
Dupont, Pierre. *Chants et poésies*, 7e édition. Paris Garnier, 1862.
Exposition universelle de 1855, Explication des ouvrages de peinture, sculpture, gravure, lithographie et architecture des artistes vivants, étrangers et français, exposés au Palais des Beaux-Arts, Avenue Montaigne, le 15 mai 1855. Paris: Vinchon imprimeur des musées, 1855.
Fay, Charles. *Souvenirs de la Guerre de Crimée 1854–1856*. Paris: Librairie militaire, 1867.
Feuilleton du Journal de la Librairie, 21 July 1855; 25 August 1855.
Flaubert, Gustave. *Correspondance*, edited by Jean Bruneau. 4 vols. Paris: Gallimard, 1980.
Forcade, Eugène. *Histoire des causes de la guerre d'Orient d'après les documens [sic] français et anglais*. Paris: Michel Lévy, 1854.
France, Anatole. *La Vie en fleur*. Paris: Calmann Lévy, 1922.
Gautier, Théophile. *L'Art dramatique en France depuis 25 ans*. Paris: Hetzel, 1859.
– *Les Beaux-arts en Europe, 1855*. 2 vols. Paris: Michel Lévy, 1855–56.
– "Introduction." *L'Univers illustré*, 22 May 1858, 1007.
– "Panorama de la prise de Sébastopol." *Le Moniteur universel*, 10 January 1861.
Gelé, Émile (Lieutenant). *Guerre d'Orient, lettres d'un Saint-Cyrien, par Émile Gelé*. Paris: Au Café parisien, 1856.

Goncourt, Edmond and Jules de. *La Peinture à l'exposition de 1855*. Paris: Dentu, 1855.

Granier de Cassagnac, Adolphe, and Paul Granier de Cassagnac. *Histoire populaire illustrée de l'empereur Napoléon III*. Paris: Lachaud et Burdin, 1874.

Grégoire, Louis. *Histoire de France: période contemporaine*, vol. 4. Paris: Garnier, 1883.

Guerre d'Orient ou Receuil des principaux actes officiels concernant les mémorables victoires de l'Alma, d'Inkermann, de la Tchernaia, du siège et de la prise de Sébastopol. Lyon: Bajat Fils, 1855.

Gyp [Sybille Riquetti de Mirbeau]. *Souvenirs d'une petite fille*, vol. 1. Paris: Calmann-Lévy, 1927.

Hamel, Ernest. *Histoire du Second Empire faisant suite à l'histoire de la Seconde République*. Paris: Furne, 1893.

Hayward, Mrs. Alfred. *The Battles of Crimea*. J.C. Ansley: Port Hope, 1855.

Herbé, Général Jean-François Jules. *Français et Russes en Crimée. Lettres d'un officier français à sa famille pendant la campagne d'Orient*. Paris: Calmann Lévy, 1892.

Houssaye, Henri. "La Peinture de batailles: le nouveau tableau de M. Meissonier. L'Exposition des oeuvres de Pils." *Revue des Deux Mondes*, troisième période, vol. 13, no. 4, 1876, 864–89.

"How Stands the Alliance between Britain and France now?" *New York Times*, 24 July 1855, 4.

Hugo, Victor. "La Guerre d'Orient." In *Actes et Paroles II. Pendant l'exil, 1852–1870*, 99–111. Paris: Michel Lévy, 1875.

– *Histoire d'un crime*. Paris: Calmann Lévy, 1877.

– *Oeuvres poétiques*, edited by Pierre Albouy. 2 vols. Paris: Gallimard, 1967.

– "Sixième anniversaire de 1848." In *Actes et Paroles II. Pendant l'exil, 1852–1870*, 117–32. Paris: Michel Lévy, 1875.

Illustrated London News, vol. XXVI, no. 726. 3 February 1855. *Illustrated London News*, vol. XXVII, no. 757. 18 August 1855.

Jaeglé, E. *La Guerre d'Orient. Pourqoi la guerre aux Cosaques? Avec notions historiques, physiques, géographique sur la Turquie et la Russie*. Paris: Durand, 1854.

Joly, Victor. *Mensonges et réalités de la Guerre d'Orient*. Brussels: J. Vanbuggenhoudt, 1855.

Kinglake, Alexander William. *The Invasion of Crimea: Its Origin and an Account of its Progress*, vol. 1. New York: Harper, 1863.

Lacan, Ernest. *Esquisses photographiques, à propos de l'Exposition universelle et la guerre d'Orient*. Paris: Grassart, 1856.

Ladimir, Jules. *Histoire complète de la Guerre d'Orient*. Paris: Librairie Populaire, 1856.

Laprade, Victor de. *Oeuvres poétiques, poèmes civiques, tribuns et courtisans*. Paris: Lemerre, 1879.

Laurencin-Chapelle, Paul Adolphe. *Nos zouaves: historique – organisations – faits d'armes – les régiments – vie intime*. Paris: J. Rothschild, 1888.

Leconte, Jules. "Souvenir de 1855." Paris: Imprimerie de J. Juteau, 1856.

Lenient, Charles. *La Poésie patriotique en France dans les temps modernes*. 2 vols. Paris: Hachette, 1894.

Leroy-Beaulieu, Paul. *Les Guerres contemporaines (1853–1866). Recherches statistiques sur les pertes d'hommes et de capitaux*. Paris: Pichon-Lamy, 1869.

Loizillon, Daniel. *Les Zouaves en Crimée. Vaudeville en un acte*. Constantine: Arcadie Imprimeur, 1854.

Loizillon, Henri. *Lettres écrites de Crimée par le Capitaine d'État-major Henri Loizillon à sa famille*. Paris: Flammarion, 1895.

Maindron, Ernest et Camille Viré. *Le Champs de Mars: 1751–1889*. Lille: Danel, 1889.

Marchal, Gustave. *La Guerre de Crimée*. Paris: Firmin-Didot, 1888.

Maynard, Félix. *Souvenirs d'un Zouave devant Sébastopol*. 2 vols. Paris: Librairie Nouvelle, 1855.

Mérimée, Prosper. *Correspondance générale*, edited by Maurice Parturier. 2 vols. Paris: Le Divan, 1941.

– "Prosper Mérimée, à propos de lettres inédites." *Revue des deux mondes*, troisième période, vol. 34, 1879, 745.

Michelet, Jules. *Journal*, vol. 2: *1849–1860*, edited by P. Viallaneix. Paris: Gallimard, 1962.

– *L'Oiseau*, 7th éd. Paris: Hachette, 1863.

Molènes, Paul de. *Les commentaires d'un soldat sur la Guerre de Crimée et le siège de Sébastopol*. Paris: Michel Lévy, 1860.

Monnier, Henri. *Mémoires de M. Joseph Prudhomme*. 2 vols. Paris: Librairie Nouvelle, 1857.

Mortemart, Général Duc de, ed. *Expédition de Crimée: lettres d'un zouave*. Paris: Firmin Didot, 1856.

Mullois, L'Abbé. *Histoire de la Guerre d'Orient des enfants*. Paris: Josse, 1859.

– *Histoire de la Guerre d'Orient*. Paris: Dillet, 1857.

Musée des Familles. *Lectures du soir*. Vol. 23, *1855–1856*. Paris, 1856.

– "Le Tableau de M. Yvon: Prise de Malakoff." October 1857.

Perret, E. *Récits de Crimée 1854–1856*. Paris: Bloud et Barral, 1888.

Rabourdin, Charles. *Nouveaux contes du bivouac*. Paris: Delgrave, 1888.

Rambaud, Alfred. "Les Russes à Sébastopol, d'après les documens publiés sous les auspices du Csarevitch." *Revue des Deux Mondes*, 3eme période, vol. 2, 1874, 497–530.

Ranken, George. *Canada and the Crimea or Sketches of a Soldier's Life. From the Journals and Correspondence of the Late Major Ranken*. London: Longman, Green, Longman and Roberts, 1862.

Rapport du Directeur de la Division des Beaux-Arts: La Politique artistique du Second Empire. Archives nationales de France, F21 487, dossier 4. Pièces diverses 1856–70.

Rochenoire, Julien de la. *Le Salon de 1855*. Paris: Matinon, 1855.
Roselat, Adrien. *Notre-Dame de France, statue colossale; fondue avec les canons pris a Sébastopol, et érigée sur le Rocher Corneille, au Puy*. Le Puy: Marchessou, Éditeur, 1860.
Roy, Just-Jean-Étienne. *Histoire du siège et de la prise de Sébastopol*. Tours: A. Mame et cie., 1856.
Sales, Pierre. *Le Sergent Renaud*. Paris: Fayard, 1898. http://www.gutenberg .org /cache/epub/17252/pg17252.html.
Sand, George. *Césarine Dietrich*. Paris: Michel Lévy, 1871.
– *Correspondance*. 25 vols. Paris: Garnier, 1964–91.
Ségur, Comtesse de. *L'Auberge de l'Ange gardien*. Paris: Hachette, 1888.
– *Le Général Dourakine*. Paris: Hachette, 1895.
Senior, Nassau. *Conversation with M. Thiers and M. Guizot and other distinguished persons during the Second Empire, 1852–1860*. 2 vols. London, 1878.
– *Correspondence and Conversations of Alexis de Tocqueville with Nassau William Senior from 1834–1859*, vol. 2, edited by M.C.M. Simpson. London: Henry S. King & Co., 1872.
Sewell, Anna. *Black Beauty; His Grooms and Companions, Autobiography of a Horse*. London: Jarrold and Sons, 1877. https://en.wikisource.org/wiki/ Black_Beauty.
Simpson, William. *The Autobiography of William Simpson, R.I. (Crimean Simpson)*, edited by George Eyre-Todd. London: Fisher Unwin, 1903.
"Some Sketches from the Present War." *Advocate of Peace*, vol. 11, no. 12 (December 1854): 185–8.
Swinburne, Algernon. *Victor Hugo*. New York: Worthington, 1886.
Taillandier, Saint-René. "L'Historien et l'histoire de la guerre de Crimée." *Revue des Deux mondes*, 3e période, vol. 27, 1878, 38–70.
Tanc, X. *Guerre d'Orient en 1854, son origine et ses causes*. Paris: Dentu, 1864.
Thoumas, Le Général. *Mes Souvenirs de Crimée, 1854–1856*. Paris: La Librairie illustrée, 1891.
Thouvenel, Louis. *Nicolas I et Napoléon III. Les Préliminaires de la guerre de Crimée*. Paris: Calmann Lévy, 1891.
Tolstoy, Leo. *Sebastopol Sketches*. Translated by David McDuff. London: Penguin, 1986.
Vairon, Ernest et Camille Viré. *Le Champs de Mars: 1751–1889*. Paris: Daniel et Beschet, 1889.
Vandam, Albert Dresden. *An Englishman in Paris (Notes and Recollections)*, vol. 2. London: Chapman and Hill, 1892.
Verne, Jules. *Aventures de trois Russes et de trois Anglais dans l'Afrique australe*. Paris: Hetzel, 1871.

– *Le Salon de 1857*. In *La Revue des Beaux arts*, vol. 8. Paris: Bureaux de la Revue des Beaux arts, 1857.
Victoria, Queen. *Leaves from a Journal, A record of the visit of the Emperor and Empress of the French to the Queen and of The Visit of the Queen and H.R.H. the Prince Consort to the Emperor of the French, 1855*. New York: Farrar Strauss, 1961.
– "La Reine Victoria d'après sa correspondance inédite." *Revue des Deux Mondes*, 5e période, vol. 42, 1907.
Vigny, Alfred de. *Les Destinées. Poèmes philosophiques*. Ed. Edmond Estève. Paris: Hachette, 1924.
Villemain, Abel-France. "Rapport sur les concours de l'année 1857." 20 August 1857. http://www.academie-francaise.fr/rapport-sur-les-concours-de-lannee-1857.
Vizitelly, Ernest Alfred. *The Court of the Tuileries, 1852–1870: Its Organization, Chief Personages, Splendour, Frivolity, and Downfall*. London: Chatto and Windus, 1907.
Wrench, Edward. "The Lessons of the Crimean War." *British Medical Journal 2*, no. 2012 (22 July 1899): 205–8.
Zola, Émile. *La Curée*. Paris: Gallimard, 1981.
– *Nouveaux contes à Ninon*. Paris: Charpentier, 1879.
– *Le Ventre de Paris*. Paris: Les Lettres modernes, 1969.
"Les Zouaves." *Revue des Deux Mondes*, March 1855, 1105–27.

Secondary Sources

Abel, Magdalena, and Henry L. Roediger. "Collective Memory: A New Arena of Cognitive Study." *Trends in Cognitive Sciences* 19, no. 7 (2015): 359–61.
Abel, Magdalena, Sharda Umanath, James V. Wertsch, and Henry L. Roediger. "Collective Memory: How Groups Remember Their Past." In *Collaborative Remembering: Theories, Research, and Applications*, edited by Michelle L. Meade, Celia B. Harris, Penny Van Bergen, John Sutton, and Amanda J. Barnier, 280–305. Oxford: Oxford University Press, 2017.
Adams, Michael. "Tennyson's Crimean War Poetry: A Cross-Cultural Approach." *Journal of the History of Ideas* 40, no. 3 (1979): 405–22.
Agulhon, Maurice. *Marianne into Battle: Republican Imagery and Symbolism in France, 1789–1880*. Cambridge: Cambridge University Press, 1981.
Anceau, Éric. *Napoléon III*. Paris: Taillandier, 2008.
Ashplant, T.G., Graham Dawson, and Michael Roper, eds. *The Politics of War Memory and Commemoration*. London: Routledge, 2000.
Assmann, Aleida. "Canon and Archive." In *A Companion to Cultural Memory Studies*, edited by Astrid Erll and Ansgar Nünning, 97–107. Berlin: Walter De Gruyter, 2010.

– *Cultural Memory and Western Civilization: Functions, Media, Archives.* Cambridge: Cambridge University Press, 2011.
– "Forms of Forgetting." Public lecture on the occasion of receiving the Dr. A.H. Heinekenprijs for historical sciences from the Royal Dutch Academy of Sciences, 1 October 2014. https://h401.org/2014/10/forms-of-forgetting.
– "Four Formats of Memory: From Individual to Collective Constructions of the Past." In *Cultural Memory and Historical Consciousness in the German-Speaking World since 1500,* edited by Christian Emden and David Midgely, 19–38. Oxford: Peter Lang, 2004.
– "Reframing Memory: Between Individual and Collective Forms of Constructing the Past." In *Performing the Past: Memory, History, and Identity in Modern Europe,* edited by Karin Tilmans, Frank van Vree, and Jay Winter, 35–50. Amsterdam: Amsterdam University Press, 2010.
– "Theories of Cultural Memory and the Concept of 'Afterlife.'" In *Afterlife of Events: Perspectives on Mnemohistory,* edited by Marek Tamm, 79–94. London: Palgrave Macmillan, 2015.
– "Transformations between History and Memory." *Social Research* 75, no. 1 (2008): 49–72.

Assmann, Jan. "Collective Memory and Cultural Identity," translated by John Czaplicak. *New German Critique* 65 (1995): 125–33.
– "Communicative and Cultural Memory." In *Cultural Memory Studies: An International and Interdisciplinary Handbook,* edited by Astrid Erll and Ansgar Nunning, 109–18. New York and Berlin: Walter de Gruyter, 2008: 109–118.

Astafieva, Elena. "L'Empire russe en Palestine, 1847–1917: aux origines de la politique russe au Proche-Orient." *The Conversation,* 4 March 2016. http://theconversation.com/lempire-russe-en-palestine-1847-1917-aux-origines-de-la-politique-russe-au-proche-orient-55542.

Bacot, Jean-Pierre. *La Presse illustrée au XIXe siècle: une histoire oubliée.* Limoges: Presses universitaires de Limoges, 2005.
– "Le rôle des magazines illustrés dans la construction du nationalisme au XIXe siècle et au début du XXe siècle." *Réseaux,* vol 3. no. 107, 2001: 265–93.

Badem, Candan, ed. *The Routledge Handbook of the Crimean War.* London: Routledge, 2021.

Baguley, David. *Napoleon III and His Regime: An Extravaganza.* Baton Rouge: Louisiana State University Press, 2000.

Baker, Ken. "The Crimean War and the Freedom of the Press." 4 February 2009. https://kenbaker.wordpress.com/2009/02/04/the-crimean-war-and-the-freedom-of-the-press.

Baldwin, Gordon, Malcolm Daniel, and Sara Greenough. *All the Mighty World: The Photographs of Roger Fenton (1852–1860).* New Haven: Yale University Press, 2004.

Bann, Stephen. *Parallel Lines: Printmakers, Painters and Photographers in Nineteenth-Century France*. New Haven: Yale University Press, 2001.

Bapst, Germain. *Le Maréchal Canrobert souvenirs d'un siècle. Tome second: Napoléon III et sa cour, La Guerre de Crimée*. Paris: Plon, 1902.

Barash, Jeffrey. *Collective Memory and the Historical Past*. Chicago: University of Chicago Press, 2016.

Barluet, Alain. "À Sébastopol, l'hommage russe aux soldats de Napoléon III tombés en Crimée." *Le Figaro*, 4 October 2020. https://www.lefigaro.fr/international/a-sebastopol-l-hommage-russe-aux-soldats-de-napoleon-iii-tombes-en-crimee-20201004.

Bartlett, Roger, and Roy Payne. "Britain's Crimean War Trophy Guns: The Case of Ludlow and the Marches." *History* 99, no. 4 (October 2014): 652–69.

Bassargette, Élisabeth. "Une imagerie éducative: Le Mouchoir illustré rouennais." *Histoire de l'éducation*, no. 30, 1986: 61–6.

Bates, Rachel. *Curating the Crimea: The Cultural Afterlife of a Conflict*. 2015. PhD diss., University of Leicester and the National Army Museum. https://www.proquest.com/docview/1827518507.

– "Negotiating a 'Tangled Web of Pride and Shame': A Crimean Case-Study." *Museum and Society* 13, no. 4 (2015): 503–21.

Baudrillard, Jean. *The Gulf War Did Not Take Place*. Bloomington: Indiana University Press, 1995.

Baumgart, Winfried. *The Crimean War, 1853–1856*. London: Arnold, 1999.

Beaux-Laffon, Marie-Germaine. "Guerre de Crimée et faïence fine: richesse et diversité des sources iconographiques." *Sèvres. Revue de la société des amis du musée national de céramique*, 13, 2004: 61–73.

Becker, Jean-Jacques. *La France, la nation, la guerre: 1850–1920*. Paris: SEDES, 1995.

Benjamin, Elizabeth. "Places and Spaces of Contested Identity in the Memorials and Monuments of Paris." *Modern and Contemporary France* 29, no. 1 (2021): 1–18.

Benjamin, Walter. *The Arcades Project*. Translated by Howard Eiland and Kevin McLaughlin. Cambridge, MA: Harvard University Press, 1999.

– "The Storyteller: Reflections on the works of Nikolai Leskov." In *Illuminations.* Translated by Harry Zohn, edited and introduction by Hannah Arendt, 83–109. New York: Harcourt Brace Jovanovich 1968.

Berman, Paul. "The International Catastrophe of Vladimir Putin." *Foreign Policy*, 13 March 2022. https://foreignpolicy.com/2022/03/13/putin-russia-war-ukraine-rhetoric-history.

Bernard, Jean-Pierre. "Des décès à l'Armée d'Orient durant la guerre de Crimée." *Histoire-Généologie*, 16 April 2009. https://www.histoire-genealogie.com/Des-deces-a-l-Armee-d-Orient?lang=fr.

Bernardy, Françoise de. "Il y a cent ans la Reine Victoria visitait Paris." *Miroir de l'Histoire*, July 1955, 160–8.

Berridge, A.L. "Off the Chart: The Crimean War in British Public Consciousness." *19: Interdisciplinary Studies in the Long Nineteenth Century* 20 (2015). http://dx.doi.org/10.16995/ntn.726.

Blier, Gérard. *Les Grands sièges de l'histoire de France*. Paris: Economica, 2012.

Bolloch Joëlle. *Photographies de guerre. De la Crimée à la Première Guerre mondiale*. Milan: Five Continents, 2004.

Boudon, Jacques-Olivier. "La Vie religieuse à la Cour de Napoléon III." In *La Cour Impérial sous le Premier et le Second Empire*, edited by Jacques-Olivier Boudon, 129–48. Paris: Éditions SPM, 2016.

Bourguilleau, Antoine. "Crimée, une guerre pour mémoire." *Slate*, 2 March 2014. http://www.slate.fr/story/84071/crimee-une-guerre-pour-memoire.

Bourke, Joanna. "Remembering War." *Journal of Contemporary History* 39, no. 4 (2004): 473–85.

Bowman, Glenn. "'In Dubious Battle on the Plains of Heav'n': The Politics of Possession in Jerusalem's Holy Sepulchre." *History and Anthropology* 22, no. 3 (2011): 371–99. https://doi.org/10.1080/02757206.2011.595008.

Bratton, J.S. "Theatre of War: The Crimea on the London Stage, 1854–5." In *Performance and Politics in Popular Drama*, edited by David Bradby and Louis James, 119–38. Cambridge: Cambridge University Press, 1980.

Braun, Marta, Regis Durant, Michel Poivert, Ulrich Keller, Pierre-Lin Renié, Thierry Gervais, Marie Chominot, Godehard Janzig, and Clément Chéroux. *L'Événement. Les images comme acteurs de l'histoire*." *Études photographiques*, vol. 21, 2007. http://journals.openedition.org/etudesphotographiques/1703.

Brown, Judy. "Great Patriotic War Memory in Sevastopol: Making Sense of Suffering in the 'City of Military Glory.'" In *War and Memory in Russia, Ukraine, and Belarus*, edited by Julie Fedor, Markku Kangaspuro, Jussi Lassila, and Tatiana Zhurzhenko, 399–428. Basingstoke: Palgrave Macmillan, 2017.

Brown, Larisa. "We'll kick Putin's backside, says Ben Wallace." *The Times*, 23 February 2022. https://www.thetimes.co.uk/article/well-kick-putins-backside-says-ben-wallace-0htn8hdps.

Burleigh, Nina. "Why Do We Forget Pandemics?" *The Nation*, 26 April 2021.

Cabourg, Gilbert. "En Crimée, les funérailles très politiques des soldats français." *La Croix*, 6 October 2020. https://www.la-croix.com/Monde/En-Crimee-funerailles-tres-politiques-soldats-francais-2020-10-06-1201117892.

Carroll, Christina. *The Politics of Imperial Memory in France, 1850–1900*. Ithaca: Cornell University Press, 2022.

Case, Lynn. *French Opinion on War and Diplomacy during the Second Empire*. Philadelphia: University of Pennsylvania Press, 1954.

Cavaignac, François. "Le Vaudeville sous le Second Empire ou le règne de Perrichon." In *Les Spectacles sous le Second Empire*. Edited by Jean-Claude Yon. Paris: Armand Colin, 2010.

Chappuis, Jean-Pierre. *Croisade en Crimée; la guerre qui arrêta les Russes*. Paris: SPL, 1978.

Charlot, Monica. *Victoria the Young Queen*. Oxford: Blackwell, 1991.

Chenu, Jean-Charles. *Rapport au Conseil de santé des armées sur les résultats du service médico-chirurgical aux ambulances de Crimée et aux hôpitaux militaires français en Turquie, pendant la campagne d'Orient en 1854–1855–1856*. Paris: V. Masson, 1865.

Childs, Elizabeth. *Daumier and Exoticism: Satirizing the French and the Foreign*. New York: Peter Lang, 2004.

Cohen, William. "Symbols of Power: Statues in 19th-c. Provincial France." *Comparative Studies in Society and History* 31, no. 3 (1989): 491–513.

Comment, Bernard. *The Painted Panorama*. New York: Harry Abrams, 2000.

Confino, Alon. "Collective Memory and Cultural History: Problems of Method." *American Historical Review* 102, no. 5 (1997): 1386–403.

– "Memory and the History of Mentalities." In *A Companion to Cultural Memory Studies*, edited by Astrid Erll and Ansgar Nünning, 77–96. Berlin: Walter de Gruyter, 2010.

Connerton, Paul. *How Modernity Forgets*. Cambridge: Cambridge University Press, 2009.

– "Seven Types of Forgetting." *Memory Studies* 1, no. 1 (2008): 59–71.

Crane, Susan, ed. *A Cultural History of Memory in the Nineteenth Century*. London: Bloomsbury, 2020.

Crivello, Maryline. "Regards sur la guerre; fragments d'histoire." *La Pensée de midi*, vol. 9, 2002, 21–31.

Dalisson, Rémi. "La Commémoration de la guerre de Crimée: propagande festive, représentations et imaginaire national sous le Second Empire (1852–1870)." Unpublished paper presented at "La Guerre de Crimée, première guerre moderne?" Paris, 7–9 November 2019.

– *Les Guerres et la mémoire*. Paris: CNRS, 2013.

Dereli, Cynthia. *A War Culture in Action: A Study of the Literature of the Crimean War Period*. Oxford: Peter Lang, 2003.

Désile, Patrick. "'Cet opéra de l'oeil': Les pantomimes des cirques parisiens au XIXe siècle." *Hors les murs*, 4 October 2011, 2–13.

Donato, Eugenio. "The Museum's Furnace: Notes towards a Contextual Reading of *Bouvard and Pécuchet*." In *Textual Strategies: Perspectives in Post-Structuralist Criticism*, edited by Josué Harari, 213–38. Ithaca: Cornell University Press, 1979.

Dosse, François, ed. *La Mémoire, pour quoi faire?* Paris: Éd. de L'Atelier, 2006.

Duberly, Frances Isabella. *Mrs. Duberly's War Journals and Letters from the Crimea, 1854–6*. Oxford: Oxford University Press, 2007.

Duflo, Pierre. *Constantin Guys: Fou de dessin, grand reporter, 1802–1892*. Paris: Armand Seydoux, 1988.

Edgerton, Robert, *Death or Glory: The Legacy of the Crimean War*. Boulder: Westview Press, 1999.

Erll, Astrid. *Memory in Culture*. Translated by S.B. Young. Basingstoke: Palgrave Macmillan, 2011.

Erll, Astrid, and Ansgar Nünning, eds. *A Companion to Cultural Memory Studies*. Berlin: Walter de Gruyter, 2010.

– *Cultural Memory Studies: An International and Interdisciplinary Handbook*. Berlin: Walter de Gruyter, 2008.

Erll, Astrid, and Ann Rigney. *Mediation, Remediation, and the Dynamics of Cultural Memory*. Berlin: Walter de Gruyter, 2009.

Favret, Mary. *War at a Distance: Romanticism and the Making of Modern Wartime*. Princeton: Princeton University Press, 2010.

Fentress, James, and Chris Wickham. *Social Memory: New Perspectives on the Past*. Oxford: Blackwell, 1992.

Figeac, Jean-Francois. "The Crimean War in French Public Opinion."" In *The Routledge Handbook of the Crimean War*, edited by Candan Badem, 69–84. London: Routledge, 2021.

Figes, Orlando. *Crimea: The Last Crusade*. London: Allen Lane, 2010.

– "Putin needs to show more restraint than hero to avoid a new Crimean war." *The Guardian*, 28 February 2014. https://www.theguardian.com/world/2014/feb/28/putin-restraint-crimea-war-ukraine-russia-nicholas.

Fredj, Claire. "Compter les morts de Crimée: un tournant sur l'identité professionnelle des médecins de l'armée française (1865–1882)." *Histoire, économie & société*, vol. 29, no. 3, 2010, 95–108.

Frenay Adrien. "The Paris Universal Exhibition, vue par *The Times*." In *L'Année 1855. La littérature à l'âge de l'Exposition universelle*, edited by Jean-Louis Cabanès and Vincent Laisney, 55–63. Paris: Garnier, 2015.

Gaubert, Henri. *Les Mots historiques qui n'ont pas été prononcés*. Paris: Spes, 1939.

Gernsheim, Helmut and Alison. *Roger Fenton, Photographer of the Crimean War: His Photographs and His Letters from the Crimea*. London: Secker and Warburg, 1954.

Gervais, Thierry. "Imaging the world. *L'Illustration*: The Birth of the French Illustrated Press and the Introduction of Photojournalism in the Mid-19th Century." *Medicographia* 27, no. 1 (2005): 97–106.

– "Witness to War: The Uses of Photography in the Illustrated Press, 1855–1904." *Journal of Visual Culture* 9, no. 3 (2010): 370–84.

Geslot, Jean-Charles. "La Guerre de Crimée dans la culture historique: images du conflit dans les ouvrages pour le grand public (deuxième moitié du XIXe siècle)." *Colloque international: La Guerre de Crimée, première guerre moderne?* Centre d'Histoire du XIXe siècle, Paris, 7–9 November 2019.

"Ghosts of Crimean War return with discovery of French cemetery." *The Journal.ie*, 23 February 2013. http://jrnl.ie/805035.

Goldfrank, David. *The Origins of the Crimean War*. New York: Longmans, 1994.

Gordon, Sophie. *Shadows of War: Roger Fenton's Photographs of the Crimea, 1855*. London: Royal Collection Trust, 2017.

Gouttman, Alain. *Le Guerre de Crimée (1853–1856)*. Paris: Perrin, 2006.

Granger, Catherine. *L'Empereur et les arts, la liste civile de Napoléon III*. Paris: École des Chartes, 2005.

Grassby, Richard. "Material Culture and Cultural History." *Journal of Interdisciplinary History* 35, no. 4 (2005): 591–603.

Grau, Oliver. "Review of Stephan Oettermann, *The Panorama: History of a Mass Medium*." *Leonardo* 32, no. 2 (1999): 143–8.

– *Virtual Art: From Illusion to Immersion*. Cambridge, MA: MIT Press, 2003.

Guffroy, Louis-Maxime. Les Fastes de l'armée française depuis la campagne de Crimée jusqu'à celle de Mexique 1854–1865. Paris: Le Bailly, 1865.

Guillaume, Laurent. "Illustrer la guerre: cent ans de gravures militaires chez Pellerin à Épinal." In *La Guerre imaginée*, edited by Philippe Buton, 121–31. Paris: Editions Seli Arslan, 2002.

Hähnel-Mesnard, Carola, Marie Liénard-Yeterian, and Cristina Marinas, eds. *Culture et mémoire: Représentations de la mémoire dans les espaces mémoriels, les arts du visuel, la littérature et le théâtre*. Paris: Éditions de l'École Polytechnique, 2008.

Halbwachs, Maurice. *Les Cadres sociaux de la mémoire*. Paris: Félix Alcan, 1925.

– *La Mémoire collective*. Paris: Albin Michel, 1997.

Hamman, Philippe. "Une entreprise de propagande bonapartiste: les assiettes à décors de Sarreguemines (1836–1870)." *Revue d'histoire moderne et contemporaine*, vol. 53–2, no. 2, 2006, 139–64.

Harari, Yuval. *Sapiens: A Brief History of Humankind*. New York: Signal, 2016.

Harrison, Mark. "The Medicalization of War – the Militarization of Medicine." *Social History of Medicine* 9 no. 2 (1996): 267–76.

Hayden, Dolores. *The Power of Place: Urban Landscape as Public History*. Cambridge, MA: MIT Press, 1997.

"Les hippodromes de spectacles à Paris au XIXe siècle." In *Le Cheval et ses patrimoines*. http://www.cheval.culture.fr/fr/page/les_hippodromes_de_spectacles_a_paris_au_xixe_siecle.

Hornstein, Katie. *Episodes in Political Illusion: The Proliferation of War Imagery in France (1804–1856)*. PhD diss., University of Michigan, Ann Arbor, 2010. Proquest, 2011. AAI3429484.

– *Picturing War in France, 1792–1856*. New Haven: Yale University Press, 2017.

Hughes, Gavin, and Jonathan Trigg. "Remembering the Charge of the Light Brigade: Its Commemoration, War Memorials, and Memory." *Journal of Conflict Archaeology* 4:, nos. 1–2 (2008): 39–58.

Huon, Jean. *Batailles et conflits oubliées*. Chaumont: Crépin-Leblond, 2018.

Hutchinson, Will, Michael Vice, and B.J. Small. *Crimean Memories: Artefacts of the Crimean War*. Atglen: Schiffer Military History, 2009.

Huyssen Andreas. *Present Pasts, Urban Palimpsests, and the Politics of Memory*. Stanford: Stanford University Press, 2003.

– *Twilight Memories: Marking Time in a Culture of Amnesia*. New York: Routledge, 1994.

Irwin-Zarencka, Iwona. *Frames of Remembrance: The Dynamics of Collective Memory*. New Brunswick: Transaction, 1994.

James, Lawrence. *Crimea 1854–1856: The War with Russia from Contemporary Photographs*. Oxford: Hayes Kennedy, 1981.

Jean-Charles Langlois 1789–1870: Le Spectacle de l'histoire. Caen: Somogy, 2005.

Johnson, Ben. "The History of the Victoria Cross." *Historic UK*. https://www.historic-uk.com/HistoryUK/HistoryofBritain/The-Victoria-Cross.

Kalifa, Dominique, Philippe Régnier, Marie-Eve Thérenty, and Alain Vaillant. *La Civilisation du journal; histoire culturelle et littéraire de la presse française au XIXe siècle*. Paris: Editions du nouveau monde, 2011.

Kansteiner, Wulf. "Finding Meaning in Memory: A Methodological Critique of Collective Memory Studies." *History and Theory* 41, no. 2 (2002): 179–97.

Kauffman, Frederick. "How Covid Breaks All the Rules of Human Narrative." *New York Times*, 23 April 2022.

Keller, Ulrich. "La Guerre de Crimée en images: regards croisés France/Angleterre." In *L'Événement, les images comme acteurs de l'histoire,* edited by Michel Poivert, 29–49. Paris: Hazan, 2007.

– "Images of War, War of Images: The Invention of Illustrated Reportage in the Crimean War." 2007. http://www.alteseite.meltonpriorinstitut.org/content/aktuell/Keller-engl.html.

– *The Ultimate Spectacle: A Visual History of the Crimean War*. Amsterdam: Gordon and Breach, 2001.

Knightley, Phillip. *The First Casualty: The War Correspondent as Hero and Myth-Maker from the Crimea to Iraq*. Baltimore: Johns Hopkins University Press, 2004.

Kozelsky, Mara. *Crimea in War and Transformation*. Oxford: Oxford University Press, 2018.

– "The Crimean War 1853–1856" [review article]. *Kritika: Explorations in Russian and Eurasian History* 13, no. 4 (2012): 903–17.

Kozintsev, Alexander. "Representing the Other in British, French, and German cartoons of the Crimean War." *Competing Eyes: Visions of Alterity*, 252–77. Budapest: L'Harmattan, 2013.

Kriegel, Lara. *The Crimean War and Its Afterlife: Making Modern Britain*. Cambridge: Cambridge University Press, 2022.

Kunzle, David. "Gustave Doré's History of Holy Russia: Anti-Russian Propaganda from the Crimean War to the Cold War." *Russian Review* 42, no. 3 (1983): 271–99.

Lalumia, Matthew Paul. *Realism and Politics in Victorian Art of the Crimean War*. Ann Arbor: UMI Research Press, 1984.
– "Realism and Anti-Aristocratic Sentiment in Victorian Depictions of the Crimean War." *Victorian Studies* 27, no. 1 (1983): 25–51.
Laurens, Stéphane, and Nicolas Roussiau, eds. *La Mémoire sociale. Identités et représentation sociales*. Rennes: Presses universitaires de Rennes, 2002.
Leanca, Gabriel, ed. *La Politique extérieure de Napoléon III*. Paris: L'Harmattan. 2011.
Lemaire, Marc. *La guerre de Crimée: Chronique et analyse d'un désastre sanitaire (1854–1856)*. PhD diss. in Military History. Montpellier: University of Montpellier, 2006.
Lerch, Dominique. "La représentation de la guerre par l'imagerie populaire (1854–1945)." *Ethnologie française*, vol. 24, no. 2 (1994): 263–75.
Levenne, François-Xavier, and Olivier Odaert. "Les écrivains au cœur des discours de la guerre." *Interférences littéraires* 9 (2009): 9–24.
Mainardi, Patricia. *Universal Expositions of the Second Empire: A Study in Art and Politics*, vols. 1 and 2. PhD thesis, City University of New York, 1984. Available from ProQuest Dissertations and Theses Global. (303288711).
Maiorova, Olga. *From the Shadow of Empire: Defining the Russian Nation through Cultural Mythology, 1855–1870*. Madison: University of Wisconsin Press, 2010.
Marcel, J.-C., and L. Mucchielli. "Un fondement du lien social: la mémoire collective selon Maurice Halbwachs." *Technologies. Idéologies. Pratiques. Revue d'anthropologie des connaissances*, vol. 13, no. 2, 1999, 63–88.
Markovits, Stefanie. *The Crimean War in the British Imagination*. Cambridge: Cambridge University Press, 2009.
– "Rushing into Print: 'Participatory Journalism' during the Crimean War." *Victorian Studies* 50, no. 4 (2008): 559–86.
Marx, Karl. *The Eighteenth Brumaire of Louis-Napoleon*. Preface to the 2nd Edition. 1869. https://www.marxists.org/archive/marx/works/1852/18th-brumaire/preface.htm.
Marx, Karl, and Friedrich Engels. *The Russian Menace to Europe: a Collection of Articles, Speeches, Letters and News Dispatches*, edited by Paul Blackstock and Bert Hoselitz. Glencoe: Free Press, 1952.
Maspéro, François. *L'Honneur de Saint-Arnaud*. Paris: Plon, 1993.
Matsuda, Matt. "Idols of the Emperor." In *States of Memory: Continuities, Conflicts, and Transformations in National Retrospection*, edited by Jeffrey K. Olick, 72–100. Durham: Duke University Press, 2003.
Mauduit, Xavier. "Les Souverains au théâtre et le spectacle dans les palais impériaux sous le Second Empire." In *Les Spectacles sous le Second Empire*, edited by Jean-Claude Yon, 21–30. Paris: Armand Colin, 2010.
Mawson, Michael Hargreave, ed. *Eyewitness in the Crimea; The Crimean Letters (1854–1856) of Lt. George Frederick Dallas*. London: Greenhill Books, 2001.
Mazurel, Hervé. "Héroïsme et exotisme: Le militaire à l'épreuve des lointains (1820–1914)." *Romantisme*, no. 161, 2013, 35–44.

McElya, Micki. "Almost 90,000 dead and no hint of national mourning. Are these deaths not 'ours'?" *Washington Post*, 15 May 2020.

Melvin, Mungo, *Sevastopol's Wars from Potemkin to Putin*. Oxford: Osprey, 2017.

Millet, Claude, ed. *Hugo et la guerre*. Paris: Maisonneuve et Larose, 2002.

Mitchell, Katharyne. "Monuments, Memorials, and the Politics of Memory." *Urban Geography* 24, no. 5 (2003): 442–59.

Montier, Jean-Pierre. "Constantin Guys selon Baudelaire: reportage et modernité." In *Littérature et Reportage*, edited by M. Boucharenc et J Deluche, 187–203. Limoges: PULIM, 2000.

Moore, Fabienne. "Gustave Doré's *Histoire de la Sainte Russie* (1854): The Invention of Graphic Rhetoric, or the Artist at War." *Dix-Neuf* 24, no. 1 (2020): 17–53.

Morris, Errol. *Believing Is Seeing (Observations on the Mysteries of Photography)*. New York: Penguin, 2014.

Moss, Walter G. "Classics Revisited: Leo Tolstoy's Sevastopol Stories." *Michigan War Studies Review*, July 2008: 1–9. https://www.miwsr.com/2008/20080702.aspx.

Myerly, Scott Hughes. *British Military Spectacle: From the Napoleonic Wars through the Crimea*. Cambridge, MA: Harvard University Press, 1996.

Napoléon III et la reine Victoria: une visite à l'Exposition universelle de 1855. Paris: Réunion des Musées nationaux, 2008.

Napoléon III et l'Europe, 1856: le congrès de Paris. Paris: Artlys, 2006. (Réunion des Musées nationaux)

Nora, Pierre. *Lieux de Mémoire*, vol. 1: *La République*. Paris: Gallimard, 1984.

Nora, Pierre, ed. *Realms of Memory*, vol. 1: *Conflicts and Divisions*. New York: Columbia University Press, 1996.

Oettermann, Stephan. *The Panorama: History of a Mass Medium*. Translated by Deborah Schneider. New York: Zone Books, 1997.

Olick, Jeffrey. *The Politics of Regret: On Collective Memory and Historical Responsibility*. London: Routledge, 2007.

Olick, Jeffrey, ed. *States of Memory: Continuities, Conflicts, and Transformations in National Retrospection*. Durham: Duke University Press, 2003.

Pao, Angela. *The Orient of the Boulevards: Exoticism, Empire, and Nineteenth-Century French Theatre*. Philadelphia: University of Pennsylvania Press, 1998.

Parsons, Christopher, and Martha Ward, eds. *A Bibliography of Salon Criticism in Second Empire Paris*. Cambridge: Cambridge University Press, 1986.

Pennebaker, James, and Becky Banasik. "On the Creation and Maintenance of Collective Memories: History as Social Psychology." In *Collective Memory of Political Events: Social Psychological Perspectives*, edited by James Pennebaker, Dario Paez, and Bernard Rimé, 3–20. Mahwah: Lawrence Erlbaum, 1997.

Pennebaker, James, Dario Paez, and Bernard Rimé, eds. *Collective Memory of Political Events: Social Psychological Perspectives*. Mahwah: Lawrence Erlbaum, 1997.

Pichois, Claude. *Le Vrai visage du general Aupick, beau-père de Baudelaire.* Paris: Mercure de France, 1956.

Plokhy, Serhii, "The City of Glory: Sevastopol in Russian Historical Mythology." *Journal of Contemporary History* 35, no. 3, 2000: 369–83.

Pointon, Marcia. "From the Midst of Warfare and Its Incidents to the Peaceful Scenes at Home: The Exposition universelle de 1855." *Journal of European Studies* 11, no. 44 (December 1981): 233–61.

Prost, Antoine. "Les Monuments aux morts." In *Les Lieux de mémoire*, edited by Pierre Nora, vol. 1, 195–228. Paris: Gallimard, 1984.

Puiseux, Hélène. *Les figures de la guerre. Représentations et sensibilités, 1839–1896.* Paris: Gallimard, 1997.

Putin, Vladimir. "Address by the President of the Russian Federation to the State Duma, March 18, 2014." http://en.kremlin.ru/events/president/news/20603.

Qualls, Karl. "The Crimean War's Long Shadow: Urban Biography and the Reconstruction of Sevastopol after World War II." Dickinson College Faculty Publications, Paper 7, 2014. https://scholar.dickinson.edu/faculty_publications/7/?utm_source=scholar.dickinson.edu%2Ffaculty_publications%2F7&utm_medium=PDF&utm_campaign=PDFCoverPages.

Rain, Pierre. "Les Relations franco-russes sous le Second Empire." *Études historiques*, 69, 1913, 629–58.

Renié, Pierre-Lin. "De l'imprimerie photographique à la photographie imprimée." *Études photographiques*, vol. 20, June 2007, 18–33.

Ricoeur, Paul. *Memory, History, and Forgetting*. Chicago: University of Chicago Press, 2004.

Rigney, Ann. "Plenitude, Scarcity, and the Circulation of Cultural Memory." *Journal of European Studies* 35, no. 1 (2005): 11–28.

– "Remaking Memory and the Agency of the Aesthetic." *Memory Studies* 14, no. 1 (2021): 10–23.

– "Remembrance as Remaking Memories of the Nation Revisited." *Nations and Nationalism* 24, no. 2 (2018): 240–57.

– "Toxic Monuments and Mnemonic Regime Change." *Studies on National Movements* 9 (2022): 7–41.

Robichon, François. "Le Panorama, spectacle de l'histoire." *Le Mouvement social* 131 (1985): 65–86.

Robichon, François, and André Rouillé. *Jean-Charles Langlois, la photographie, la peinture et la guerre. Correspondance inédite de Crimée (1855–1856)*. Nîmes: Jacqueline Chambon, 1992.

Robins, Colin. "Cholera and Dysentery in the Crimean War: A Layman's View." *Journal of the Society for Army Historical Research* 75, no. 304 (Winter 1997): 240–5.

Royle, Trevor. *Crimea: The Great Crimean War, 1854–1856*. New York: St. Martin's Press, 2000.

Roynette, Odile. "Pour une histoire culturelle de la guerre au XIXe siècle." *Revue d'histoire du XIXe siècle*, vol. 30, no. 1, 2005, 11–18.

Russell, William H. *Russell's Despatches from Crimea (1854–1856)*, edited by Nicholas Bently. New York: Hill and Wang, 1966.

Sabourin, Lise. *Alfred de Vigny et l'Académie française*. Paris: Honoré Champion, 1998.

Samuels, Maurice. "Regarding the Crimean War: History, Spectacle, Modernity." *Dix-Neuf* 6, no. 1 (2006): 26–41.

– *The Spectacular Past: Popular History and the Novel in Nineteenth-Century France*. Ithaca: Cornell University Press, 2004.

Schellino, Andrea. *Baudelaire et Paul de Molènes. Autour du projet théâtral du Marquis du 1er Houzard*. Paris: Kimé, 2014.

Schlesser, Thomas. "Les Beaux-Arts à l'Exposition universelle," in *L'Année 1855. La littérature à l'âge de l'Exposition universelle*, edited by Jean-Louis Cabanès and Vincent Laisney, 39–48. Paris: Garnier, 2015.

Seaman, Rebecca. "Cholera: Dread Disease of the Crimean War, 1854–1855." In *Epidemics and War: The Impact of Disease on Major Conflicts in History*, edited by Rebecca Seaman, 83–95. Santa Barbara: ABC Clio, 2018.

Sémur, François-Christian. *MacMahon ou la gloire confisquée (1808–1893)*. Paris: J.C. Gawsewitch, 2005.

Smith, Karen E. *Constantin Guys: Crimean War Drawings 1854–1856*. Cleveland: Cleveland Museum of Art, 1978.

Smits, Thomas. *The European Illustrated Press and the Emergence of a Transnational Visual Culture of the News, 1842–1870*. London: Routledge, 2019.

Solnit, Rebecca, "The Monument Wars." *Harper's Magazine*, January 2017. https://harpers.org/archive/2017/01/the-monument-wars.

Sontag, Susan. *Regarding the Pain of Others*. New York: Picador, 2004.

Spinney, Laura. *Pale Rider: The Spanish Flu of 1918 and How It Changed the World*. London: Jonathan Cape, 2017.

Stein, Richard. "Roger Fenton's Killing Fields." *Nineteenth-Century Contexts* 4, no. 2 (2020): 181–200.

Strauss, Julia. "Heroism of the Light Brigade still shines." *The Telegraph*, 25 October 2004.

Sweetman, John. *The Crimean War, 1854–1856*. London: Routledge, 2001.

Tamm, Marek, ed. *Afterlife of Events: Perspectives on Mnemohistory*. London: Palgrave Macmillan, 2015.

– "Beyond History and Memory: New Perspectives in Memory Studies." *History Compass* 11, no. 6 (2013): 458–73.

Tate, Trudi. "Sebastopol: On the Fall of a City." *19: Interdisciplinary Studies in the Long Nineteenth Century* 20 (2015). https://doi.org/10.16995/ntn.720.

Temperly, Harold. "The Treaty of Paris of 1856 and Its Execution." *Journal of Modern History* 4, no. 3 (September 1932): 387–414.

Teukolsky, Rachel. "Novels, Newspapers, and Global War: New Realisms in the 1850s." *Novel* 45, no. 1 (2012): 31–55.

Thoma, Julia. *The Final Spectacle: Military Painting under the Second Empire, 1855–1867*. Berlin: Walter de Gruyter, 2019.

– "Panorama of War: The *Salle de Crimée* in Versailles." *Nineteenth-Century Art Worldwide* 15, no. 1 (2016). https://www.19thc-artworldwide.org/index.php/spring16/thoma-on-panorama-of-war-salle-de-crimee-versailles.

– "Writing History: Horace Vernet's Oeuvre under the Second Empire." In *Horace Vernet and the Thresholds of Nineteenth-Century Visual Culture*, edited by Daniel Harkett and Katie Hornstein, 90–108. Hanover: Dartmouth College Press, 2017.

Tilmans, Karin, Frank Van Vree, and Jay Winter, eds. *Performing the Past: Memory, History, and Identity in Modern Europe*. Amsterdam: Amsterdam University Press, 2010.

Trapp, Frank. "The Universal Exhibition of 1855." *Burlington Magazine* 107, no. 747 (1965): 300–5.

Trouillot, Michel-Rolph. *Silencing the Past: Power and the Production of History*. Boston: Beacon Press, 1995.

Truesdell, Matthew. *Spectacular Politics, Louis-Napoléon Bonaparte and the "Fête impériale" 1849–1870*. Oxford: Oxford University Press, 1997.

Varley, Karine. *Under the Shadow of Defeat: The War of 1870–71 in French Memory*. New York: Palgrave Macmillan, 2008.

– "Under the Shadow of Defeat: The State and the Commemoration of the Franco-Prussian War, 1871–1914." *French History* 16, no. 3 (2002): 323–44.

Verbeke, Lise. "Qui est ce Zouave, vigie des crues de Paris?," 26 January 2018. https://www.franceculture.fr/histoire/le-zouave-du-pont-de-lalma-scrute-par-les-parisiens.

Viaud, Jean. "Contribution à l'actualisation de la notion de mémoire collective." In *La mémoire sociale. Identités et représentationas sociales*, edited by S. Laurens and N. Roussiau, 37–47. Rennes: Presses universitaires de Rennes, 2002.

Vidal, Philippe Jean. "Peinture militaire." In *Dictionnaire du Second Empire*, edited by Jean Tulard, 986–90. Paris: Fayard, 1995.

Vignon, Claude [Noémie Cadiot]. *Exposition universelle de 1855: Beaux-arts*. Paris: A. Fontaine, 1855.

Vincent, Robert. "Lois, censure et liberté." In *La Civilisation du journal, histoire culturelle et littéraire de la presse française au XIXe siècle*, edited by Dominique Kalifa et al., 61–95. Paris: Nouveau Monde, 2011.

Vinitzky-Seroussi, Vered, and Chana Teeger. "Unpacking the Unspoken: Silence in Collective Memory and Forgetting." *Social Forces* 88, no. 3 (March 2010): 1103–22.

Voir, ne pas voir la guerre; Histoire des représentations photographiques de la guerre. Paris: Somogy, 2001.
Vottero, Michaël. "Autour d'Isidore Pils et les peintres de l'Alma, la peinture au service de Napoléon III." In Gabriel Leanca, *La politique extérieure de Napoléon. III*, 197–212. Paris: L'Harmattan, 2011.
War Monuments in Canada. https://www.cdli.ca/monuments/pq/crimee.htm.
Wasserman, Jerry. "Transcultural Cross Dressing: Zouave Performance from the Crimea to Michael Jackson." *Alt.Theatre* 8, no. 3 (March 2011).
Waters, Catherine. *Special Correspondence and the Newspaper Press in Victorian Print Culture, 1850–1886*. London: Palgrave, 2019.
Wertsch. J.V. "Collective Memory." In *Memory in Mind and Culture*, edited by P. Boyer and J.V. Wertsch, 117–37. Cambridge: Cambridge University Press. 2009.
Wertsch, James V., and Henry L. Roediger III. "Collective Memory: Conceptual Foundations and Theoretical Approaches." *Memory* 16, no. 3 (2008): 318–32.
Winter, Jay. *Sites of Memory, Sites of Mourning: The Great War in European Cultural History*. Cambridge: Cambridge University Press, 1995.
Woodham-Smith, Cecil. *The Reason Why*. London: Constable, 1953.
Yon, Jean-Claude. "Les Mises en scène du pouvoir imperial." In *Napoléon III et l'Europe, 1856: le congrès de Paris*, 130–3. Paris: Artlys, 2006.
Yon, Jean-Claude. ed. *Les Spectacles sous le Second Empire*. Paris: Armand Colin, 2010.
Young, James. *The Texture of Memory: Holocaust Memorials and Meaning*. New Haven: Yale University Press, 1993.
Zarobell, John. "Jean Charles Langlois 1789–1870. Le Spectacle de l'histoire." *Nineteenth-Century Art Worldwide* 5, no. 1 (Spring 2006). http://www.19thc-artworldwide.org/spring06/163-jean-charles-langlois-1789-1870-le-spectacle-de-lhistoire.

Selected Poetry on the Crimean War

A***B***. *Chant lyrique sur la Guerre d'Orient*. Marseille: Camoin Frères, 1858.
Barandéguy-Dupont. *La Nicolaïde ou la Guerre d'Orient*. Montmartre: Pilloy, 1854.
Barbe, Philibert. *Odes sur la Guerre d'Orient*. Toulouse: Gibrac, Ouvriers réunis, 1854.
– *Poésies sur la Guerre d'Orient. Au Profit des soldats de la Crimée*. Carcassonne: P. Labau, 1855.
Bazan, P. *La Guerre d'Orient, poème nationale*. Cherbourg: A. Coupey, 1859. (Ancien agent administratif des Directions de Travaux de la Marine, Chevalier de la Légion d'Honneur.)
Bisson, E. *La Guerre de Crimée, poème*. Montmartre: Pilloy et Perrault, 1858.

Bornier, Henri de. *La Guerre d'Orient, poème*. Paris: Taride, libraire, 1858. (Sous-bibliothécaire de la Bibliothèque Sainte-Geneviève.)

Bouvier Fils. *Guerre d'Orient. Odes sur l'agression de la Russie, l'intervention de la France, la bataille d'Alma*. Lyon: Boursy, 1854.

Carré, Michel, and A. Adam. *Victoire!!! Cantate, à l'occasion de la prise de Sébastopol. Chantée sur le Théâtre impérial de l'Opéra-Comique dans la Représentation gratuite donnée par l'ordre de S.M. l'Empereur*. http://gallica.bnf.fr/ark:/12148/bpt6k5431301j/f2.image.

Casse, M. le Baron du. *La Guerre d'Orient, poème*. Paris: Dentu, 1858.

Charlemagne, Hippolyte de. *La Guerre d'Orient, souvenir de Béranger*. Paris: Chez les principaux libraires, 1858.

Charousset, M. *La Guerre de Crimée*. Perpignan: J.B. Alzine, 1856. (Capitaine au 21e de ligne).

Colombey, Théodore Pernot de. *La Guerre d'Orient*. Paris: Bénard et cie., 1858.

Coti, F. *La Guerre d'Orient, poésies*. Paris: Boucquoin, 1856.

Coutures, Owinski. *La Guerre d'Orient, poème*. Villeneuve-sur-Lot: Guillaume Leygue, 1857.

Dallaire, Julien. *La Guerre d'Orient. Pièce qui a remporté le prix de poésie décerné par l'Académie française*. Paris: Firmin Didot, 1858.

Defosse, J.-C. *À nos jeunes soldats partant pour la guerre d'Orient: strophes patriotiques*. Rouen: Lecointe, 1854.

Deshayes, M. l'abbé. *La Vérité aux Français, Episode sur la Guerre d'Orient. Prose et vers*. Tours: J. Bouserez, 1855.

Dumas, Adolphe. *La Guerre d'Orient, poème*. Paris: Taride, Libraire, 1858.

Dupont, Pierre. *Chants et chansons, poésie et musique*, vol. 3. Paris: Alexandre Hussiaux, 1854.

– *Chants guerriers, paroles et musique*. Paris: Arnaud de Vresse, 1855.

Faurie, J.B. *La Guerre d'Orient, poème*. Paris: Ch. Lahure et Cie. Typographe, 1858.

Fauvel, A.E. *Guerre d'Orient, poesies*. Metz: Imprimerie Mayer Samuel, 1854.

Garaudel, Eugène. "Le Chant des conscrits ou le Départ pour la Turquie." Paris: Duval-Poignée, 1854.

Gérard, A.-F. "La Guerre d'Orient." In *Odes*. Vitry: F.-V. Bitsch, 1856.

Jonquet, Dr. *La Guerre d'Orient, poème en huit chants*. Blois: Chez tous les libraires du Département, 1856.

Laprade, Victor de. *Oeuvres poétiques. Poèmes civiques, tribuns et courtisans*. Paris: Lemerre, 1879.

Lys, C. "L'Ovation. Paris, 29 décembre 1855." Paris: Félix Malteste et Cie, 1855.

M… (Ancien Officier de l'ex grande Armée impériale). *Épopée sur la guerre actuelle d'Orient et de la Baltiques de 1853–1854*. Amiens: Alfred Caron, Typographe, 1854.

Pourille, Stanislas. *La Critique européenne ou Chansons nouvelles sur La Guerre d'Orient*. Paris: Gauvin, 1854.

Rabourdin, Charles. *Le Siège de Sébastopol. Poème en six chants*. Paris: Delagrave, 1890.

Tampucci, Hippolyte. *La Guerre d'Orient, souvenir de Béranger*. Paris: Chez les principaux librairies, 1858. (Précédé par "A M. Villemain, Lettre sur les concours de l'Académie française.")

Touillon, L. *La Chute de Sébastopol, poème dédié à l'armée d'Orient*. Paris: Garnier, 1857.

Index

About, Edmond: *L'Homme à l'oreille cassée*, 146, 180n69; *Maître Pierre*, 37; review of Universal Exhibition of 1855, 113; review of Salon of 1857, 129
Académie Française: poetry competition "La Guerre d'Orient," 49–50
active and passive memory, 24–5
Agulhon, Maurice, 153
Allais, Alphonse, 37
Alma (battle): 14, 16, 26, 15; paintings, 110–13, *112*, 122, 124–5, *125*, 127, 129
Assmann, Aleida, 23, 24, 25, 41, 74, 99, 152, 154–5, 167–8
Assmann, Jan, 7, 22–3, 166
Aupick, Jacques, 13, 54
Autran, Joseph, 45

Balaclava (battle), 16–17, 58–9. *See also* Charge of the Light Brigade
battle paintings, 109–11, 112, 125, 128–9, 130–1, 134, 136, 137
Baudelaire, Charles: and Constantin Guys, 55–6, 132–4, 176nn 48, 49; and Jacques Aupick, 54; and Paul de Molènes, 87–88; publication of first *Fleurs du Mal*, 54–5; translations of Edgar Allan Poe, 54
Beaumont-Vassy, Edouard-Ferdinand, vicomte de, 89, 95
Bedarrides, J.B., *Journal humoristique du Siège de Sébastopol par un artilleur*, 42
Benjamin, Walter, on the panorama, 136, 139
Bingham, Robert Jefferson, 130
Bocher, Charles, *Lettres de Crimée, Souvenirs de Guerre*, 43, 147, 148, 162
Bonnassieux, Jean-Marie, 5
Bosquet, Pierre, 41, 73, 85, 113, 145
Boulevard de Sébastopol, 96–8, *96, 97, 98*
British army: conditions of, 10, 156; compared to French army, 11, 146–7

Cabasson, Guillaume-Alphonse, *Apotheosis of Napoleon III*, 109, 180n68
Camp du Drap d'or (the Field of the Cloth of Gold) summit, 63, 77
Canrobert, François Certain de, 36–7, 73, 85, 87, 134, *135*
Cardigan, James Thomas Brudenelle, Earl of, 16–17, 156
caricatures, 54, 102, 113, *114*, 115, *115*, 117, *126*, 128, 131

Catholic Church and Crimean War 13, 144, 149, 153, 167, 171nn10–11
Cham (pseud. of Charles Amédée de Noé): caricatures by, 102, 115, *126*, 128, *128*, 131, *133*
Charge of the Light Brigade, 41, 158; films and songs about, 18; Tennyson's poem, 17, 35, 58–9, 172n17
Charivari, Le, 54, 102, 115
Chavet, Victor Joseph, *68*, *69*
Chenu, Jean-Charles, 158, 162, 182n88
cholera, 10, 14, 36, 40–2, 50–1, 57, 62, 95, 157, 160–2, 171n12, 175n43, 182nn89–90
Confino, Alan, 140
Connerton, Paul, 23
Courbet, Gustave, Pavilion of Realism, 112; *L'Atelier du peintre, allégorie réelle déterminant une phase de sept années de ma vie artistique*, 112; *Tableau de figures humaines, historique d'un enterrement à Ornans*, 131; *Demoiselles au bord de la Seine*, *133*
Crémazie, Octave: "Sur les ruines de Sébastopol," 45–6
Crimea, Russian annexation in 2014, 6, 21, 23
Crimean War: confusion about, 144–5; disease, 10, 36, 40–2, 57, 156, 160, 162; impact in Britain, 18–19; impact in Russia, 19–20; lack of impact in France, 147; origins, 13–16, 149–51; outcome 16, 147
Crimean War Memorial, Waterloo Place, 3–4, 19, 27, 155, 166
Crusade, 46, 49– 50, 57, 153
cultural memory, 7, 22–3, 25, 33, 35, 59, 76, 95, 99, 156, 158, 165, 168

Daudet, Alphonse, 37
Daumier, Honoré: *Les Cosaques pour Rire: album de quarante caricatures; Chargeons les Russes: Album de quarante caricatures*, 54, 75, 115, *115*
Defence of Sebastopol (film), 20
Delacroix, Eugène, 65, 103, 137, 180n69
Descaves, Lucien: *La Colonne*, 13, 39–40, 42, 53, 62, 162; *Les Sous-Offs*, 174n34
Doin, Ernest: *Le Conscrit ou le Retour de Crimée*, 75–6, 153
Doré, Gustave: battle paintings, 111, 113, 124; illustrations 115, *116*, *117*, 118; *Histoire pittoresque, dramatique et caricaturale de la Sainte Russie*, 113, *114*
Du Camp, Maxime: review of Salon of 1857, 129; review of Salon of 1861, 126; *Souvenirs littéraires*, 135, 179n66; *Orient et Italie*, 159–60, 162–3, 175n44,
Dumas, Alexandre, 37, 65, 176n52
Dupont, Pierre, "La Nouvelle Alliance," "Le Siège de Sébastopol," "La Prise de Sébastopol," 47–8
Durand-Brager, Jean-Baptiste Henri: illustrations, 119, *120*, *121*, 123; paintings of Siege of Sebastopol, 127, 131, *132*

epidemics and war, 160–4
equestrian spectacles, 76–9

Fay, Charles, 85–6
Fet, Afanasy, 19
Fenton, Roger: photographs by, 80, 119, 121, 122, *123*, *124*, 181n73; self-portrait as a Zouave, *81*

Flaubert, Gustave, 34, 143, 147, 175n44
forgetting, 23, 126, 156, 165–6
France, Anatole, 91
Franco-Prussian War, 152–4
French army: advanced efficiency compared to British army, 11, 156; fraternity with Russians, 146–7; losses, 10, 160–3

Gautier, Théophile: on illustrated press, 118; on the panorama, 137, 139–40
Giraudoux, Jean, 22
Goncharov, Vasili, 20
Goncourt, Edmond de, 37
Goncourt, Edmond and Jules de, 111
Grassot, Paul, 8, 38, 173n32
Great Storm of 14 November 1854, 170n5, 172n15
Guérard, Eugene-Charles-François, 122; *Queen Victoria's Entry into Paris, 18 August 1855*, *66*
Guys, Constantin, drawings of Crimean War, *34*, 55–9, 123, 132, *134–5*, 176nn48–9
Gyp (pseud. of Sibylle Riquetti de Mirabeau), *Souvenirs d'une petite fille*, 36–7

Halbwachs, Maurice, 165
Herbé, Jean-Jules, 147, 156
Hippodrome, 76–8
Holy Sites dispute, 13–14, 167
Hugo, Victor, 13, 14, 50, 145, 160; "Saint-Arnaud," 50–2; Speech, 24 February 1855, 52–5, 73–4

Illustrated London News, 55, *58*, 63, 71–2, 77, 83–5, *84*, 97, 119, 121, 134, 175n46
Illustration, journal universel, L', *78*, 90–1, 118–19, *121*, 175n46, 180n72
Ingres, Jean-Auguste-Dominique, 103; *Apotheosis of Napoleon I*, 105, *108*, 109
Inkermann (battle), 16, 52–3

Keller, Ulrich, 8, 59, 159
Kinglake, Alexander William, 161
Kipling, Rudyard, "The Last of the Light Brigade," 17
Kriegel, Lara, 10, 12

Lacan, Ernest, 119, 181n74
Ladimir, Jules, 151, 164
Lami, Eugène, 111; *Souper offert par Napoléon III en l'honneur de la Reine Victoria dans la salle de l'Opéra de Versailles, 25 août 1855*, *71*
Langlois, Jean-Charles: career, 134–7; panorama, *Prise de Sébastopol*, 137–40, *138*
Laprade, Victor de, "L'Hymne à l'Épée," 46
Lassalle, Emile, *72*
Laurencin-Chapelle, Paul Adolphe, 82–3
Leroy-Beaulieu, Paul, 162
Lys, C., "L'Ovation," 48

MacMahon, Patrice de, 8, 29, 30, 151, 152, 155
Malakoff, the taking of: 16, 151, 152, 163; chocolate, 27, *28*; commemorative towers, 27–8; paintings and illustrations, *80*, 101–3, *102*, *103*, 122, 127, 129–31, *150*
Marchal, Gustave, 41
Marx, Karl, 49, 149
Maupassant, Guy de, 37
Maykov, Apollon, 19
Maynard, Félix, 43
Méhédin, Léon, 137, *138*
Mérimée, Prosper, 93, 149–50, 179n64

Millet, Claude, *Des Glaneuses*, 129, 131, 181n78
Mitchell, Katharyne, 67, 170n8
Molènes, Paul de, 80, 87–8
Monnier, Henri, *Mémoires de M. Joseph Prudhomme*, 37–8
Mullois, l'abbé, 82, 167
Musée des Familles (journal), 94, 130
Musée français-anglais, Le (journal), 116–18
Musée Historique de Versailles, 124, 126, 130, 136, 157

Napoleon I (Napoleon Bonaparte), 13, 16, 19, 57, 103, 105, 108–9, *108*, 149, 159, 179n62, 180n68
Napoleon III: Catholic support, 4–5, 13, 144, 153; Crimean War, 13–15, 149–50; and Queen Victoria, 63–7, *72*; theatricality, 61–3; and Tsar Nicholas I, 171n13; Universal Exhibition of 1855, 101–3, 105, 109; "le Petit," 51, 103, 149, 180n67
Nekrasov, Nikolay, 19
Nieuwerkerke, Alfred Émilien, comte de, 111, 124, 125
Nightingale, Florence, 3, 16, 17, 18, 31, 155
Nora, Pierre, 152, 167
Notre Dame de France Puy-en-Velay, 5, 6, 35

Panoramas: *Battle of Navarino*, 136; *Battle of Sedan*, 153, 181n84; *Defence of Sebastopol*, 20; *Taking of Sebastopol (Prise de Sébastopol)*, 137–40
Paris, Treaty of, 10, 16, 75, 113, 147
Paris Commune, 39, 40, 90, 108
Pays, Le (Journal de l'Empire), 54, 69–70
Philipon, Charles, 115, 117
Pils, Isidore, battle paintings, 109–11, *110*, *112*, 125, 127, 129
plays about the Crimean War, 74–7, 153
Pont de l' Alma, 28–32, *30*
Presse, La (newspaper): on Napoleon III, 61; on Queen Victoria's visit to France, 67, 72–3
Pruche, Clément: illustrations by, *89*, *92*, 127
Punch (magazine), 61–2

Queen Victoria, visit to France: ceremonial events and entertainments, 65–8; diary entries, 67, 68; diplomacy, 70–1; paintings and illustrations of the visit, *66*, *68*, *69*, *70*, *71*, *72*; state ball at Versailles, 67–9

Rabourdin, Charles, 43, 44–5
Raglan, Fitzroy James Henry Somerset, Baron, 10, 16, 17, 161
Rain, Pierre, 145, 149
Renan, Ernest, 166
Renié, Pierre-Lin, 101, 121–2
return of French troops into Paris (29 December 1855), 90–5; illustrations, *89*, *91*, *92*, *96*
Revue des deux mondes (journal), 54–5, 80, 130
Richebourg, Pierre Ambroise, 97–8, 130; photograph by, *97*
Ricoeur, Paul, 23
Rigney, Ann, 18, 22, 42, 154, 158, 165
Roubaud, Franz, panorama, *Defence of Sebastopol*, 20
Roynette, Odile, 22
Russell, William, 17, 19, 121, 144, 155, 156, 158, 182nn85–6

Russian cannons from Sebastopol, 3, 5, 6, 25, 27, 34, 166
Russian Orthodox Church, 13, 149, 171nn10–11

Saint-Arnaud, Jacques Leroy: military career, 10, 14, 26–7, *26*, 171n12; poem by Victor Hugo, 50–1
Sales, Pierre, *Le Sergent Renaud*, 37
Salle de Crimée (Musée historique de Versailles), 124–6, *125*, 157–8
Salon of 1857, paintings and reviews, 126–31; satirical guidebook, 128
Salon of 1859, paintings of the Crimean War, 131–2
Sand, George, 37, 75, 92–3
Sebastopol, siege of, 4, 6, 8, 11, 16, 38–9, 42, 70, 83, 163, 167; French commemoration of victory, 79, 96–8; paintings, 127, 131, 132; poems, 44–5, 47; in Russian national imagination, 20–1; toponymy (France), 169n3
Sebastopol monument (Welsford-Parker Monument), 25, *26*
Sebastopol Sketches (Tolstoy), 19–20, 146
Ségur, Sophie Rostopchine, Countess of, *L'Auberge de l'ange gardien*, *Le Général Dourakine*, 34–5
Senior, Nassau William, 9, 11, 145, 149, 150
Sewell, Anna, *Black Beauty*, 18
Siege of Silistria, equestrian spectacle, 76–9, *78*
Swinburne, Algernon, 52

Tabar, François, *Guerre de Crimée, Fourrageurs*, 132
Tennyson, Alfred, "The Charge of the Light Brigade," 16, 17, 35, 41, 58, 158, 172n17
Théâtre de Constantine, 79
Théâtre de la Gaîté, 74–5
Théâtre des Délassements-Comiques, 74
Théâtre des Variétés, 79, 81
Théâtre du Vaudeville, 74
Théâtre Imperial du Cirque, 76–7
Third Republic, 152–3, 167–8
Times, The (newspaper), war reports, 155, 157
Tocqueville, Alexis de, 9, 11, 145; 149
Tolstoy, Leo, *Sebastopol Sketches*, 19–20, 34, 35, 146
Tsar Alexander II, 20
Tsar Nicholas I, 13, 21
typhus, 10, 40–1, 53–4, 160, 162–3, 182n90
Tyutchev, Fyodor, 19

Universal Exhibition of 1855: battle paintings, 109–13, *110*, *112*, 113, 124; display of art, 102–3; reviews, 109–11, 113

Verne, Jules: *Aventures de trois Russes et de trois Français dans l'Afrique australe*, 38–9; review of Salon of 1857, 127, 129–30
Vernet, Horace: battle paintings, 8, 57, *80*, 103, 111, 124, 127, 129, *150*, 180n69; *Apotheosis of Napoleon I*, *108*, 109
Victoria Cross, 27, 155
Vigny, Alfred de: on indifference to the war, 21, 43–4, 50, 140, 174n36, 174n40; "Wanda, histoire russe," 44
Vizitelly, Ernest, 14, 67

Yvon, Adolphe: *Prise de la Tour Malakoff,* 101, *102,* 125, 127, 129–31; travel to Crimea, 137

Zola, Émile: on deployment of French soldiers to Crimea, *Nouveaux contes à Ninon,* 35–6; on Franco-Prussian War, 154; mention of Crimean War in novels of *Les Rougon-Macquart,* 36, 154
Zouaves: mythical reputation of, 28, 80–1, 82, 173n29, 177n57; theatrical productions, 79, 81, 82, 178n58
Zouave statue on Pont de l'Alma, 28–31, *30*
Zouave theatre at Inkermann, 81–7, *84, 85*

Milton Keynes UK
Ingram Content Group UK Ltd.
UKHW051827040324
438897UK00020B/126/J